Jewish-Christian Debates

~

God, Kingdom, Messiah

by
JACOB NEUSNER
and
BRUCE CHILTON

Fortress Press
Minneapolis

JEWISH-CHRISTIAN DEBATES
God, Kingdom, Messiah

Cover design: Michael Mihelich
Cover graphic: David Hiser, Tony Stone Images
Interior design: The HK Scriptorium

Library of Congress Cataloging-in-Publication Data

Neusner, Jacob, 1932–
    Jewish-Christian debates : God, kingdom, messiah / Jacob Neusner and Bruce Chilton.
        p.   cm.
    Includes bibliographical references and index.
    ISBN 0-8006-3109-9 (alk. paper)
    1. God (Judaism).   2. Judaism—Doctrines.   3. God.   4. Theology, Doctrinal.   5. Kingdom of God—Biblical teaching.   6. Jesus Christ—Kingship.   7. Messiah—Judaism.   8. Jesus Christ—Messiahship.   9. Judaism—Relations—Christianity.   10. Christianity and other religions—Judaism.   I. Chilton, Bruce.   II. Title.
    BM610.N483   1998
    296.3—dc21   97-48643
                                                                              CIP

Manufactured in the U.S.A.   AF 1-3109
02   01   00   99   98   1   2   3   4   5   6   7   8   9   10

Contents

~

Preface

~

THIS BOOK PRESENTS a theological dialogue between Judaism, represented by its classical statement, and Christianity, formulated in
terms of its initial canon. We cover three dimensions of the religious
life: knowing God, living life in accord with God's will, and hoping in
God. Both Judaic and Christian theological structures assign to these
aspects of the religious life a critical and central role, for, beyond the
affirmation of its truth, each religion insists upon the expression—in
concrete action as well as in prevailing attitude—of the truth that is
affirmed. Since each religion concerns itself with just these matters, we
propose to explain to the faithful of each group precisely how loyal
Judaists (practitioners of the religion, Judaism, as distinct from Jews,
members of an ethnic group) and Christians make their lives with God.

To a believing Judaist, Christianity bears some resemblance to
Judaism, yet on closer inspection it differs radically; consequently, the
Christian family of religions is exceedingly difficult for a Judaist to
understand. And, while persons of good will often prefer not to say so,
Judaism ought to be readily understood by Christians, being the religion of "the Old Testament"; but in fact, Judaism as they see it is so different from what the Old Testament leads one to expect as to be
beyond all comprehension. If Christianity were wholly unlike Judaism,
then any dialogue with Christianity on the part of Judaism would begin
with the recognition that the other is wholly other: beyond all parallels,
comparisons, and contrasts. And if Judaism were totally unrelated to
Christianity, then any dialogue with Judaism on the part of Christianity

would also commence with the understanding that the Christian stood utterly out of relationship with the Judaist. But, we maintain, the categorical structures of the two religions correspond to one another, and, in these pages we mean to show that the system of the one addresses questions critical to the system of the other. Dialogue is possible because, we hold, each of us out of the resources of our own faith can make some (if not entire) sense of the religion of the other.

That is because Judaism and Christianity, along with Islam, rest upon a single, shared conviction: God is one, unique, known to humanity through the prophets of ancient Israel, beginning with the patriarchs and extending through Moses at Sinai. For the two thousand years now drawing to a close for Christianity, no less than for the fourteen hundred years of Islam, not to mention the fifty-seven hundred years Judaism counts from the creation of the world as accounted for by the Torah, these three great religions have declared to humanity their belief in one and the same God. Yet, even as this morning's headlines attest, the three faiths have found it exceedingly difficult to explain to one another anything about that one God whom all have known, whom all have proclaimed, from Sinai, by Jesus Christ, through the seal of the prophet Muhammad.

So all have known that one God, whether in the person of Jesus Christ, God incarnate, or in the revelation of the one whole Torah given by God to Moses at Sinai, or in the Qur'an, "the word of God in the strictest sense of the term—not only as example and admonition but as a decree coming from the very mouth of God."[1] But despite believing in one and the same God, appealing to one and the same story of creation, sharing prophets in common (such as Abraham and Moses), and referring to shared revelation (from Sinai and the prophets), they have sustained for most of their lives on earth a certain loathing for one another and an utter incapacity to communicate. So they have turned inward, each religion talking to its own audience, none proposing to speak beyond its own walls, except to explain to the others how misguided about God they are. At best each offers outsiders tolerance, bestowed perforce; but often a malign relativism—declaring each is right for its own—masks mutual incomprehension.

Even now, whether one religion wishes to talk with another is not altogether clear—but that the world will listen is beyond doubt. Now, when each party has gained something of what it has long wanted, the time to talk has come. Islam is no longer under the heel of Christian

Europe and its far western provinces; Christianity is no longer beset in Europe by a strong, well-entrenched alternative in communism; Judaism is no longer bereft of place, a social order for which it states the norm. Working out centuries-old problems at home, whether for Islam in the Near and Middle East, the part of the Indian subcontinent now called Pakistan, Malaya, and Indonesia and Islamic sub-Saharan Africa; or for Christianity in Europe, Africa, and the Americas; or for Judaism in the ancient homeland, now the State of Israel, and North America and Western Europe, the three religions that call Abraham and Sarah father and mother find respite. And they can look beyond themselves.

But for what? Judaism on its own makes no sense of Jesus Christ, God incarnate, in terms Christians can recognize as authentic to their faith; Christianity, on its own, cannot grasp Israel, God's first love, in terms holy Israel can comprehend; and Islam, so far as we in the West can reckon, has yet to frame a theory of the other religions of the book in terms that do not claim supersession. Election and incarnation, keystones of the faith of Judaism and Christianity, respectively, will stand for mutual hatred unless they are mutually understood. So if the moment presents its opportunity, it can only be to accomplish what the faiths of the one God—known through Abraham, the Torah, Christ, and the Prophet Muhammad, respectively—have never before achieved. And that is not so grand a thing as to make sense of difference, to understand how the one God whom all of us worship, love, and serve could have said so many contradictory things to us: church, Israel, Islam. Perhaps another age will work its way toward that deep question, beyond our searching out. For us, a great step forward will be the simple journey toward understanding: the possibility, even, of conversation. For a long time, perhaps for all time, we three have not conversed at all. The time has come to talk.

The first step clearly leads Judaism to undertake dialogue with Christianity, and Christianity with Judaism. Such dialogue as took shape before our own day consisted of two self-serving monologues. Neither took a keen interest in the other; both found in making up a message for the other essentially an occasion for reaffirming itself. In fact, neither could make sense, in its terms, of the other, and neither tried. A genuine argument requires that different people argue about the same thing, appeal to the same facts, invoke the same canons of thought and reasoned argument. So dialogue makes contradictory demands: (1) thinking about the other in one's own terms, and yet (2) framing one's thought in terms that the other can also grasp. An authentic effort at mutual comprehension—leading even to understanding and respect at the deepest layers of consciousness—demands: (1) making sense of the other in one's own framework, yet making sense of the other (2) so that the other will recognize that sense too. The identification of shared categories in the two distinct systems, Judaic and Christian, meets these conditions; talking about the same things, the two religions can make sense of their differences.

Obviously, that kind of thinking beyond the limits of oneself proves difficult even under the benign circumstances of discourse among relatives or friends. Among religions it is much more difficult, since our religions, at least—Islam, Christianity, Judaism—claim to know God through God's own revelation. So the same God who tells Jews and Muslims not to eat pork or carrion tells the Christian in the Pauline tradition that food makes no difference; and the same God who tells the (Roman Catholic) Christian that Rome is the rock on which to build has told Islam about a different rock altogether. Clearly, the message is confused. And yet we do worship one and the same God, each religion by its own admission, and we do value, among other writings, the same Scriptures.

Not only so, but we three together—Islam, Judaism, Christianity—stand at the end of dreadful trials and look forward with well-founded confidence to a world that will now hear us out and that asks us to answer questions long addressed not to heaven but to earth. If we speak intelligibly—if, even, we find some one thing to say together—we shall be heard where until now we have been dismissed or ignored But for the moment nothing suggests that we understand one another so well that we may talk together, and much shows that we do not. Whether anyone has ever known how to think about the other in a way authentic to one's own viewpoint but also plausible to the other's self-understanding, few until now have tried to find out. It is time to try to talk. And no two religions in history have found more in common about which to talk than Judaism and Christianity.

So if we have not negotiated theological truth except through dissimulation, and if we will not desist from the effort to come to terms with one another either, what task lies before us? It is to ask questions not of belief but of attitude, emotion, and feeling: to ask whether each side may be able to form a newfound sympathy for the other. Insofar as sympathy rests on mutual understanding, in these pages we mean to lay foundations for a future of mutual good will. What we mean is a sympathy resting not on guilt and regret for a bloody past (on the Christian side) or on resigned recognition of the facts of life and power (on the Judaic side). Such attitudes—shame and guilt, or resignation rich in resentment at what cannot be changed—distort relationships. Sympathy flows from an understanding, out of one's own resources of religious understanding, of what proves critical to the life of the other. In this book we each undertake to explain ourselves in terms the other can grasp; we take up, specifically, three critical components common to the religious systems of Judaism and Christianity, as we explain in the Introduction.

We call attention to a three-volume companion[2] to this work, which compares the theological structures of Judaism and Christianity, with special attention to the formative categories. Here we deal with the working of two religious systems, and in the counterpart volumes we set forth the principal components of the two religious structures. By "system" we mean how the religion works, and by "structure" we mean what the religion says. Obviously our work on these projects runs along similar lines, but each project accomplishes its own goals, treating its own topics in a distinctive way.

The two projects are readily distinguished. In the other one, we compare and contrast the principal components of the counterpart structures of Judaism and Christianity, and in this, we do the same for the counterpart systems of the two traditions. In the present volume we explain how they function in comparable, sometimes parallel, ways. What we contribute in these pages is an account of how each brings about communion with God, how each defines the worldly life of the faithful under God's dominion, and how each addresses the issue of teleology through the medium of eschatology.

Each religious tradition sets forth its definition of revelation; each defines the social order to whom God has spoken, that God called into being in God's service; and each knows where and how, in this world, we meet God in human encounter. It follows that in those three volumes, in contrast to the present one, we identify and spell out in an elementary way the three principal areas of communion among—and therefore conflict between—the heirs of the same Scripture:

1. Revelation as God's self-manifestation: how and what we know about God; that is, the character of scriptural revelation.
2. The people of God: who constitutes the people to whom God is made manifest; that is, the definition of the body of the faithful.

3. God in the world: where and through whom we meet God in this world; the this-worldly traits we identify as godly; what it means for humanity to be "in our image, after our likeness," encompassing also the issue of incarnation.

We focus here on the classical and definitive documents of the two traditions. For Judaism our concern is the Torah as it took shape in the first six centuries of the Common Era. The systematic issues we address in Judaism are: meeting God within the power of God's rationality in the Torah (chapter 1); living in accord with the rules and regulations of the holy life (chapter 3); and the coming of the Messiah as the result of the humble acceptance of God's rule (chapter 5). For Christianity, the counterpart categories concern engaging with God through Christ by means of practices grounded in the New Testament (chapter 2); the experience of God's primordial rule as remaking the world (chapter 4); and the bodily presence of God in Christ (chapter 6). As the Torah, traditionally defined, is our foundation for the understanding of Judaism, so the New Testament is the basis on which we explain Christianity.

Both authors elect to limit discussion to the classical writings, in the clear recognition that both religions unfolded through time, so that later writers expanded and recast the classical definitions and even categories. But we maintain that, however things changed through time, the classical formulation remains the paramount one.[3] All translations of Talmudic literature are by Jacob Neusner unless otherwise noted.

The authors express thanks to their academies, Bard College for both and the University of South Florida for Jacob Neusner, for ongoing support for their scholarly work. Each author has found for himself ideal conditions for a life of scholarship, and neither takes for granted the gifts that he receives in these centers of higher learning. Jacob Neusner completed the second draft of his part of the book as Research Professor at Åbo Akademi Forskningsinstitut, in Åbo/Turku, Finland, and wishes to thank the Akademi and its research institute for providing ideal working conditions for the summer of 1993.

Both express thanks, also, to Dr. Marshall Johnson, formerly of Fortress Press, for his commitment to this project and his guidance in bringing it to fruition. If we achieve our goal of a sustained theological encounter of an illuminating character, it is because of his guidance and long-term commitment to this project.

~

Introduction

~

A THEOLOGICAL DIALOGUE between Christianity and Judaism finds its justification in a simple fact. The two religions agree in principal assertions: God is one; God is made manifest through revelation, part of which, at least, is contained in the Hebrew Scriptures of ancient Israel; God orders history and rules the lives of humanity; God and humanity respond to one another and are covenanted to one another. These are among many fundamental, shared affirmations. The most important from a comparative perspective is that Christianity and Judaism appeal in common to the Hebrew Scriptures of ancient Israel (called, variously, Old Testament or written Torah) in their definition of their authoritative writings, the Bible (Old Testament and New Testament) and the Torah (written and oral). Since the Bible of Christianity and the Torah of Judaism record how humanity knows God, the appeal to a common source of facts and truth suggests they share much. Moreover, a massive tradition of morality and ethics, beginning with the Ten Commandments, joins them together. Both view history in the same framework, as a medium for the expression of God's will. They concur that God's chief demand concerns love of neighbor as of self, and that morality and ethics form the highest priority of the good and holy life. Both accept that the pattern of human experience is a matter of a covenant with God.

Not only sharing many ideas in common, but formed also in accord with a single pattern, they share a common categorical structure.

1

Both traditions form their religious systems in these categories: (1) the self-manifestation of God in revelation (Scripture); (2) the social entity called into being at the service of God (Israel, church); (3) the conception that, in this world, we meet and know God. These three formidable categories define the principal foci of both religious traditions: revelation, the definition of the body of the faithful, and meeting with God. Because of the correspondence of structure and important components of their respective canonical writings, people have found ample reason to speak of a "Judeo-Christian tradition."

But, by that expression, they have ordinarily meant a single tradition expressed by partners to the same religion, separated by trivialities. As we demonstrate here, dialogue uncovers enormous areas of difference between the two mutually (but partially) comprehending parties. Like the language differences between the British and the Americans, we find ourselves separated from one another by supposing that by the same words we mean the same things, when that is not at all the case. So we can disagree because we agree, but, in agreeing, we find we really do not understand one another very well. That is quite natural. After all, if Judaism and Christianity formed a single "Judeo-Christian tradition," encompassing not only this-worldly morality and ethics but transcendent issues of religious truth and belief, then why have the faithful of the two perspectives formed distinct and conflicting communities for two millennia?

Consequently, the integrity and autonomy of both religions have found themselves compromised by allegations that what the two have in common vastly outweighs (and renders negligible) what separates them. The notion of a single tradition in two parts, though rich in validating evidence, leads people to two false notions. This fact explains why we—long-time friends, each a faithful practitioner of his religion—have come together to write this book. We mean to spell out important points of difference, points that at the same time permit us to understand each other in terms each party can grasp. Because we agree on premises and facts and modes of thought and argument, we can disagree. But because we disagree, we find ourselves compelled to explore our own convictions—the structure and system of our respective faiths—in search of the intellectual resources for the understanding of the other. That is to say, we know the other, but we do not understand the other. Solely by appeal to our own principles of explanation and rational inquiry, can we understand anything that is different. But in the case of Christianity, the Judaic believer can find principles of explanation that yield understanding of the Christian; and in the case of Judaism, the Christian believer can discover in Christianity grounds for a sympathetic understanding of the Judaist.

If we concede at the outset that vast areas of consensus are apparent in the two religious traditions' moral and ethical teachings, beginning with the Ten Commandments and the commandment to love God with all our heart, soul, mind, and might, what is wrong with the present state of affairs, the notion of a "Judeo-Christian tradition"? It is not that there is no such shared tradition; it is that the formulation of what is shared distorts and misrepresents the integrity of the two religions. First, people who trivialize enormous differences assume that Judaism is the same as the religion of the Old Testament, superseded by the New; then Christians find it difficult to explain to themselves why Judaism should exist at all. Second, some assume that Christianity is just the daughter religion of Judaism, and so deny to Christianity its own autonomy. Consequently, an anti-Christian polemic emerges, which maintains that Jesus was a Jew (meaning, not in the ethnic but in the religious sense), and only that, from birth to death; Christianity was the invention of someone else (commonly, the apostle Paul). It must follow that authentic disciples of Jesus must practice Judaism, not Christianity.

Each of these contradictory positions serves the apologetic needs of those who maintain it—the former, Christianity, which for nearly its entire recorded history has found Israel's faith incomprehensible, because surpassed and fulfilled in Jesus Christ; the latter, Judaism, which never accorded recognition to Christianity at all, denying anything had changed on earth by reason of its advent. But principal components of Christianity today have let go of supersessionism—the doctrine that, with the advent of Jesus Christ, Israel was superseded—and have come to respect the faithfulness of eternal Israel to its covenant with God. And in the twentieth century, some Judaic theologians have come to grips with the fact of Christianity not solely in this-worldly and adventitious terms but in the framework of Sinai.

Half-truths such as we have mentioned—that Judaism is the same as the Old Testament religion, that Christianity is just a degenerate Judaism—do rest on certain facts, making it difficult to dismiss out of hand what is actually a distortion. It is true that Judaism is the religion of the Old Testament, but then so is Christianity. Both religions appeal to revelation in addition to the Old Testament: the oral Torah and the New Testament, respectively. And both read the Hebrew Scriptures through the light of these further revelations. It also is true that Christianity began in the heart of the Jewish people. But even as the faith began to take shape, Christianity formulated its own statement and in no way accepted dependent status on the prior religious tradition of Israel, the holy people. It follows that these characterizations are both right and wrong—and therefore misleading, since Judaism appeals to the Torah, which includes, but is not exhausted by, "the Old Testament," and since Christianity is not just "Judaism plus the Messiah."

If these two religions compare so extensively and present contrasts of such illuminating character, how are we to proceed to understand them? The answer is that each can best be read not only in its own terms but also in comparison and contrast with the other. The work of comparison and contrast, in a spirit of mutual respect, is what we undertake in this book. Here we set forth what each religious tradition teaches on fundamental questions, which both religions define in much the same way but answer very differently, according to their respective natures. We offer this modest dialogue as an example of what it means to try to understand the other by appeal to the resources of one's own faith. Each of us knows what it means to commune with God, to live in the realm of heaven, and to sustain the hope in God's ultimate salvation of humanity. So when one tells the other about his formulation of these matters and explains how his religious system works to solve the principal questions of human existence under the aspect of God's presence in history and dominion in eternity, each author speaks of what the other can grasp. The categories are the same, so too the stakes. That is why we mean to be mutually comprehensible, and, in understanding one another, we hope to stand for eternal Israel and for the church in her fullness in a quest for amity and this-worldly collaboration.

As we consider how the two religious traditions deal with three generative questions, our comparisons and contrasts concern how the traditions work. Our description of the religions' structure, as distinct from the system considered here, is in another series of works (see Preface, note 2). What we want to know here are answers to these questions:

1. Communion with God: How, in everyday life, do we enter into dialogue with God, not just to know about God, but to meet God?
2. The kingdom of God: What does it mean to enter, or to live in, God's kingdom? Where do we find that kingdom realized, and how do we live our lives within it?
3. The mystery of the Messiah: What is our goal and purpose, the teleology of our lives and work, and when and how will the tensions and imperfections of existence, both personal (represented by death) and social (symptomized by oppression and injustice) come to resolution?

These questions, concerning religious aspiration, service, and anticipation, strike us as critical to both religious systems (or sets of religious systems), and we think that because of their topical cogency, they constitute a valid program of systemic comparison and contrast. Both religious traditions insist, in the tradition of the Pentateuch and the Prophets, that God is present in the here and now, and that we can meet and know God in this world. Each then explains where and how that meeting, that "community with God," takes place.

A closely correlated idea concerns life under God's rule or dominion. Both traditions share the conviction that to be "Israel" or "church" is to live in another realm of being, one in which allegiance belongs to God and loyalty to God's law. Both, indeed, use much the same language, with Judaism speaking of "the kingdom of heaven" (a euphemism for God), and Christianity teaching the mystery of the kingdom of God. And both maintain that, at the end of days, God will save humanity by sending the Messiah, or Savior.

At issue are theological teachings, and so we undertake theological comparison and contrast. We describe the positions, in the classical and formative documents, of the two religions, and then point to traits of commonality (ordinarily: structural) and disagreement (commonly: functional). These traits of a working religious system describe the everyday life of the faithful, telling them how theological teaching infuses the workaday world with a new light. Understanding the functional categories of the respective systems leads us deep into the human realities of the faiths before us. The issues concern knowing God, living with God, and hoping in God; communion, the kingdom of God, and the Messiah standing for those encompassing dimensions of the religious life. This comparison does not require us to debate who is right, or by what governing criteria one or another party is right. We take the position that God will determine questions of theological truth; our task is only to pursue our respective rationalities, and to do so as rigorously and uncompromisingly as we can.

Having referred to "Judaism" and "Christianity," we have to specify with greater precision what we mean by these protean terms. Both of us mean to characterize the religions as they are set forth in their classic writings; our account speaks only of the formative age, the earliest centuries of the Common Era (C.E. = A.D.).

In the case of Judaism, we speak here of the Judaism of the dual Torah, set forth in the Scripture and the documents of the oral Torah, that is, the Mishnah (ca. 200 C.E.), the Talmuds (the Talmud of the Land of Israel and the Talmud of Babylonia, which explain the Mishnah, ca. 400 and 600, respectively), and the Midrash compilations (which explain Scripture, ca. 200–600). The books cited here, other than Scripture, are then the Mishnah, the two Talmuds, and some of the compilations of exegeses of Scripture, with special attention to those that reached closure at about the same time as the first of the two Talmuds, that of the Land of Israel, in the fifth century.

The Judaic religious system portrayed in these foundational documents of the oral Torah functions around two poles: sanctification in the here and now, and salvation at the end of time. Sanctification in the here and now involves making holy such commonplace and worldly actions as have to do with food, clothing, shelter, procreation; vocation and avocation; family life and relationships—the simple things that constitute what we know of life. Communion takes place in the Torah, God's self-manifestation; when we pray, we speak to God, but when we study, God speaks to us. The kingdom of God defines where we mean to live; a Yiddish song goes, roughly: "The British think that their king is a king, and the Germans think that their Kaiser is a Kaiser, but our King is the King of Kings, the Holy One, who is blessed." Holy, eternal Israel lives in the intangible but real realm governed by God: God's law rules, God's will defines, God's word determines how things ought to be. But what are the signs of the kingdom? Where do we find it? What kind of life do the subjects of that realm lead? And, finally, faced with this world's disappointments and humiliations, what does holy Israel expect in time to come, and for what does holy Israel hope? The issues then concern knowledge of God, sanctification, and salvation.

How does Judaism formulate its position on the questions of a working religious system that we take up in this book? In the categories of communion, piety, and hope, we examine how Judaism worked and what it produced. When we know how faithful Israel communed with God, how Judaic practitioners expressed their love for God through acts of piety, and how they formulated their sense of the future and the basis for their stout hope, we know why Judaism succeeded, for its entire history, in sustaining the Jewish people and retaining their loyalty. For the stakes in Judaism are transcendent, surpassing all this-worldly consideration. Judaism is a religion of mind and heart, but also of family and community, one that asks entire devotion to God, not only in the parts of life God can command, the life of the people together in community, but especially in the secret places of existence not subject to God's will but only to one's own will.

In the case of Christianity, our focus is the New Testament. Those twenty-seven documents were composed at the moment of Christianity's emergence from early Judaism, and prior to the systematic definition of the new movement (which occurred preeminently during the second century). But the relative absence of formal doctrine in the New Testament, as compared to later formulations, has not impeded its universal recognition as the classic work of the religion. Here we can learn of the first message concerning Jesus, which was called a "gospel," the news of God's triumph. That primitive preaching is combined with Jesus' own teaching and presented in the books we call Gospels (especially Matthew, Mark, and Luke), which were programs of instruction for the first Christians of the Greco-Roman world. The Bible obviously contains books that are older, but none that are closer to the defining energy of the new faith.

The force of claims regarding Jesus is so great as to be difficult to comprehend at times. For that reason, documents of the New Testament that are more reflective, but still implicated in the development of the initial movement, such as John's Gospel, can be helpful in understanding how the movement emerged and understood itself. On the other hand, controversial works such as Paul's letters are instructive of the fundamental struggle concerning Christian identity that was characteristic of the church during the mid-first century C.E. The attempt of later writings (such as Acts) to package the struggle as a familial argument within a unified movement is touching but unconvincing. What is clear, however, is that Christianity had emerged by the end of the first century as a movement separate from Judaism and in search of another identity.

Later centuries would see identities come and go. From the second century, Christians might claim to be the true philosophers of the Roman Empire, or heroic ascetics in Syria. The adoption of Christianity by Constantine as a religion of state transformed the church radically, and the sudden change from being persecuted to wielding power was as heady as it was dangerous. The notion of a hierarchical core in the midst of society nonetheless survived through the Middle Ages, and is by no means defunct today. Hierarchy gave a sense of purpose and cohesion to medieval society, just as the challenge of hierarchy by human reason gave us a Renaissance and a Reformation. The busy centuries since then have seen reason in a more analytic mode produce a self-described Enlightenment, a vaunted technology, and a belief that religion itself might be explained rationally and subsumed within ideology. But after two hundred years of explanation, many of us feel a cultural loss of control, a helplessness before inhuman and destructive forces within humanity.

Our cultural crisis has arrived in tandem with Christianity's crisis. The church's mere survival has been a victory; the fact that it has any word to say, after centuries of persecution, triumphant hegemony, scorn, division, more persecution and more triumph, is startling. But there can be no masking the fact that Christianity as a faith has been more challenged by the cultural relativism that is its product than any other religion has been. The problem is not merely one of unbelief; the problem is that the difference between belief and unbelief is itself problematic.

The New Testament does not define Christianity, but it maps the forces that propelled it from being a movement within early Judaism to being a religious community widely represented in the Mediterranean basin. Those forces, the systemic drive of a fresh perspective regarding how humanity might worship and live in communion with one God, moved some people to practices, feelings, and beliefs they had never known before. The system of the religion preceded its systematic expression, and only an appreciation of the system will prevent Christianity from being confused with the cultural forms it has assumed in history.

Unless Christianity is understood as a system of religion, whether by its practitioners or by those who need to grapple with it, it cannot be understood at all. The issues of the Jewish-Christian debate are irreducibly important, because they bring us directly to the point of the generative systems that gave us one religion and another. If there is to be a humane analysis and practice of religion, it will develop on that basis.

We believe that mutual understanding leads to good will, and our goal is to clarify for believing Jews the ways in which Christianity is less alien than it seems, and to clarify for believing Christians the ways in which Judaism is less exotic than it appears. That goal is not reached by dismissing difference or negotiating theological truth. It is reached by trying to clarify, in terms of logic and structure such as all parties can affirm, the points of common conviction and the shared affirmation, thus exposing issues of contention as well. It is exceedingly difficult for Judaic believers to understand Christianity, and the converse is likewise true; each finds the convictions of the other incomprehensible. We believe that by showing the structural and systemic commonalities, we render each intelligible within the framework of the structure and system of the other, and that strikes us as an intellectually constructive effort at mutual understanding. For in the end, the Judaic believer can grasp Christianity only within his or her categorical structure and system, and the same is so for the Christian.

For whom do we write this book? In the end it is not for those who seek to diminish religious conflict, but for those who want increase of religious commitment in their own tradition. We mean to speak to Jews and Christians who want to better understand their own religious traditions, not only (or even mainly) those of outsiders. In our view, when we identify the issues that theological teachings address and understand the alternative positions on those issues that classical thinkers have adopted, we treat religion as vital. We cease to regard as self-evident the views we hold, but grasp that they represent decisions among alternatives, choices people have made in full consideration of other possible choices. Then our respective religions take on weight and consequence and become living choices among alternative truths.

Contention forms the highest compliment, the deepest reinforcement of the faith. Only by seeing the options that have faced the framers of Judaism and Christianity in their classical writings shall we understand how, in full rationality and with entire awareness of issues and options, the founders of our respective traditions took the paths they did. Judaism represents choices on conflicted issues, decisions made in full rationality between contradictory positions, and so does Christianity. It does no good to pretend the two religions are saying the same thing in different language; they are saying different things. But we aim to show, also, that each religion indeed can understand the other, and the faithful of one religion have the power to view the other with sympathy, if not with empathy; with respect and not with condescension, such as mere tolerance conveys.

It is therefore our intent to make Judaic believers and Christian ones alike firmer, each in his or her own faith, by demonstrating the options that people deriving from a single tradition—that of ancient Israel—exercised. In doing so, we simply transcend empty assertions of agreement where there is none. When religion is reduced to platitudes and banalities, lifelessly repeating things deemed to be self-evident, it loses all consequence and forms a mere chapter in the conventions of culture. But from Judaism and Christianity stretching backward centuries beyond counting, faithful Israel, on the one side, and the living body of Christ, on the other, drew sustenance and found the strength to endure.

Let us not at the end lose sight of the remarkable power of these religions in times past and in our own day. The world did not make life easy for Judaism through its history in the West; and, in the age of militant secularism on the one side, and violently anti-Christian communism on the other, Christianity has found itself back in the catacombs. The century that now closes has afforded to the faith of Israel and of Christ no honor, and to the Israelite and to the Christian no respect by reason of loyalty to that vocation. Christianity outlived communism in the USSR and its colonies. At the sacrifice of home and property, even at the price of life itself, Israel resisted the world's corrosive insistence that Israel cease to exist; Israel has reaffirmed its eternal calling. Whatever the choice of private persons, that social order formed by Israel on the one side, the church of Jesus Christ on the other, has endured, against it all, despite it all, through all time and change. The act of defiance of fate in the certainty of faith in God's ultimate act of grace is the one thing God cannot have commanded, but it is what, in times of terrible stress, Judaic and Christian faithful have given freely and of their own volition. God said, "Serve me," but God could only beseech, "And trust me too."

Not even God can coerce trust. God cannot command love. God can only win trust, earn respect, and—so Scripture says on nearly every page—yearn for our love. We, humanity to whom knowledge of God has been vouchsafed, play the principal role in the divine-human transaction. That is why eternal, holy Israel and the church could give what God could only ask but not compel: the gifts of the heart, love and trust, given freely. And that is what Israel, in response to Sinai, and Christendom, in response to the empty tomb, willingly gave, and by their loyal persistence freely give today. These facts of human devotion tell us the power of the faiths that in these pages meet for a theological comparison. The stakes then are very high indeed.

Part One

~

COMMUNION WITH GOD

~

1

Meeting God in the Torah

JACOB NEUSNER

Theology is not philosophy, and philosophy is not a substitute for religious convictions. But whereas religion can exist without philosophy, and philosophy without religion, theology cannot exist without recourse to each of the other two. It rationally reflects on questions arising in pre-theological religious experience and the discourse of faith; and it is the rationality of its reflective labor in the process of faith seeking understanding which inseparably links it with philosophy. For philosophy is essentially concerned with argument and the attempt to solve conceptual problems, and conceptual problems face theology in all areas of its reflective labors.
Ingolf U. Dalferth, *Theology and Philosophy* [1]

IN JUDAISM, we commune with God by studying the Torah, which is God's self-manifestation, set forth in God's own language and wording. So we begin our dialogue with the fundamental issue of theology: how we know God. The answer, for Judaism, is that we meet God in the Torah. That is where God speaks to us, and, therefore, it is where we learn whatever we are ever going to know about God. But that is a great deal. The language of the Torah portrays the language of God: all the words of God we have. We meet God in the intellectual labor of finding the rules that form of words sentences, of sentences coherent thoughts, and of coherent thoughts, the sum of God's mind so far as in the Torah we know and gain access to it. In the intelligent reading of the Torah we meet God; in the rules of reading we uncover the theology of Judaism. The logic of God—the theology of Judaism—that affords knowledge that

15

God has manifested, then, consists in identifying the Torah's hermeneutics and articulating its principles in accessible, theological language.

We can understand the Torah, God's Word in God's own words, because our minds and God's mind work in the same way, ours being "in [God's] image, after [God's] likeness." Since we think in accord with the same categories and rules, we can understand one another; since the rules of reasoning that dictate what is rational to God govern our minds as well, we can communicate, and in a very exact sense indeed. "Our sages of blessed memory"—the saints who wrote down the originally oral Torah—do not concede that the Author's original meaning and intent cannot be recapitulated. They maintain, to the contrary, that the very language used, on the one side, and the character of the document, on the other, together afford ready access to the divine Author's wording, therefore to God's original meaning and intent. Sages begin with the firm conviction that they know that meaning because they know how to find it out. When we follow them from their reading upward to the rules that manifestly govern that reading, and when we then recapitulate those rules in the setting not of reading but of believing—the implications for knowledge of the mind of God, the modes of thought of God, the rationality of God—then through God's self-manifestation in the Torah we know God. Or, more to the point, we know whatever it is about God that God wishes us to know. From the fact that God gave the Torah, all things flow. To the fact that God gave the Torah, all things return.

Theology in Hebrew Scriptures

The method of that theology of Judaism was to speak by indirection, through hermeneutics to convey reasoned and coherent knowledge of God. The first principle, then, was: God is made manifest in the Torah. Then what is the Torah and how is it to be read? The answer is to be found in the hermeneutics of pure rationality that guide the right reading of the Torah, written and oral, Scripture and the Mishnah in concrete terms. A clear definition of theology is required at the outset. For that purpose we reverse the elements of the definition provided by Dalferth at the head of this chapter. The predicate becomes the subject: Where we have rational reflection on questions arising in religious experience and the discourse of faith, there we have theology. When we find reflective labor on the rationality—the cogency, harmony, proposition, coherence, balance, order, and proper composition—of statements of religious truth, of truth revealed by God, then we have identified a theological writing. And, as a matter of acknowledged fact, the Talmud forms the sustained, rigorous, open-ended activity of rational reflection on the sense and near-at-hand significance of the Torah.

That writing is characterized by concern with argument and the attempt to solve conceptual problems. By themselves, of course, these traits do not mark a writing as theological. Argument concerning conceptual problems yields theology when the argument deals with religion, when the conceptual problems derive from revelation. Only the source of the givens of the writing—revelation, not merely reasoned analysis of this world's givens—distinguishes theology from philosophy, including philosophy of religion. But that suffices. Take for example that splendid formulation of religion as philosophy, the Mishnah.

The Mishnah states its principles through the method of natural history, sifting the traits of this-worldly things, demonstrating philosophical truth—the unity of one and unique God at the apex of the natural world—by showing on the basis of the evidence of this world, universally accessible, the hierarchical classification of being. That is a philosophical demonstration of religious truth. The Talmud of Babylonia states its principles through right reasoning about revealed truth, the Torah. The Torah (written or oral) properly read teaches the theological truth that God is one, at the apex of the hierarchy of all being. That is a theological re-presentation of (the same) religious truth. But that representation in the two Talmuds (and in the Midrash compilations, not treated here) also exhibits the traits of philosophical thinking: rigor, concern for harmonies, unities, consistencies, points of cogency, sustained argument and counterargument, appeal to persuasion through reason rather than coercion through revelation.

That explains how and why, for Judaism in its classical, Talmudic statement, the methods of philosophy applied to the data of religious belief and behavior produced theology. By these criteria deriving from propositions of general intelligibility, I maintain that the second of the two Talmuds, the Talmud of Babylonia, formed a massive and sustained work of theology, in which the method of philosophy shapes the message of religion into a restatement characterized by rationality and integrity. Through that second Talmud in particular Judaism states its theology. Because of the distinctive character of that Talmud, the power of its modes of analytical inquiry, that theology defined the intellect of Judaism: the Torah for generations to come.

Let me explain the specific, historical, and literary terms I have used. We start with the end product, the Torah as defined at the end of the formation of Judaism. That Torah, called in due course "the one whole Torah of Moses, our rabbi," was formulated and transmitted by God to Moses in two media, each defining one of the components, written and oral. The written Torah is Scripture as we know it, encompassing the Pentateuch, Prophets, and Writings. The oral part of the Torah came to be written down in a variety of works, beginning with the Mishnah, ca. 200 C.E. The canon of the Judaism the theology of which is described here is made up of extensions and amplifications of these two parts of the Torah. The written part is carried forward through collections of readings of verses of Scripture called Midrash compilations. The oral part is extended through two sustained, selective commentaries and expansions, called Talmuds, the Talmud of the Land of Israel, also known as the Yerushalmi (ca. 400 C.E.), and the Talmud of Babylonia, also known as the Bavli (ca. 600 C.E.).

The second Talmud's distinctive hermeneutics, which contains within itself the theology of the Judaism of the dual Torah, is exposed not in so many words but in page-by-page repetition. It is not articulated but constantly (even tediously) instantiated; we are then supposed to draw our own conclusions. The unique voice of the Talmud, which bears that hermeneutic, speaks with full confidence of being heard and understood, and that voice is right—we never can miss the point. For the hermeneutic itself—insistence on the presence of philosophy behind jurisprudence, law behind laws, total harmony among premises of discrete and diverse cases pointing to the unique and harmonious character of all existence, social and natural—properly understood, bears the theological message of the unity of intellect, the integrity of truth.

As the Mishnah had demonstrated the hierarchical classification of all natural being, pointing at the apex to the One above, so the second Talmud demonstrated the unity of the principles set forth in the Torah. The upshot is that Judaism would set forth the religion that defined how humanity was formed "in [God's] image, after [God's] likeness," not to begin with but day by day: in the rules of intellect, the character of mind. We can be like God because we can think the way God thinks, and the natural powers of reason carry us upward to the supernatural origin of the integrity of truth. That sentence sums up the theological consequence of the Talmud's hermeneutics. The place where God and humanity meet, therefore, is in the Talmud above all: the place in which the entire Torah is set forth in a manner fully accessible to the shared rationality of God and humanity.

The Talmud of Babylonia therefore forms the pinnacle and the summa—what we mean when we speak of "Judaism"—because from the time of its closure to the present day it defined not only Judaic dogma and its theological formulation but also Judaic discourse that carried that dogma through to formulation in compelling form. The entire documentary heritage of the first six centuries of the Common Era was recast in that Talmud. And that body of writing was itself a recapitulation of important elements of the Hebrew Scriptures and in its basic views indistinguishable in theological and legal character from elements of the Pentateuch's and Prophets' convictions and requirements. Scripture itself ("the written Torah") would reach coming generations not only as read in the synagogue on the Sabbath and festivals, but also, and especially, as recast and expounded in the Talmud in the schoolhouses and courts of the community of Judaism. That re-presentation was accomplished through one medium: a governing, definitive hermeneutics, the result of applied logic and practical reason when framed in terms of the rules of reading a received and holy book.

Since the Talmud sets forth its entire composition as a commentary to the Mishnah, and since the Mishnah itself is a philosophical law code, the vast legal system of the Judaism of the dual Torah served as the theological statement of Judaism. All contemporary expositions of the theology of the Judaism of the dual Torah recapitulate that fact, insisting that it is in the Talmud that theological norms, extending not only to right thought but also right action and therefore to matters of law or halakhah as much as of faith or aggadah, come to full expression. The halakhah, the faith lived in deeds, as much as the aggadah, the faith expressed in attitudes and sentiments and conveyed by words, began in the Talmud and appealed to the Talmud. For the most part, therefore, the systematic and cogent statement of Judaism would take a form scarcely accessible to those to whom the Talmud was alien, since the modes of thought and the media of discourse—dialectical, analytical argument concerning the harmonization of discrete principles—rested upon, and constantly referred to, the norms set forth in the Talmud.

Idiom Alien to Language of Philosophy

Expressing its theology only in the adumbration of hermeneutics, Judaism did not put forth theological statements in the idiom and media familiar to its monotheistic companions, Christianity and Islam. That mode of expression had the advantage of allowing the faithful to draw their own conclusions through their own intellects; they could not err or fall into schism or heresy, since they read the Torah as the Talmud defined the Torah and they explicated the Torah following the signals given by the Talmud for the reconstitution (re-presentation) of the reading and interpretation of the Torah. But it had the disadvantage of not bringing to clear and articulated propositional formulation the truths of the Torah; too much was left unsaid.

The problem was not that Judaism lacked systematization and philosophical grounding of its religious convictions, such as theology in propositional form as well as in argument provides for Islam and Christianity. The Talmud provides such a systematization and philosophical grounding: that on every page defined its authors' purpose, and that is what they accomplished. The problem rather was that the modes of theological discourse proved particular and did not correspond to the more accessible ones familiar in the other two heirs of the Greco-Roman intellectual traditions. All three drew upon the received philosophical heritage of the Greco-Roman tradition, whether Aristotelian or Platonic. But while Christianity and Islam adhered to the categorical structure of the received philosophy and explicitly accommodated themselves to its method and discipline, the Judaic heirs spoke in an idiom quite alien to the generalizing language of philosophy, even while exploring profoundly philosophical issues.

As a result, the philosophical character of the Mishnah's program does not enjoy the recognition that the counterpart thought and expression in Christian and Muslim theology do. Discourse in an openly and blatantly philosophical mode—that is, freestanding, not exegetical in form; generalizing, not particular to cases; yielding unarticulated principles of a philosophical character in agenda—would not enter into the theology of Judaism for centuries after the formation of the Talmud. Because of the nature of revelation in Judaism—the Torah alone as unique and final—theology in Judaism would insist for a very long time upon exegetical form, on the one side, and hermeneutical character of expression, on the other: always cases, rarely generalizations, and never articulated abstract principles, except when right thinking produced knowledge of precisely those principles of high abstraction that conveyed the integrity of truth.

What accounts for the particularity of the medium chosen by the theology of Judaism? The answer is clear from what has already been said. Since, for Judaism, the task of theology was to define and explain the Torah, because God was made manifest solely in the Torah by God's own action, hermeneutics formed the correct medium of expression. It was through guiding the reading of the Torah, beginning with the definition of canon (in secular language) that reasoned inquiry into faith would go forward, and that was at the first (but only at the first) step a hermeneutical task. By contrast, Christianity knew God through the person of Jesus Christ, God incarnate. The Bible recorded the faith, but it is to be distinguished, in its place and function in Christianity (of all kinds) from the Torah; the Torah dictated by God to Moses at Sinai formed the sole and exhaustive account of everything that God wished to tell humanity. True, the person of the sage as much as the oral and written components of the Torah formed the medium of conveying the whole Torah of Sinai. But that is a generic claim concerning the sage, not the specific claim concerning Jesus Christ that the church put forth. So while alike, the media prove profoundly different in conception and expression. The person of Christ, not the Bible, formed the counterpart. So the church, the living body of Christ, and the tradition that it preserved, as much as the Bible, carried the burden of the faith. The Bible did not, and could not, be represented as the sole and exhaustive account of Christ. Other media for theological discourse stood side by side with the exegetical ones, and hermeneutics formed the child of theology, not its father, as was the case for Judaism.

The Flow of Dialectical Argument

Of precisely what elements, thought and expression alike, did this theology expressed through hermeneutics consist? Where and how do we identify its principal formulation? And what is the theological statement made through the hermeneutics at hand? The answer is, through a particular mode of argument, the dialectical kind. There the true encounter with God takes place: God and humanity argue in accord with the same rules of thought about the same principles applied to the same cases.

Dialectical argument—the movement of thought through contentious challenge and passionate response, initiative and counterploy—characterizes the Talmud of Babylonia in particular, but finds a limited place in other Rabbinic documents as well. A definition of that trait of important writings therefore is called for. The dialectical, or moving, argument is important because, in the sustained conflict provoked by the testing of proposition in contention, argument turns fact into truth. Making a point forms of data important propositions. The exchanges of propositions and arguments, objects and ripostes, hold together, however protracted. While the Talmud of Babylonia forms the principal arena for dialectics in Rabbinic literature, the same mode of thinking and writing also occurs elsewhere in the halakic literature, from the Mishnah onward to the Talmud of the Land of Israel. But all of our cases will derive from the Bavli.

Dialectical means moving or developing an idea through questions and answers, sometimes implicit, but commonly explicit. What "moves" is the flow of argument and thought, from problem to problem. The movement is generated specifically by the raising of contrary questions and theses. What characterizes the dialectical argument in Rabbinic literature is its meandering, its moving hither and yon. It is not a direct or straight-line movement, not simply thesis, antithesis, synthesis. Rather, the Rabbinic dialectical argument—the protracted, sometimes meandering, always moving flow of contentious thought—raises a question and answers it, then raises a question about the answer, and, having raised another question, it gives an answer to that question, and it continues in the same fashion. So it moves hither and yon, flowing across the surface of the document at hand.

Those second and third and fourth turnings differentiate a dialectical from a static argument, much as the bubbles tell the difference between still and sparkling wine. The always-sparkling dialectical argument is one principal means by which the Talmud or other Rabbinic writing accomplishes its goal of showing the connections between this and that, ultimately demonstrating the unity of many "thises and thats." These efforts at describing the argument serve precisely as well as program notes to a piece of music: they tell us what we are going to hear; they cannot play the music.

The dialectical argument opens the possibility of reaching out from one thing to something else, not because people have lost sight of their starting point or their goal in the end, but because they want to encompass, in the analytical argument as it gets under way, as broad and comprehensive a range of cases and rules as they possibly can. The movement from point to point in reference to a single point that accurately describes the dialectical argument reaches upward toward a goal of proximate abstraction, leaving behind the specificities not only of cases but of laws. It carries us upward to the law that governs many cases, the premises that undergird many rules, and still higher to the principles that infuse diverse premises; then we reach the principles that generate other, unrelated premises, which, in turn, come to expression in other, still-less intersecting cases. The meandering course of argument comes to an end when we have shown how things cohere.

The passage that we consider here occurs at the Babylonian Talmud Baba Mesia 5B–6A, which is to say, Talmud to Mishnah Baba Mesia 1:1-2. Our interest is in the twists and turns of the argument and what is at stake in the formation of a continuous and unfolding composition:

> [5B] IV.1.A.   This one takes an oath that he possesses no less a share of it than half, [and that one takes an oath that he possesses no less a share of it than half, and they divide it up]:

The rule of the Mishnah, which is cited at the head of the sustained discussion, concerns the case of two persons who find a garment. We settle their conflicting claim by requiring each to take an oath that he or she owns title to no less than half of the garment, and then we split the garment between them.

Our first question is one of text criticism: analysis of the Mishnah-paragraph's word choice. We say that the oath concerns the portion that the claimant alleges he possesses. But the oath really affects the portion that he does not have in hand at all:

> B.   Is it concerning the portion that he claims he possesses that he takes the oath, or concerning the portion that he does not claim to possess? ["The implication is that the terms of the oath are ambiguous. By swearing that his share in it is not 'less than half,' the claimant might mean that it is not even a third or a fourth (which is 'less than half'), and the negative way of putting it would justify such an interpretation. He could therefore take this oath even if he knew

that he had no share in the garment at all, while he would be swearing falsely if he really had a share in the garment that is less than half, however small that share might be.]

C.   Said R. Huna, "It is that he says, 'By an oath! I possess in it a portion, and I possess in it a portion that is no more than half a share of it.'" [The claimant swears that his share is at least half (Daiches).]

Having asked and answered the question, we now find ourselves in an extension of the argument. The principal trait of the dialectical argument is now before us: (1) but (2) maybe the contrary is the case, so (3) what about—that is, the setting aside of a proposition in favor of its opposite. Here we come to the definitive trait of the dialectic argument: its insistence on challenging every proposal with the claim, "maybe it's the opposite?" This pestering question forces us back upon our sense of self-evidence; it makes us consider the contrary of each position we propose to set forth. It makes thought happen. True, the Talmud's voiced "but"—the whole of the dialectic in one word!—presents a formidable nuisance, but so does all criticism. Only the mature mind will welcome criticism. Dialectics is not for children, politicians, propagandists, or egoists. Genuine curiosity about the truth shown by rigorous logic forms the counterpart to musical virtuosity. So the objection proceeds:

D.   Then let him say, "By an oath! The whole of it is mine!"

Why claim half when the alleged finder may as well demand the whole cloak?

E.   But are we going to give him the whole of it? [Obviously not, there is another claimant, also taking an oath.]

The question contradicts the facts of the case: Two parties claim the cloak, so the outcome can never be that one will get the whole thing.

F.   Then let him say, "By an oath! Half of it is mine!"

Then—by the same reasoning—why claim "no less than half," rather than simply half?

G.   That would damage his own claim [which was that he owned the whole of the cloak, not only half of it].

The claimant does claim the whole cloak, so the proposed language does not serve to replicate his actual claim. That accounts for the language that is specified.

> H.   But here too is it not the fact that, in the oath that he is taking, he impairs his own claim? [After all, he here makes explicit the fact that he owns at least half of it. What happened to the other half?]

The solution merely compounds the problem.

> I.   [Not at all.] For he has said, "The whole of it is mine!" [And, he further proceeds,] "And as to your contrary view, By an oath, I do have a share in it, and that share is no less than half!"

We solve the problem by positing a different solution from the one we suggested at the outset. Why not start where we have concluded? Because if we had done so, we should have ignored a variety of intervening considerations and so should have expounded less than the entire range of possibilities. The power of the dialectical argument now is clear: It forces us to address not the problem and the solution alone, but the problem and the various ways by which a solution may be reached; then, when we do come to a final solution to the question at hand, we have reviewed all of the possibilities. We have seen how everything flows together; nothing is left unattended.

The dialectical argument in the Talmud and in other Rabbinic writings therefore undertakes a different task from the philosophical counterpart. What we have here is not a set piece of two positions, with an analysis of each, such as the staid philosophical dialogue exposes with such elegance; it is, rather, an analytical argument, explaining why this, not that, then why not that but rather this; and so on. When we speak of a moving argument, this is what we mean: it is not static and merely expository, but dynamic and always contentious. It is not an endless argument, an argument for the sake of arguing, or evidence that process but not position is important to the Talmud and other writings that use the dialectics as a principal mode of dynamic argument. To the contrary, the passage is resolved with a decisive conclusion, not permitted to run on.

The dialectical composition proceeds, continuous and coherent from point to point, even as it zigs and zags. We proceed to the second cogent proposition in the analysis of the cited Mishnah-passage, which asks a fresh question: Why an oath at all?

2.   A.   [It is envisioned that each party is holding on to a corner of the cloak, so the question is raised:] Now, since this one is possessed of the cloak and standing right there, and that one is possessed of the cloak and is standing right there, why in the world do I require this oath?

Until now we have assumed as fact the premise of the Mishnah's rule, which is that an oath is to be taken. But why assume so? Surely each party now has what he is going to get. So what defines the point and effect of the oath?

B.   Said R. Yohanan, "This oath [to which our Mishnah-passage refers] happens to be an ordinance imposed only by rabbis,
C.   "so that people should not go around grabbing the cloaks of other people and saying, 'It's mine!'" [But, as a matter of fact, the oath that is imposed in our Mishnah-passage is not legitimate by the law of the Torah. It is an act taken by sages to maintain the social order.]

We do not administer oaths to liars; we do not impose an oath in a case in which we may end up with one of the claimants taking an oath he knows to be untrue. Since one party really does own the cloak, the other really has grabbed it. The proposition solves the problem but hardly is going to settle the question. On the contrary, Yohanan raises more problems than he solves. So we ask how we can agree to an oath in this case at all:

D.   But why then not advance the following argument: since such a one is suspect as to fraud in a property claim, he also should be suspect as to fraud in oath-taking?

Yohanan places himself in the position of believing in respect to the oath what we will not believe in respect to the claim on the cloak; for, after all, one of the parties before us must be lying! Why sustain such a contradiction: gullible and suspicious at one and the same time?

E.   In point of fact, we do not advance the argument: since such a one is suspect as to fraud in a property claim, he also should be suspect as to fraud in oath-taking, for if you do not concede that fact, then how is it possible that the All-Merciful has ruled, "One who has conceded part of a claim against himself must take an oath as to the remainder of what is subject to claim"?

If someone claims that another party holds property belonging to him or her, and the one to whom the bailment has been handed over for safekeeping, called the bailee, concedes part of the claim, the bailee must then take an oath in respect to the rest of the claimed property, that is, the part that the bailee maintains does not belong to the claimant at all. So the law itself—the Torah, in fact—has sustained the same contradiction. That fine solution, of course, is going to be challenged:

> F.   Why not simply maintain, since such a one is suspect as to fraud in a property claim, he also should be suspect as to fraud in oath-taking?
> G.   In that other case, [the reason for the denial of part of the claim and the admission of part is not the intent to commit fraud, but rather,] the defendant is just trying to put off the claim for a spell.

We could stop at this point without losing a single important point of interest; everything is before us. One of the striking traits of the large-scale dialectical composition is its composite character. Starting at the beginning, without any loss of meaning or sense, we could stop at the end of any given paragraph. But the dialectics insists on moving forward, exploring, pursuing, insisting; and were we to remove a paragraph in the middle of a dialectical composite, all that follows would become incomprehensible. That is a mark of the dialectical argument: sustained, continuous, and coherent, yet perpetually in control and capable of resolving matters at any single point.

Now, having fully exposed the topic, its problem, and its principles, we take a tangent indicated by the character of the principle before us: when a person will or will not lie or take a false oath. We have a theory on the matter; what we now do is expound the theory, with special reference to the formulation of that theory in explicit terms by a named authority:

> H.   This concurs with the position of Rabbah. [For Rabbah has said, "On what account has the Torah imposed the requirement of an oath on one who confesses to only part of a claim against him? It is by reason of the presumption that a person will not insolently deny the truth about the whole of a loan in the very presence of the creditor and so entirely deny the debt. He will admit to part of the

debt and deny part of it. Hence we invoke an oath in a case in which one does so, to coax out the truth of the matter."]

I.   For you may know, [in support of the foregoing], that R. Idi bar Abin said R. Hisda [said]: "He who [falsely] denies owing money on a loan nonetheless is suitable to give testimony, but he who denies that he holds a bailment for another party cannot give testimony."

The proposition is now fully exposed. A named authority is introduced, who will concur in the proposed theoretical distinction. He sets forth an extralogical consideration, which the law always will welcome; the rational goal of finding the truth overrides the technicalities of the law governing the oath.

Predictably, we cannot allow matters to stand without challenge, and the challenge comes at a fundamental level, with the predictable give-and-take to follow:

J.   But what about that which R. Ammi bar Hama repeated on Tannaite authority: "[If they are to be subjected to an oath,] four sorts of bailees have to have denied part of the bailment and conceded part of the bailment, namely, the unpaid bailee, the borrower, the paid bailee, and the one who rents."

K.   Why not simply maintain, since such a one is suspect as to fraud in a property claim, he also should be suspect as to fraud in oath-taking?

L.   In that case as well, [the reason for the denial of part of the claim and the admission of part is not the intent to commit fraud, but rather,] the defendant is just trying to put off the claim for a spell.

M.   He reasons as follows: "I'm going to find the thief and arrest him." Or: "I'll find [the beast] in the field and return it to the owner."

Once more, "if that is the case" provokes yet another analysis; we introduce a different reading of the basic case before us, another reason that we should not impose an oath:

N.   If that is the case, then why should one who denies holding a bailment ever be unsuitable to give testimony? Why don't we just maintain that the defendant is just trying to put off the claim for a spell. He reasons as follows: "I'm going to look for the thing and find it."

O.   When in point of fact we do rule, He who denies hold-

ing a bailment is unfit to give testimony, it is in a case in which witnesses come and give testimony against him that at that very
moment, the bailment is located in the bailee's domain, and he fully
is informed of that fact, or, alternatively, he has the object in his possession at that very moment.

The solution to the problem at hand also provides the starting point for
yet another step in the unfolding exposition. Huna has given us a different resolution of matters. That accounts for No. 3, and No. 4 is also predictable:

> 3.   A.   But as to that which R. Huna has said [when we have a
> bailee who offers to pay compensation for a lost bailment rather
> than swear it has been lost, since he wishes to appropriate the article
> by paying for it, (Daiches)], "They impose upon him the oath that
> the bailment is not in his possession at all,"
>
> B.   why not in that case invoke the principle, since such a
> one is suspect as to fraud in a property claim, he also should be sus-
> pect as to fraud in oath-taking?
>
> C.   In that case also, he may rule in his own behalf, I'll give
> him the money.
>
> 4.   A.   Said R. Aha of Difti to Rabina, "But then the man clearly
> transgresses the negative commandment: 'You shall not covet.'"
>
> B.   "You shall not covet" is generally understood by people
> to pertain to something for which one is not ready to pay.

Yet another authority's position now is invoked, and it draws us back to
our starting point: the issue of why we think an oath is suitable in a case
in which we ought to assume lying is going on. Our return to our starting point comes via a circuitous route:

> 5.   A. [6A]   But as to that which R. Nahman said, "They impose
> upon him [who denies the whole of a claim] an oath of induce-
> ment," why not in that case invoke the principle, since such a one is
> suspect as to fraud in a property claim, he also should be suspect as
> to fraud in oath-taking?
>
> B.   And furthermore, there is that which R. Hiyya taught on
> Tannaite authority: "Both parties [employee, supposed to have
> been paid out of an account set up by the employer at a local store,
> and storekeeper] take an oath and collect what each claims from the
> employer," why not in that case invoke the principle, since such a
> one is suspect as to fraud in a property claim, he also should be sus-
> pect as to fraud in oath-taking?

C.   And furthermore, there is that which R. Sheshet said, "We impose upon an unpaid bailee [who claims that the animal has been lost] three distinct oaths: first, an oath that I have not deliberately caused the loss, that I did not put a hand on it, and that it is not in my domain at all," why not in that case invoke the principle, since such a one is suspect as to fraud in a property claim, he also should be suspect as to fraud in oath-taking?

We now settle the matter:

D.   It must follow that we do not invoke the principle at all, since such a one is suspect as to fraud in a property claim, he also should be suspect as to fraud in oath-taking.

What is interesting is why walk so far to end up where we started. Do we invoke said principle? No, we do not. What we have accomplished on our wanderings is a survey of opinion on a theme, to be sure, but opinion that intersects at our particular problem. The moving argument serves to carry us hither and yon; its power is to demonstrate that all considerations are raised, all challenges met, all possibilities explored. This is not, as I said, merely a set-piece argument, where we have proposition, evidence, analysis, conclusion. It is a different sort of thinking altogether, purposive and coherent, but also comprehensive and compelling for its admission of possibilities and attention to alternatives.

Religious Encounter in Worldly Form

What then is at stake in the dialectical argument? I see three complementary results. All of them, in my view, prove commensurate to the effort required to follow these protracted, sometimes tedious disquisitions.

First, we test every allegation by a counterproposition, so serving the cause of truth through challenge and constant checking for flaws in an argument.

Second, we survey the entire range of possibilities, which leaves no doubts about the cogency of our conclusion.

Third, quite to the point, by the give-and-take of argument, we are enabled to go through the thought processes set forth in the subtle markings that yield our reconstruction of the argument. We not only review what people say, but how they think: the processes of reasoning that have yielded a given conclusion. Sages and disciples become party to the modes of thought; in the dialectical argument, they are required to replicate the thought processes themselves. This is the point at which the encounter of God and humanity takes over. By making ourselves party not only to the conclusion but to the mode of argument, we enter into those transactions concerning what is rational that flow from the Torah; we find our way into the processes of reasoning that are God's as revealed in the Torah.

While deeply religious in context, the encounter takes a worldly form. Let me give a single example of the power of the dialectical argument to expose the steps in thinking that lead from one end to another: principle to ruling, or ruling to principle. In the present instance, the only one we require to see a perfectly routine and obvious procedure, we mean to prove the point that if people are permitted to obstruct the public way, if damage was done by them, they are liable to pay compensation. First, we are going to prove that general point on the basis of a single case. Then we shall proceed to show how a variety of authorities, dealing with diverse cases, sustain the same principle.

Babylonian Talmud Baba Mesia 10:5/O–X

O.   He who brings out his manure to the public domain—

P.   while one party pitches it out, the other party must be bringing it in to manure his field.

Q.   They do not soak clay in the public domain,

R.   and they do not make bricks.

S.   And they knead clay in the public way,

T.   but not bricks.

U.   He who builds in the public way—

V.   while one party brings stones, the builder must make use of them in the public way.

W.   And if one has inflicted injury, he must pay for the damages he has caused.

X.   Rabban Simeon b. Gamaliel says, "Also: He may prepare for doing his work [on site in the public way] for thirty days [before the actual work of building]."

We begin with the comparison of the rule before us with another Tannaite position on the same issue, asking whether an unattributed, therefore authoritative, rule stands for or opposes the position of a given authority; we should hope to prove that the named authority concurs. So one fundamental initiative in showing how many cases express a single principle—the concrete demonstration of the unity of the law—is to find out whether diverse, important authorities concur on the principle, each ruling in a distinctive case; or whether a single authority is consistent in ruling in accord with the principle at hand, as in what follows:

> I.1   A.   May we say that our Mishnah-paragraph does not accord with the view of R. Judah? For it has been taught on Tannaite authority:
>
> B.   R. Judah says, "At the time of fertilizing the fields, a man may take out his manure and pile it up at the door of his house in the public way so that it will be pulverized by the feet of man and beast, for a period of thirty days. For it was on that very stipulation that Joshua caused the Israelites to inherit the land" [Talmud Baba Mesia 11:8E–H].
>
> C.   You may even maintain that he concurs with the Mishnah's rule [that while one party pitches it out, the other party must be bringing it in to manure his field]. R. Judah concedes that if one has caused damage, he is liable to pay compensation.

In line with the position just now proposed, Judah will turn out to rule every which way on the same matter. And that is not an acceptable upshot.

> D.   But has it not been taught in the Mishnah: If the storekeeper had left his lamp outside the storekeeper is liable [if the flame caused a fire]. R. Judah said, "In the case of a lamp for Hanukkah, he is exempt" [Mishnah Baba Qama 6:6E–F], because he has acted under authority. Now surely that must mean, under the authority of the court [and that shows that one is not responsible for damage caused by his property in the public domain if it was there under the authority of the court]!

The dialectic now intervenes. We have made a proposal. Is it a good one? Of course not; were we to give up so quickly, we should gain nothing:

> E.   No, what it means is, on the authority of carrying out one's religious obligations.

By now, the reader is able to predict the next step: "But isn't the contrary more reasonable?" Here is how we raise the objection.

> F.   But has it not been taught on Tannaite authority:
> G.   in the case of all those concerning whom they have said, "They are permitted to obstruct the public way," if there was dam-

age done, one is liable to pay compensation. But R. Judah declares one exempt from having to pay compensation.

H. So it is better to take the view that our Mishnah-paragraph does not concur with the position of R. Judah.

The point of interest has been introduced: whether those permitted to obstruct the public way must pay compensation for damages they may cause in so doing. Here is where we find a variety of cases that yield a single principle:

2. A. Said Abayye, "R. Judah, Rabban Simeon b. Gamaliel, and R. Simeon all take the position that in the case of all those concerning whom they have said, 'They are permitted to obstruct the public way,' if there was damage done, one is liable to pay compensation.

B. "As to R. Judah, the matter is just as we have now stated it."

Simeon b. Gamaliel and Simeon now draw us to unrelated cases:

C. "As to Rabban Simeon b. Gamaliel, we have learned in the Mishnah: Rabban Simeon b. Gamaliel says, 'Also: He may prepare for doing his work [on site in the public way] for thirty days [before the actual work of building].'

D. "As to R. Simeon, we have learned in the Mishnah: A person should not set up an oven in a room unless there is a space of four cubits above it. If he was setting it up in the upper story, there has to be a layer of plaster under it three handbreadths thick, and in the case of a stove, a handbreadth thick. And if it did damage, the owner of the oven has to pay for the damage. R. Simeon says, 'All of these measures have been stated only so that if the object did damage, the owner is exempt from paying compensation if the stated measures have been observed'" [Mishnah Baba Batra 2:2A–F].

We see then that the demonstration of the unity of the law and the issue of who stands (or does not stand) behind a given rule go together. When we ask who does or does not stand behind a rule, we ask about the principle of a case, which leads us downward to a premise, and we forthwith point to how that same premise underlies a different principle yielding a case—so how can X hold the view he does, if that is his premise, since at a different case he makes a point with a principle that rests on a contradictory premise? The Mishnah and the Talmud are comparable to the moraine left by the last ice age, fields studded with boulders. For the Talmud, reference is made to those many disputes that litter the pages and impede progress. That explains why much of the Talmud is taken up not only with sorting out disputes, but also with showing their rationality. Reasonable people have perfectly valid reasons for disagreeing about a given point, since both parties share the same premises but apply them differently; or they really do not differ at all, since one party deals with one set of circumstances, the other with a different set of circumstances.

The Unity of Laws in Law: God's Unity

At issue in the meeting with God in the processes of intellect, however, is not process alone or principally, but proposition. The dialectical argument aims at proving a point, not merely playing a game. The dialectical argument proves the ideal medium for the assertion, through sustained demonstration, of the union of laws in law. It is the way in which, in our minds, we undergo the demonstration (and the experience) of God's unity and the unity of all being in God and through God. This takes the form of the demonstration of the wholeness and coherence of the laws of life: the social, historical, and natural rules that describe how things really are.

Specifically, if all we know is laws, then we want to find out: What is at stake in them? Accordingly, the true issues of the law emerge from the detailed rulings of the laws. Generalization takes a variety of forms, some yielding a broader framework into which to locate a case, others a proposition of consequence. Let me give an obvious and familiar instance of what is to be done. Here is an example of a case that yields a principle:

Talmud Baba Mesia to 9:11

A. (1) A day worker collects his wage any time of the night.

B. (2) And a night worker collects his wage any time of the day.

C. (3) A worker by the hour collects his wage any time of the night or day.

I.1 A. Our rabbis have taught on Tannaite authority:

B. How on the basis of Scripture do we know, A day worker collects his wage any time of the night?

C.   "[You shall not oppress your neighbor or rob him.] The wages of a hired servant shall not remain with you all night until the morning" (Lev. 19:13).

D.   And how on the basis of Scripture do we know, and a night worker collects his wage any time of the day?

E.   "[You shall not oppress a hired servant who is poor and needy] . . . you shall give him his hire on the day on which he earns it, before the sun goes down" (Deut. 23:14-15).

F.   Might I say that the reverse is the case [the night worker must be paid during the night that he does the work, in line with Lev. 19:13, and the day worker by day, in line with Deut. 23:15]?

G.   Wages are to be paid only at the end of the work [so the fee is not payable until the work has been done].

What do we learn from this passage? Specifically, two points:

1. Scripture yields the rule at hand;
2. Scripture also imposes limits on the formation of the law; but one generalization, that the law of the Mishnah derives from the source of Scripture.

If we take a small step beyond this, we learn that the two parts of the Torah are one. The hermeneutics instructs us to ask: How on the basis of Scripture do we know. . . ? Its premise then is that Scripture forms the basis for rules not expressed with verses of the written Torah. The theological principle conveyed in the hermeneutics expressed in the case is that the Torah is one and encompasses both the oral and the written parts; the oral part derives its truths from the written part.

If I had to identify the single most important theological point that the Talmud and other writings that use dialectics set forth, it is this: The laws yield law; the truth exhibits integrity, all of the parts—the details, principles, and premises—holding together in a coherent manner. To understand how generalizations are attained, however, we cannot deal only with generalizations. So we turn to a specific problem of category formation: namely, in the transfer of property, whether we distinguish between a sale and a gift. In both instances property is transferred, but the conditions of transfer clearly differ; in the one case there is a quid pro quo, in the other, not. Does that distinction make a difference? The answer to that question will have implications for a variety of concrete cases; for example, transfers of property in a dowry, divisions of inheritances and estates, the required documents and procedures for effecting transfer of title. If, then, we know the correct category formation, we form a generalization that will draw together numerous otherwise unrelated cases and (more to the point) rules.

One way to accomplish the goal is to identify the issue behind a dispute; this leads us from the dispute to the principle that is established and confirmed by the dispute on details—that is, whether the principle applies, and, if it does, how it does. In this way we affirm the unity of the law by establishing that all parties to a dispute really agree on the same point; then the dispute itself underlines the law's coherence:

Talmud Baba Batra 1:3

> A. He whose [land] surrounds that of his fellow on three sides,
>
> B. and who made a fence on the first, second, and third sides
>
> C. they do not require [the other party to share in the expense of building the walls].
>
> D. R. Yosé says, "If he built a fence on the fourth side, they assign to him [his share in the case of] all [three other fences]."

In the following dispute, we ask what is subject to dispute between the two named authorities, B–C.

> 2. A. It has been stated:
>
> B. R. Huna said, "All is proportional to the actual cost of building the fence [Simon: which will vary according to the materials used by the one who builds the fence]."
>
> C. Hiyya bar Rab said, "All is proportionate to the cost of a cheap fence made of sticks [since that is all that is absolutely necessary]."

To find the issue, we revert to our Mishnah-rule. The opinions therein guide the disputing parties. Each then has to account for what is subject to dispute in the Mishnah-paragraph. The point is that the Mishnah's dispute is not only rational, it also rests upon a shared premise, affirmed by all parties. That is the power of D:

> D. We have learned in the Mishnah: He whose [land] surrounds that of his fellow on three sides, and who made a fence on the first, second, and third sides—they do not require [the other

party to share in the expense of building the walls]. Lo, if he fences the fourth side too, he must contribute to the cost of the entire fence. But then note what follows: R. Yosé says, "If he built a fence on the fourth side, they assign to him [his share in the case of] all [three other fences]." Now there is no problem from the perspective of R. Huna, who has said, "All is proportional to the actual cost of building the fence [Simon: which will vary according to the materials used by the one who builds the fence]." Then we can identify what is at issue between the first authority and R. Yosé. Specifically, the initial authority takes the view that we proportion the costs to what they would be if a cheap fence of sticks was built, but not to what the fence-builder actually spent, and R. Yosé maintains that under all circumstances, the division is proportional to actual costs. But from the perspective of Hiyya bar Rab, who has said, "All is proportionate to the cost of a cheap fence made of sticks [since that is all that is absolutely necessary]," what can be the difference between the ruling of the initial Tannaite authority and that of R. Yosé? If, after all, he does not pay him even the cost of building a cheap fence, what in the world is he supposed to pay off as his share?

We now revert to the dialectics, but a different kind. Here we raise a variety of possibilities, not as challenges and responses in a sequence, but as freestanding choices; the same goal is at hand, the opportunity to examine every possibility. But the result is different: not a final solution but four suitable ones, yielding the notion that a single principle governs a variety of cases. That explains why we now have a set of four answers, all of them converging on the same principle:

> E.   If you want, I shall say that what is at issue between them is the fee to be paid for a watchman. The initial authority holds that he pays the cost of a watchman, not the charge of building a cheap fence, and R. Yosé says that he has to pay the cost of building a cheap fence.
>
> F.   But if you prefer, I may say that at issue between them is the first, second, and third sides, in which instance the initial Tannaite authority has the other pay only the cost of fencing the fourth side, not the first three, and R. Yosé maintains he has to pay his share of the cost of fencing the first three sides too.
>
> G.   And if you prefer, I shall maintain that at issue between them is whether the fence has to be built by the owner of the surrounding fields or the owner of the enclosed field if the latter pays the cost of the whole. The initial Tannaite authority says that the

consideration that leads the owner of the enclosed field to have to contribute at all is that he went ahead and built the fourth fence, so he has to pay his share of the cost of the whole; but if the owner of the surrounding fields is the one who went ahead and did it, the other has to pay only the share of the fourth fence. For his part, R. Yosé takes the position that there is no distinction between who took the initiative in building the fourth fence, whether the owner of the enclosed field or the owner of the surrounding field. In either case the former has to pay the latter his share of the whole.

H.   There are those who say, in respect to this last statement, that at issue between them is whether the fourth fence has to be built by the owner of the enclosed field or the surrounding fields so that the former has to contribute his share. The initial Tannaite authority holds that, even if the owner of the surrounding fields makes the fourth fence, the other has to contribute to the cost, and R. Yosé maintains that if the owner of the enclosed field takes it on himself to build the fourth fence, he has to pay his share of the cost of the whole, because through his action he has shown that he wants the fence, but if the owner of the surrounding fields builds the fourth side, the other pays not a penny [since he can say he never wanted a fence to begin with].

The premise of E is that the owner of the land on the inside has a choice as to the means of guarding his field, but he bears responsibility for the matter. F agrees that he bears responsibility for his side, but adds that he also is responsible for the sides from which he enjoys benefit. G concurs that the owner of the inner field is responsible to protect his own property. H takes the same view. What we have accomplished is, first, to lay a foundation in rationality for the dispute of the Mishnah-paragraph; and, further, to demonstrate that all parties to the dispute affirm the responsibility to pay one's share of that from which one benefits. Justice means "no free lunch."

Quest for Consensus and Rationality of Dispute

Thus far we have shown how the laws of the Torah are coherent. In what follows, the unity of the law extends from agreements behind disputes to a more fundamental matter: identifying the single principle behind many, diverse cases. What do diverse cases have in common?

Along these same lines, that same hermeneutics wants us to show how diverse authorities concur on the same principle, dealing with diverse cases; how where there is a dispute, the dispute represents schism versus consensus, with the weight of argument and evidence favoring consensus; where we have a choice between interpreting an opinion as schismatic and as coherent with established rule, we try to show it is not schismatic; and so on. All of these commonplace activities pursue a single goal: to limit the range of schism and expand the range of consensus, both in political, personal terms of authority and, more to the point, in the framework of case and principle. If I had to identify a single hermeneutical principle that governs throughout, it is the quest for harmony, consensus, unity, and, above all, the rationality of dispute: reasonable disagreement about the pertinence or relevance of established, universally affirmed principles.

Here is a fine instance of the working of the hermeneutics that tells us to read the texts as a single coherent statement, episodic and unrelated cases as statements of a single principle. The principle is: It is forbidden for someone to derive uncompensated benefit from somebody else's property. That self-evidently valid principle of equity—"Thou shalt not steal" writ small—then emerges from a variety of cases; the cases are read as illustrative. The upshot of demonstrating that fact is to prove a much-desired goal. The law of the Torah—here, the written Torah, one of the Ten Commandments no less!—contains within itself the laws of everyday life. So one thing yields many things; the law is coherent in God's mind, and retains that coherence as it expands to encompass the here and now of the social order. The details as always are picayune, the logic practical, the reasoning concrete and applied; but the stakes prove cosmic in a literal sense of the word. The problem involves a two-story house, owned by the resident of the lower story. The house has fallen down. The upstairs tenant has nowhere to live. The landlord does not rebuild the house. The tenant has the right to rebuild the downstairs part of the house and to live there as long as the landlord has not completed the rebuilding of the house and also has not refunded to the tenant the cost of rebuilding the part that the tenant has reconstructed for himself. Judah rejects this ruling, and, in doing so, invokes a general principle, by no means limited to the case at hand. Then the Bavli will wish to show how this governing principle pertains elsewhere.

Mishnah-tractate Baba Mesia 10:3
and Talmud Baba Mesia 117A–B

A.   A house and an upper story belonging to two people which fell down—

B.   [if] the resident of the upper story told the householder [of the lower story] to rebuild,

C.   but he does not want to rebuild,

D.   lo, the resident of the upper story rebuilds the lower story and lives there,

E.   until the other party compensates him for what he has spent.

F.   R. Judah says, "Also: [if so,] this one is [then] living in his fellow's [housing]. [So in the end] he will have to pay him rent.

G.   "But the resident of the upper story builds both the house and the upper room,

H.   "and he puts a roof on the upper story,

I.   "and he lives in the lower story,

J.   "until the other party compensates him for what he has spent."

At issue is a principle that settles the case at hand: whether one may gratuitously derive benefit from someone else's property. We shall now show that Judah repeatedly takes that position in a variety of diverse cases:

I.1   A.   [117B]   Said R. Yohanan, "In three passages R. Judah has repeated for us the rule that it is forbidden for someone to derive benefit from somebody's else's property. The first is in the Mishnah-passage at hand. The next is in that which we have learned in the Mishnah."

The case that is now introduced involves an error in dyeing wool. The premise of the rulings is that dyeing always enhances the value of wool, whether it is dyed one color or another. On that basis, the following is quite clear:

B.   He who gave wool to a dyer to dye it red, and he dyed it black, or to dye it black, and he dyed it red—

C.   R. Meir says, "The dyer pays him back the value of his wool."

D.   And R. Judah says, "If the increase in value is greater than the outlay for the process of dyeing, the owner pays him back for the outlay for the process of dyeing. And if the outlay for the process of dyeing is greater than the increase in the value of the wool, the owner pays him [the dyer] only the increase in the value of the wool" [Mishnah Baba Qama 9:4G–K].

E.   And what is the third? It is as we have learned in the Mishnah:

F.   He who paid part of a debt that he owed and deposited the bond that has been written as evidence covering the remaining sum with a third party, and said to him, "If I have not given you what I still owe the lender between now and such-and-such a date, give the creditor his bond of indebtedness," if the time came and he has not paid,

G.   R. Yosé says, "He should hand it over."

H.   And R. Judah says, "He should not hand it over" [Mishnah Baba Batra 10:5A–E].

I.   Why [does it follow that Judah holds that it is forbidden for someone to derive benefit from somebody else's property]? Perhaps when R. Judah takes the position that he does here, it is only because there is blackening of the walls.

J.   [Freedman: the new house loses its newness because the tenant is living there, so the house owner is sustaining a loss, and that is why the tenant has to pay rent];

K.   as to the case of the dyer who was supposed to dye the wool red but dyed it black, the reason is that he has violated his instructions, and we have learned in the Mishnah:

L.   Whoever changes [the original terms of the agreement]— his hand is on the bottom [Mishnah Baba Mesia 6:2E–F]. [That is to say, the decision must favor the other party, the claim of the one who has changed the original terms being subordinated.]

M.   And as to the third case, the one who has paid part of his debt, here we deal with an enticement, and we infer from this case that R. Judah takes the position that in the case of a come-on, there is no transfer of title.

Yohanan's observation serves the purpose of showing how several unrelated cases of the Mishnah really make the same point: You shall not steal. The voice of the Talmud—that is to say, the dialectics itself—then contributes an objection and its resolution, making Yohanan's statement plausible and compelling, not merely an observation that may or may not be so.

An ideal way of demonstrating the unity of the law is to expose the abstract premise of a concrete rule, and to do so without regard to the number of discrete cases that establish that rule. Here is a case in which the theological principle—that a stipulation may not be made contrary to what is written in the Torah—is shown to form the premise of a concrete case. Then the case once more merely illustrates the principle of the Torah, which delivers its messages in just this way, through exemplary cases. 2.A commences with a common attributive formula, "said X . . . said Y. . . ." This bears the meaning, "said X in the name of Y (and on his authority)." Judah is then the tradent of the opinion or ruling, and Samuel the original source. Such an attributive formula may encompass three or more names and is common in both Talmuds.

> 2.   A.   And said R. Judah said Samuel, "He who says to his fellow, '. . . on the stipulation that the advent of the Seventh Year will not abrogate the debts'—the Seventh Year nonetheless abrogates those debts."
>
> B.   May one then propose that Samuel takes the view that that stipulation represents an agreement made contrary to what is written in the Torah, and, as we know, any stipulation contrary to what is written in the Torah is a null stipulation? But lo, it has been stated:
>
> C.   He who says to his fellow, "[I make this sale to you] on the stipulation that you may not lay claim of fraud [by reason of variation from true value] against me"—
>
> D.   Rab said, "He nonetheless may lay claim of fraud [by reason of variation from true value] against him."
>
> E.   Samuel said, "He may not lay claim of fraud [by reason of variation from true value] against him."
>
> F.   Lo, it has been stated in that connection: said R. Anan, "The matter has been explained to me such that Samuel said, 'He who says to his fellow, "[I make this sale to you] on the stipulation that you may not lay claim of fraud [by reason of variation from true value] against me"—he has no claim of fraud against him. [If he said,] ". . . on the stipulation that in the transaction itself, there is no aspect of fraud," lo, he has a claim of fraud against him.'"
>
> G.   Here too, the same distinction pertains. If the stipulation was, "on condition that you do not abrogate the debt to me in the Sabbatical Year," then the Sabbatical Year does not abrogate the debt. But if the language was, "on condition that the Sabbatical Year itself does not abrogate the debt, the Sabbatical Year does abrogate the debt."
>
> *Talmud to Makkot 1:1L–N, 1:2, 1:3/I.2*

The Power of Language in the Torah

What is at stake in this issue is not only jurisprudential principles but theological truth, concerning the power of language. In the Torah, language is enchanted; it serves, after all, for the principal medium of the divine self-manifestation: in words, sentences, paragraphs, a book: the Torah. So what one says forms the foundation of effective reality; it makes things happen, not only records what has happened.

But what happens if one makes a statement that ordinarily would prove effective, but the contents of the statement contradict the law of the Torah? Then such a stipulation is null. Why? Because the Torah is what makes language work, and if the Torah is contradicted, then the language is no more effective—changing the world to which it refers, the rules or conditions or order of existence—than it would be if the rules of grammar were violated. Just as, in such a case, the sentence would be gibberish and not convey meaning, so in the case at hand, the sentence is senseless and null.

The main consequence of formation of thought through dialectical arguments, more than through any other mode of thought and writing, is simply stated. It is the power of that mode of the representation of thought to show us—as no other mode of writing can show—not only the result but the workings of the logical mind. By following dialectical arguments, we ourselves enter into those same thought processes, and our minds then are formed in the model of rigorous and sustained, systematic argument. The reason is simply stated. When we follow a proposal and its refutation, the consequence thereof, and the result of that, we become partners to the logical tensions and their resolutions; we are given an opening into the discourse that lies before us. As soon as matters turn not upon tradition, to which we may or may not have access, but reason—specifically, challenge and response, proposal and counterproposal, "maybe matters are just the opposite?"—we find an open door before us.

For these are not matters of fact but of reasoned judgment. The answer, "Well, that's my opinion," in its traditional form—namely, "That is what Rabbi X has said, so that must be so"—finds no hearing. Moving from facts to reasoning, from propositions to the process of counterargument, the challenge resting on the mind's own movement, its power of manipulating facts one way rather than some other and of identifying the governing logic of a fact—that process invites the reader's or the listener's participation. The author of a dialectical composite presents a problem with its internal tensions in logic and offers a solution to the problem and a resolution of the logical conflicts.

The dialectical argument opens the possibility of reaching out from one thing to something else, and the path's wandering is part of the reason. The wandering is not because people have lost sight of their starting point or their goal in the end, but because they want to encompass, in the analytical argument as it gets under way, as broad and comprehensive a range of cases and rules as they can. The movement from point to point in reference to a single point that accurately describes the dialectical argument reaches a goal of abstraction. At the point at which we leave behind the specificities not only of cases but of laws, sages carry the argument upward to the law that governs many cases, the premises that undergird many rules, and still higher to the principles that infuse diverse premises; then the principles that generate other, unrelated premises, which, in turn, come to expression in other, still less intersecting cases. The meandering course of argument comes to an end when we have shown how things cohere that we did not even imagine were contiguous.

The dialectical argument forms the means to an end. The distinctive character of the Talmuds' and other documents' particular kind of dialectical argument is dictated by the purpose for which dialectics is invoked. Specifically, the goal of all argument is to show in discrete detail the ultimate unity of the law. The hermeneutics of dialectics aims at making manifest how to read the laws in such a way as to discern that many things really say one thing. The variations on the theme then take the form of detailed expositions of this and that. Then our task is to move backward from result to the reasoning process that has yielded said result: through regression from stage to stage to identify within the case not only the principles of law that produce that result, but the processes of reasoning that link the principles to the case at hand. And, when we accomplish our infinite regression, we move from the workings of literature to its religious character and theological goal: it is to know God in heaven, represented on earth by the unity of the law, the integrity of the Torah, where we encounter God's true power: God's rationality, which is ours too.

A Christian's Response to a Judaist's Communion with God

BRUCE CHILTON

⁓

SOME YEARS AGO, a Christian scholar wrote a study of *Avoth* ("Fathers"), the tractate that is an addition to the Mishnah.[1] The scholar worked at a time when theologians were just coming to grips with the fact that, when the Torah was invoked within Judaism, the reference was not to a legalistic form of justification by works, as in Saint Paul's attack on the faith from which he converted. Partially in order to distance himself from that apologetic definition of Torah, the scholar entitled his book *Study as Worship*. He wanted to show that devotion, rather than legalism, constituted the center of the Rabbinic ethos. There have been many similar attempts in the intervening years, all of them designed to help Christians see that Paul was making an argument, not describing a system of religion, and that his terms of reference, shaped at least as much by his new perspective as from his former experience, could not be used to generate an accurate or sympathetically critical vision of Judaism.

The problem any Christian has in understanding Judaism, however, is not just that "Torah" does not mean "law." "Study" also does not mean "study," nor does "worship" mean "worship." A Christian can read no source that could be described as manifesting "the sum of God's mind" (so Neusner, p. 15). But Professor Neusner can say, "In Judaism, we commune with God by studying the Torah, which is God's self-manifestation, set forth in God's own language and wording" (p. 15). It follows that "study" in Judaism (for example, in an academy of study, a *beth*

45

midrash) is not aimed only at learning in the usual sense, but represents a recapitulation of God's own thoughts, as one thinks through the categorical hierarchy of the Mishnah and enjoys the return to unity by means of the dialectical reasoning that Talmud embodies. Such a worshipful recognition of divine synthesis (see p. 44) is as far from worship in the usual sense as the intellectual labor of Talmud is from study in the usual sense and as Torah is from law in the usual sense. Because Judaism is a system of religion, distinct from Christianity, there is practically no term of reference that can be transferred from one perspective to the other without a change of meaning.

The need for an adjustment in the received meaning of words in order to understand Judaism itself merits attention. We who speak of religions and attempt to analyze what they are and how they function stand within the mainstream of a Western philosophical tradition. That tradition has known its Platonic and its Aristotelian moments, and those alternatives have their representatives in the study of religion. For every Otto, Eliade, or Campbell to maintain a Platonic analysis involving changeless ideals,[2] there is a Robertson Smith, a Durkheim, or a Geertz to stand proxy for Aristotle in an insistence upon logical process.[3] The battle is as perennial—and as derivative—as the contest between Jungians and Freudians in psychology. The persistence with which modern schools of thought and analysis may be appreciated as extensions of Platonic or Aristotelian approaches is typically taken as a sign of the enduring vitality of those philosophical alternatives. However commendable our reverence for the classical past may be, another reading of the situation is possible: It may be that modern thought is much more repetitive than it likes to think of itself as being. Judaism's lack of fit with the received categories of Western philosophy—and with their shadows in the language of common sense—therefore poses a challenge to the way in which we normally look upon intellectual activity.

In a recent, heated debate, Professor E. P. Sanders has taxed Professor Neusner with an imprecise use of language—even "double talk"—in describing Judaism as a philosophy.[4] His attack illustrates the tendency of Western Christianity to marginalize Judaism and Judaic thinkers as anomalies that appear confusing within received categories. Judaism is not a Christianity, with claims about God and humanity that may be accommodated within one philosophical system or another, because Judaists decline to embrace those systems. At the same time, they present their perspective as a comprehensive account of the categorical thinking of the Creator, such that God's fashioning of the world corresponds to Mishnah's system of purity; discussion of that system, the hermeneutical task of Talmud, amounts to replicating the intentions and reflections of God.

Because Judaism is neither a religion in the sense of Christianity nor a philosophy in the sense of Aristotle, it is no accident that the pogroms of Europe became more persistent and vicious as European thought increasingly evolved into a synthesis of Christianity and Aristotle.[5] Issues of power, race, and ideology were subsidiary to the central threat posed by Judaism to Christian Europe: It spoke its own philosophical language of God's way with the world just as Europeans were developing their own voice. "The Jew" was the threatening other whose learning was gibberish, whose religion was godless, whose work was commerce, whose loyalty was to the tribe, whose knowledge was magic. Everything, in short, that Europe wished to cease being was summed up in "the Jew," and that atavistic terror still demands its victims.

"Systematization and philosophical grounding" (p. 20) are the aim and the achievement of the Talmudic Torah, which relates the phenomenal and the noumenal, as well as what God makes and what people do, into a single, embracing account of the mind of God. That account is no simple reading of the Hebrew Bible, nor is it a religion completely different from Christianity. Neither a brother nor a stranger, Judaism has been treated as a heresy, that bastard son among religions. Some of the most exacting work of Christian scholarship in the field of Judaism has been conducted as much in the attempt to convert Jews as to understand the milieu of primitive Christianity. But the Judaic "other" has been a determined survivor.

That survival has been a function of Judaic heroism and loyalty to identity, but there is also another force at work in the phenomenon. However much Christians indulged their anti-Semitism, Judaism was irreducibly implicated in the emergence of Christianity itself. A recent story in *The Jerusalem Post* describes the experience of a Jewish schoolgirl in Germany after her class had been catechized that the Jews had killed God's son. The anguish and betrayal of such lessons can scarcely be exaggerated, and similar stories have been told (literally, scandalously) millions of times. Yet even here—in an appalling example of what can be done with texts of the New Testament—there is a sign of the armor that would make Judaism proof against destruction at the hands of Europeans. Finally, even the anti-Semite must recognize in the Scriptures of Christianity a clear identification of the people of God. Although they might be cast in the role of God's recalcitrant and undeserving children, they are God's nonetheless. The same Paul who lamented his own Judaism also hoped that the sight of Gentiles converting to Christianity would convince Jews to join out of jealousy, "and so all Israel will be saved" (Rom. 11:26). Insofar as European anti-Semitism is a product of its Christianity, it would naturally be less successful in its genocide than the campaigns against South American, North American, and African peoples. However much your Jewish neighbor confused you, however little regard you might have for that person, actual denigration to the point of treating him or her as not a human being cannot be justified on the basis of the New Testament.

And so Christianity has been unable to shake its double. Judaism is always there, not quite destructible, but usually unacceptable in polite company. Present as a rival for the affections of Hellenistic culture throughout the period of the New Testament, as a competitor for the claim of spiritual rationality in the formative debates of theology during the period of the church fathers, Judaism became the bogeyman of Europe during the Middle Ages, a friendlier poltergeist of learning and disputation after the Reformation. Since the Enlightenment, polite company with Jews has been encouraged, but on the condition that Judaism itself is as carefully concealed as the Christianity of well-bred hosts. If only we could forget about religion completely (perhaps preserving a few vestiges for the sake of ethnic pride), we all might live together in peace. . . .

As I write these words, the end result of a religious policy of deliberate oblivion is being computed in the corpses, the wounds, the atrocities, the unyielding agonies of Bosnia and Herzegovina. I visited Yugoslavia in the summer of 1967, sponsored by an organization called The World Youth Forum, which had been established by the old *Herald Tribune* and later supported by the Columbia Broadcasting System. Its only purpose was good civic works, and it flew a group of us to Europe to meet with leaders of government, industry, the arts, and education. Yugoslavia was most impressive among the countries we visited in the evident enthusiasm of its young people for the society they were in the thick of building. Yes, they told us, the social tension we had read about had been a problem, but since World War II Tito's reforms had given Yugoslavs a new vision of who they were and where they were going. Only the older generation clung to the religious and ethnic forms of a time that was quickly passing away. More than a quarter century later, what has passed away (and what has not) would have been a surprise to most observers in the summer of 1967.

What went so cruelly wrong? The Balkan tragedy will require generations to resolve, and may never be understood in all its complexity, but something seems plain: The role of religion in fomenting violence did not diminish as a result of a national campaign to dissuade people from religious practice. Indeed, it might be argued that religion becomes more virulent in its social manifestation the more institutions of state seek to stigmatize it. Upwardly mobile people are typically willing to tailor their behavior, including their religious practice and orientation, to their ambition; those whose goal is status and/or power often, under an incentive as slight as a passing fashion, put religious loyalties behind them. But religion is not simply or primarily a matter of the affiliations of those who wish to get along and get ahead. Religious systems are by nature pre-institutional, and they function most explicitly in settings in which social organizations do not demand ultimate loyalty. A great error of many Marxist analyses of religion has been that they confuse religion itself with institutions of religion. They imagine there would be no Catholics without the Vatican, no Muslims without pilgrimages, no Judaism without Zion. So Stalinist policies broke papal power within national borders, prevented pilgrimage, barred emigration to Israel, and the analysts waited for religion to disappear. Their patience rewarded them with the experience of religious movements the like of whose ferocity has not been seen since the Enlightenment in the West.

The politics of religious oblivion have been shown to be worse than bankrupt. Such programs actually exacerbated social tensions, in that religious differences, supplanted by proudly secular ideologies in public discourse, are repressed to the level of the prejudice and taste of the groups defined by each religion. Our Christianity, our Judaism, or our Islam becomes whatever we say it is, and we say it against whoever is not of us. Because religion is what forms and transforms the cultures of groups, to remove religion from public discourse is, inadvertently but inexorably, to authorize social fragmentation. The violence that goes under the name of cleansing, ethnic or otherwise, will be the inevitable result when the groups that are products of fragmentation share territory. Since shared territory has become common and ideologies of state are weakening, the Balkans are the mirror of our broken selves, the failed utopias and the programmatic ignorance of the past three hundred years.

Recent experience insists that our rivals are doubles who will not go away. In their early life together, "cleansing" might have been the actual result of tensions between Christianity and Judaism, but neither side was fully up to the task. Judaism once dissociated from Christians, so that Rome persecuted fledgling Christianity for its refusal to recognize the divinity of the emperor, a right only Jews could claim. But Rome was too slack, and Judaism too diverse, for that policy to be effective. Christians, too, missed their chance at imperial triumph; it was a nearer miss, but finally the humanity of Jews and Muslims could not be denied long enough for them to be eliminated. A recognition of Jews and Christians is built into the Qur'an, so that Muslims have always been badly placed finally to destroy their rivals.

Religious conflict has nonetheless been a perennial, often deadly problem in the West, a perceived threat to social order. The comparatively recent solution of the Enlightenment, the denial of religion as such and its replacement with a deification of the state or an ideology, has been shown to be what it is by the holocaust of the Third Reich on the right and the holocaust of Yugoslavia on the left. The politics of destruction can only destroy us; the politics of enlightened oblivion only puts off the politics of destruction. The more religious rivals are ignored, the more they are scorned, and the more we and they supplant civility with mounting wrath. And because that wrath is not definitive, because Christianity and Islam and Judaism finally do not wish to invoke murder as the final solution, each must see that the ignorance, the scorn, the wrath are a crime and must stop.

Such wisdom as Christianity offers is not the product of idealistic toleration. It has tried and failed to end its rivalry with Judaism by means of fratricide, and did not quite manage to bring the crime off. What it offers, however, is not simply the spectacle of a failure that is superior to the success it sought; the wisdom of its failure is the recognition that Judaism could not be destroyed any more than Christianity would destroy itself. The scandal of Judaism was that Jews could have been Christians, and chose not to be; Judaism was a religious alternative to Christianity, not a superstition believed for want of something better. Reluctantly and painfully, Christian thinkers have come to see Judaism as a religion, to recognize its formative and transformative power over culture.

American scholars, Erwin Goodenough and George Foot Moore prominent among them,[6] have contributed signally to the realization that Judaism can only be rightly understood as religion, an insight more grudgingly admitted in Europe, where the ashes of a different sort of solution still smolder. With the development of Jacob Neusner's work, Judaism has itself contributed, not only to its self-understanding, but to its understanding by at least one chastened brother in religion. The challenge to Christian thinkers, in turn, is to appreciate Judaism as religion rather than rival, and then to become self-aware of Christianity's system of religion. The systemic understanding of other and self, self and other, is the alternative to fratricide.

The example cited from Baba Mesia 5B-6A (pp. 23–30) is an excellent case in point. How can the ownership of a garment found by two persons be settled? The grounding question of the Mishnah (Baba Mesia 1:1-2) seems clear enough, and Talmud's reflection upon the nature of Mishnah's answer is involved but lucid. What we do not find is an explanation of why we should be interested in such issues. In the absence of an explanation, one easily assumes that the entire discussion is arbitrary, and Talmudic Judaism is then dismissed as the province of a legalistic elite. That process of assumption and dismissal is often repeated when people are introduced to sources of Rabbinic Judaism. The force of the process can appear visceral, as gut-level as the anti-Semitism to which it is related. Westerners are commonly disaffected—literally and acutely—by the claim that matters such as the ownership of garments whose owners could not be bothered to keep track of them are of divine concern.

What is the foundation for that common reaction? The grounds of the common disaffection may be analyzed along the lines of two perspectives. Viewed from the first perspective, the discussion of ownership is annoying because the answer to the question posed is obvious, a matter of common sense. Indeed, insofar as the parties in dispute wind up dividing the garment in Mishnah, the rule of common sense seems to be acknowledged. According to the first perspective of disaffection, then, the whole of the discussion in Talmud is a monumental irrelevance; after all, the nature of the oaths involved can scarcely be pertinent, when the claims asserted are simply ignored in the division of the property. How can we be serious about a discussion in Talmud concerning oaths that are implicitly treated as beside the point in Mishnah?

The second perspective of disaffection is related to the first, but it is more profoundly felt. The typically Western impatience with Rabbinic literature stems not only from the supposition that "common sense" has already answered many of the questions discussed in Mishnah and Talmud, but also from the unexpressed conviction that "common sense" should govern the relations among people, *and should not be subjected to questions that might undermine its authority.* There is no virtue, and certainly no religion, in using convoluted arguments in order to tell people to do what they should intuitively and spontaneously put into practice, without the forethought and afterthought that impede action.

Both of these perspectives are generated from typically Christian constructions of morality. As a system, the movement that came to be called Christianity practiced its communion with God, as we will see, by means of the imitation of Christ in respect of baptism, prayer, ethics, and communion. The systemic focus was so tight that teachers within the canonical sources frequently warned Christians away from philosophical speculation. In a passage that will concern us further in chapter 6, a representative warning appears in Colossians (2:6-11a):

> As you, then, received Christ Jesus the Lord, walk in him, rooted and built up in him and established in faith—just as you were taught, abounding in thanksgiving. See to it lest anyone make prey of you by means of philosophy and empty deceit: the tradition of men and the elements of the world, and not Christ. For in him all the fullness of deity dwells bodily, and you are fulfilled in him, who is the head of every principality and authority. In him also you were circumcised with a circumcision made without hands. . . .

The readiness with which philosophy and deceit are equated is arresting, and suggests why the quasi-philosophical investigations of Mishnah and Talmud will seem a nuisance to the heirs of Christian culture. Indeed, the irony is that precisely those heirs of the culture who do not identify themselves as Christians will be all the more annoyed. For them, common sense—usually defined by some loose invocation of the principle of love and the rule of the majority—is all that is left of systemic Christianity.

When it emerged as a system of religion, Christianity did not attempt to frame a comprehensive alternative to understandings of the world that were then current. There were Christians who were also Stoics, and Platonists, and Aristotelians, just as there were Christians who were also Jews. As the passage from Colossians suggests, attempts to construct Christianity in expressly philosophical terms were viewed with suspicion. The practitioners of the religion assumed that the systemic concern with the imitation of Christ should not be identified with a particular form of philosophy. Because the focus of the system was in that sense practical, Christians could live with varying understandings of common sense, and permit those understandings to govern their normal relationships, provided they were consistent with the imitation of Christ.

For that reason, Christianity was articulated in Stoic terms during the second century, and then entered a predominantly Platonic cycle prior to the victory of Aristotle in the great synthesis of Thomas Aquinas in the thirteenth century.[7] The Reformation inherited a resurgence of Platonism from the Renaissance, consistent with the Reformers' fascination with Augustine, the influential thinker of the fifth century, but also—and more fatefully—their appeal to rationality fomented a new interest in the role of scientific reason. The emphasis on reason, of course, revolutionized the apprehension of religion and culture during the Enlightenment, as historical method became fundamental within the humanities. Since the Enlightenment, the transitions of our culture have made it unclear what our present phase is, but that is only natural for people living within a philosophical synthesis. Outsiders of a later period will more readily see what is going on now.

Nonetheless, it is apparent that reason has been challenged as an irreducible and determinative force, because human beings themselves have been explained in terms of the three great materialist philosophies of the recent past. The evolutionary materialism of Charles Darwin, the psychological materialism of Sigmund Freud, and the historical materialism of Karl Marx have all had their day in offering accounts of why and how people are as they are. Of the three, only Darwinism shows much vitality, and by no means remains unchallenged. Whatever becomes of materialism, it seems plain that, although it successfully dislodged reason as the self-evident center of humanity, it has not managed to produce cogent accounts of what makes people human. The recent fashion of linguistic philosophies, in the end too self-referential themselves to produce such an account, would suggest that the next dominant concern of philosophical activity will focus on issues of cognition. The shaping of human perception and action, no longer according to Platonic forms or Aristotelian contingencies, but along the lines of systems of meaning people themselves appear to construct in community, could prove to be the central issue of public discourse in the period after the Cold War.

Whether or not the cognitive issues of the meaning of perception and activity prove to be central in the years to come, a single generalization remains: Christianity has not only tolerated philosophical structures not of its own making, it has required them. Without Israel's Scriptures, the Stoics' morals, Platonic idealism, Aristotelian realism, the Renaissance's obsession with the source of knowledge and beauty, the reason of science and its materialist offspring, it is impossible to understand what Christianity has become. One source of the perceived threat of Rabbinic Judaism is that it has framed a comprehensive account of how human reality as such is to be classified and understood, while Christianity has let those tasks be accomplished within the philosophies it has embraced as commonsense understandings of the world. An acceptance of the Rabbinic account of God would mean the dissolution of Christianity as it has evolved, because no sense would remain under the aspect of the common. Judaism locates God's concerns within the realm of human society; mundane issues such as ownership are elevated to questions of divine moment. On such an understanding, what would God not be directly involved in? Would there be any room for a world separate from God? Both God and the world have received careful attention among Christian thinkers, but any serious consideration of Judaism would involve a searching and radical redefinition of their relationship, and of the character of Christianity itself.

The dialectical argument over ownership, the Mishnaic classification and the Talmudic hermeneutics, is therefore threatening to Christianity, precisely because such matters are held to be discussed within the mind of God. Christians typically find it easier to express affection for other religious traditions, especially Buddhism, because it is possible to conceive of them as offering the sort of alternative constructions of reality in a philosophical vein that Christianity has thrived on. As soon as one sees, however, that the philosophy involved is not an alternative, but the way a given religious system declares that things are, ardor is likely to diminish. Rabbinic Judaism usually does not have to suffer diminished ardor, because the disaffection that has already been discussed tends to govern the Western response from the beginning.

Because the Christian West finds itself between philosophies, however, a critically appreciative reading of Judaism has become possible (if not likely). The matter of ownership is, after all, not as straightforward as one might think; the wording of oaths is far from unambiguous; common sense appears all too uncommon. The importance of those issues, from the point of view of Christianity, is self-evident: how we think of what we own, how we affirm ownership, and where disputes might be settled are in fact structurally vital matters in our relations with others. My neighbor is my neighbor, however I conceive of his or her property, but what I do in respect of that property is structured by my understanding of ownership.

However important the issue of ownership may be, I have just shown that for Christianity its significance lies in the arena of social structure, not system. That is, I discover that there is a challenge to any social philosophy in the systemic imperative to love my neighbor, and that challenge has resulted in a long history of social experimentation within Christianity, from feudalism to communism. But that very history would suggest that Christianity as a religious system offers no philosophy of ownership, even in an incipient form. In his first letter to the Corinthians, Paul raises the issue of Christians with legal claims against one another (1 Cor. 6:1-11). His only advice is to settle such matters out of court in order to avoid scandal; without the enunciation of a single principle, he tells his readers that, since they are to be involved in the final judgment of the world, they ought to be able to regulate their own affairs. Here again, Judaism is different in a way that reveals what in comparison to other religions is a missing element in Christianity. Christians have typically preferred to dismiss Judaism rather than to ask why their own religion has not developed in the same way as others.

If we compare the passages from Baba Mesia 1:1-2 (together with its Talmudic discussion) with the passage from 1 Corinthians 6, we see that what is in the medium of system for the one religion is in the medium of social structure for the other. The reading of Baba Mesia by a Christian, as by an atheist or a Buddhist, must therefore involve a disciplined act of the imagination. The discipline is not to believe that such things as ownership matter; they do for all communities, at one point or another. The discipline is to see the system within the discussion, to appreciate that, for this system, the minutiae of ownership may be explored, and can only be rightly known, within the mind of God.

The example of Baba Mesia 10:5 with its Talmudic discussion (pp. 31–34) is therefore pointed, and for two reasons. More trivially, and yet inescapably, I have to observe: If God can care about manure on paths, what might God not attend to? And Talmud implicitly responds: If you can conceive of a more minute concern, what makes you think God has not already turned God's attention to it? Because Judaism is a system, its concerns have been thought through, applied, thought through again, applied afresh, usually in several cycles before anything like the texts of Mishnah and Talmud as we know them emerged. The questions I might bring to bear, as a Christian theologian who has wandered outside his own religion (partly to understand Christianity better and partly to try to grasp what religion itself might be), will only rarely be coincident with the central concerns of that system. Religions are the engines of culture, including the cultural activity we call philosophy. So we can ask any question we like of any system we like, but we should not be offended if our questions are not quite taken seriously. If I ask the text, Why are you boring me with this stuff? it replies: Who told *you* to read me?

The second feature of pointedness in the discussion of manure is the more telling. The apparently plain provisions of Mishnah are, within the Talmudic discussion, deliberately contrasted with the views of Rabbi Judah. That contrast then opens a consideration of how to weigh the obligation to keep a public way clear against other imperatives. After all, manure may be piled to be trodden, not in an obstructive way. As we have seen, that is only the beginning. The rule is then weighed against what one might do on the authority of courts or under religious obligation. Even when the discussion appears simply to confirm the initial statement of the Mishnah, the deeper accomplishment of Talmud is to relate the variety of its considerations to the single claim of unity within the mind of God.

Where the Christian is instructed to be minded with the intentions of Christ, and to work out what that might mean, the Judaist is provided with an enormous range of instances of what God's mind is, expressed in tangible matters of detail. There can be no doubt regarding how to be a neighbor to your employee (Baba Mesia 9:11), or how propertied neighbors should divide the cost of setting up fences (Baba Batra 1:3). Only a poet in the Protestant tradition could have written "Something there is that doesn't love a wall. . .";[8] property means walls, and if their construction is not a matter of agreement, offense is the likely result.

How is it that the United States, in many ways the successful colony of Protestant Christendom, is the most litigious nation in the world? The same students who will tell me that Judaism is legalistic because it tells people how to share their property, as in the discussion of Baba Mesia 1:3, will take their landlords to court over a tank of heating oil. Members of my congregation who would dismiss as beneath the concerns of religion the discussion (in the same passage) of how to distribute the value added to products will nonetheless find a way to balance the advantage of income that might be derived from their church's property against the liability for taxation that results from commercial use. Neither my students nor my congregants are any more hypocritical than human beings generally, but neither are they exempt from the tendencies of the cultural system (which is, at the end of the day, a religious system, be they theists or not) that shapes and drives them.

So I read a Judaist's account of his communion with God, and it is evidently not simply a matter of personal piety. It implies personal devotion, of course, because the account identifies the workings of the mind of God, and simple integrity requires that people attend to the truths they identify. But the truth of Professor Neusner's account is a matter of the very system of Judaism. A systemic encounter with God, mediated by Mishnah and Talmud, for Judaism illuminates the whole of human experience, especially our experience in society. As a Christian observer, I can learn in two ways from what I see.

First, the relative agnosticism of my own religion in the realm of social structure becomes apparent. Paul and others content themselves with telling the church to be minded with Christ and run things accordingly, leaving the development of coherent philosophy to another day. Paradoxically, faith makes us more certain of what we cannot see than of what we can.[9] The nature of God, the divine call to humanity through Jesus Christ, our daily living with God (baptized with Christ in the spirit, conscious of our heavenly Father in prayer, enacting the love of our Lord, eating the food of our Savior)—these are the realia of Christian faith. What is commonly called the real world is a land of shadows, not in a Platonic sense alone (although it has been and remains that for some Christians), but in the sense that our achievements of love (the great and the humble) are the silhouettes of Christ, our true light.

Christianity has frequently been called a supernatural religion, but it might be more helpful to think of it as metasocial. Although it undertakes the transformation of societies it touches (as religions generally do), it stubbornly refuses to provide a template of what we are to be. "Beloved, now we are God's children, and it has not yet appeared what we shall be; we know that, when he appears, we shall be like him, for we shall see him exactly as he is" (1 John 3:2, ca. 100 C.E.). Such statements do not represent sudden attacks of vagary; they attest a refusal to spell out what can only be enacted in God's time.

Second, the account of a Judaist's communion with God is a vigorous reminder that the studied agnosticism of Christianity leaves certain aspects of experience open, not to deny them their role, but so that they might be developed. The pretense that social relations do not matter is an invitation for the further predations of the new legalism that inhibits the progress of social life in the West. Paul's advice is sound, after all: If we hope to be a part of the kingdom that is to be all in all, how can we live as vassals to institutions which deny that kingdom? As long as their system of religion lasts, Christians will never legislate the kingdom, since that prerogative is not theirs. But neither, at their more lucid moments, will they deny that the very neighbors they are commanded to love as if each of them were Christ (see Matt. 25:31-46) live in neighborhoods that are defined by the sorts of consideration embodied in Mishnah and Talmud.

2

Engaging with God through Christ

BRUCE CHILTON

Certain it is, and proved by holy scripture, that God hath a fatherly and loving affection toward us, far passing the love of bodily parents to their children. Yea, as far as heaven and earth is asunder, so far his love exceedeth the love of natural parents to their children. . . . "Can a wife forget the child of her womb, and the son whom she hath borne? And though she do forget him, yet I will not forget thee."[1] Here are shewed the affections and unspeakable love which God beareth towards us.—Hugh Latimer, "Sermons on the Lord's Prayer" (1552)

Introduction

C HRISTIANS COMMONLY ASSERT their communion with God in four ways. At baptism, they are identified with Christ, who stood in relation to God as a beloved child to a father. In prayer, that filial consciousness is enriched after the pattern given by Jesus. Ethically, Christians are called to follow the example of Christ. And in the Eucharist, which is also called communion, they understand that the Christ who made communion with God possible becomes available again in his reconciling presence. The means of communion are clearly referred to in the New Testament, but the documents involved stand at the end of a definite process of formation. The process needs to be appreciated before the documents themselves can be understood.

The writings of the New Testament were produced at discrete stages within the development of early Christianity. All the documents assume that an initial, usually oral, preaching about Jesus has been heard and accepted at some point in the past, whether recently or long ago. That predominantly oral message, the triumphal news or "gospel" (*euanggelion*) of God's victory, is only indirectly attested in the documents of the canon. The term *Gospel* came to be applied to specific documents because they presuppose and build upon the message concerning Jesus. The intended audience is composed of believers.

The first three Gospels, Matthew, Mark, and Luke, represent a second stage, following acceptance of the message of the initial gospel that their audiences had heard. They are written as catechesis (elementary instruction), in order to prepare sympathetic hearers of the gospel of Jesus for genuine membership in the church, a membership marked by baptism. John's Gospel represents a more advanced, third stage; it presupposes that its readers have been catechized in a way comparable to that laid out in the earlier Gospels and are prepared to develop their faith in the face of perceived threats to the survival and welfare of the community.

The Letters or Epistles (from the term *epistole*) of the New Testament, mostly from Paul, address particular issues in communities of baptized followers. In the vehemence of much of the correspondence, a fourth stage, controversy within the movement, is clearly reflected. In some instances the epistolary form is used to address matters of more general and doctrinal concern. The aspiration to speak to the church at large (that is, "catholic") marks the fifth stage. The stage of catholic synthesis speaks through several sorts of writing—for example, the Acts of the Apostles, the first history of the new movement; and the Revelation (or Apocalypse) of John, the preeminent example of predictive prophecy in the New Testament.

The dates of individual documents will be indicated here, following a largely conventional scheme,[2] but it should be stressed from the outset that, from the point of view of understanding any system of religion, what is of determinative importance in the evaluation of a document is not its chronology, but the stage of the movement it represents. After all, the movement produced the documents and framed their governing concerns. The principal stages represented in the New Testament, then, are (1) evangelization, a largely oral phase now known only by inference; (2) catechesis, which the first three Gospels are designed to serve; (3) theological reflection upon catechesis, as in the Gospel according to John; (4) controversy, which the Epistles amply attest; and (5) catholic synthesis, which is attempted in idioms as different as those of Acts (the genre of history) and Revelation (the genre of prophecy).

In that the first three Gospels emerge from the catechetical stage of the movement, when candidates were prepared for baptism, they provide the best indications of the governing concerns of the movement as it initiated new members. The first three Gospels are commonly called "synoptic," because they may be viewed together when they are printed in columns. Unfortunately, their obviously literary relationship has caused scholars to presume that they were composed by scribes working in isolation who copied, one from another. A comparative approach,[3] served by an understanding of the development of tradition into documents within both early Judaism and Christianity, has brought us to the point where deviations of one document from another, related document, are not assumed to be purely scribal changes. Rather, agreement and disagreement provide opportunities to grasp accurately the social function and meaning of a given document by referring to the distinct ways it construes a program shared with comparable documents.

Within such an approach, material agreement among the Gospels is no surprise, because documents of early Judaism and Rabbinic Judaism also present synoptic relationships, sometimes with greater verbal similarity, and often with more than three documents involved. What *is* notable in the synopticity of the first three Gospels is that the orders of passages can be compared regularly; that justifies their literary characterization as the "Synoptics." But once their function within catechesis is appreciated, the cause of their agreements and their deviations becomes evident: What we see in the first three Gospels are the methods of baptismal initiation followed in three influential, nearly contemporaneous but separate churches.[4] There is a reasonable degree of consensus that Mark was the first of the Gospels to be written, around 71 C.E. in the environs of Rome. As convention has it, Matthew was subsequently composed, near 80 C.E., perhaps in Damascus or elsewhere in Syria, while Luke came later, say in 90 C.E., perhaps in Antioch.

Baptism

What is it that the Synoptic Gospels are designed to show us about our prospects for communion with God? In aggregate, they initially highlight baptism, a single moment of communion that is both public and private. They address that moment by relating the baptism of Jesus at the hands of John the baptist (Matt. 3:13-17/Mark 1:9-11/Luke 3:21-22). Here Jesus is addressed unequivocally by God as "my Son," and from that point the spirit that descends upon him governs Jesus' actions. The emphasis on the latter motif is such that Jesus, after the baptism, is portrayed as being brought by the spirit into the wilderness for his temptation (Matt. 4:1/Mark 1:12/Luke 4:1). His baptism commences his public ministry and his spiritual dynamism.

The claims made for Jesus' baptism are all the more dramatic against the background of what may be surmised of the ministry of John the baptist. According to Josephus, John practiced ablutions and preached righteousness in the wilderness (*Antiquities* 18 §§ 116–19). John's practice of generic baptism, dipping people in water so that they might become pure in their commitment to righteous repentance, seems quite distinct from the experience of Jesus as conveyed by the Synoptics. By the time the first three Gospels were composed, baptism had been appropriated within Jesus' movement.

In a passage commonly regarded as a reflection of a truly evangelical, oral tradition, Peter in the book of Acts preaches in the house of the Roman centurion Cornelius and begins the gospel of Jesus with reference to the baptism preached by John (Acts 10:37-38). The result of his preaching is that the Holy Spirit falls upon those present (v. 44), and Peter proceeds to baptize them with water (vv. 46c-48). Peter is here portrayed as authorizing the baptism of Gentiles, despite the astonishment of his companions, who are "of the circumcision" (v. 45). The Synoptic Gospels are telling the story of Jesus' baptism for people who themselves could be baptized because the movement's membership was no longer exclusively Jewish. The content of baptism had been changed: It was now baptism "in the name of Jesus Christ" (v. 48, a formulation found frequently in Acts).

The notion of baptism into Jesus' name represents a transformation of John's program of ritual and ethical purification. It is impossible, on the face of the texts of the Synoptic Gospels, to determine what "happened" to Jesus, as distinct from what happened in the practice of predominantly Gentile Christians. That indeterminacy between what occurred in the past and what is appropriated in the present is enshrined within the texts themselves. At the crucial moment, when it concerns the experience of being baptized, the Synoptic Gospels present interesting (and distinctive) qualifications:

> Matthew 3:16: Having been baptized, immediately Jesus arose from the water; and lo, the heavens were opened, and he saw God's spirit descending as a dove, coming upon him.

> Mark 1:9c-10: . . . and he was baptized in the Jordan by John. And immediately, arising from the water, he saw the heavens split, and the spirit as a dove descending upon him.

> Luke 3:21b-22: . . . and Jesus having been baptized, while he was praying, heaven was opened, and the Holy Spirit descended in bodily form as a dove upon him.

Although the Synoptic Gospels are comparable here, there is no question of a verbatim identity among them. Nonetheless, each presents the baptism as a function of Jesus' own experience, as well as of what was said and done. In Matthew, the statement is made that the heavens were opened, but then the descent of the Spirit is described as what Jesus—and, apparently, Jesus alone—saw. Mark's wording presents both the heavenly tear[5] and the descent of the dove of the Spirit as matters to which only Jesus could have attested. Luke's language might seem to refer to objective events, but what is related is cast as a matter of what transpired while Jesus was praying after his baptism.

What is the reason for such frustrating indeterminacy? Why not merely state what happened and what it means? Scholars of the New Testament commonly appeal to what are taken to be the looser standards of ancient historiography, but such explanations are superficial. The catechumen who was prepared for full admission into the society of Christians in Damascus (by Matthew) or Rome (by Mark) or Antioch (by Luke) was to be baptized into Jesus Christ's name, and therefore to receive the Spirit of God. The narrative of Jesus' baptism was naturally presented as a paradigm of what the catechumen was to experience. The voice that addresses Jesus as the divine Son, in whom God is well pleased (Matt. 3:17/Mark 1:11/Luke 3:22b), is saying what Jesus, God, and the church know, but what Jesus' contemporaries are said not to have grasped. The Gospels deliberately speak out of time, in order to convey their timely knowledge to the catechumen.

The indeterminacy between what might be said of Jesus and what may be said by the follower at baptism is, then, no quirk of the Synoptic Gospels, nor a matter of literary presentation alone. This is not just an unfortunate confusion, but a systemic feature of Christianity: the narrative identification in baptism between the believer and Jesus Christ. We may briefly cite instances of similar claims of the identification in other documents of the New Testament, whose genres are different from the Synoptics', and which emerged at different stages.

The Gospel according to John (written in Ephesus ca. 100 c.e.) does not refer to Jesus' baptism, although it presupposes that Jesus belonged to the group around John the baptist.[6] John the baptist is chiefly important within the fourth Gospel as a witness (cf. 1:6-8), and he is the vehicle of claims made in the Synoptics by means of Jesus' baptism. He is portrayed as attesting that Jesus is "the lamb of God," on the basis of John's own vision of the Spirit descending as a dove and resting upon Jesus (1:29-32). The baptist goes on to explain that "He who sent me to baptize with water said to me, Upon whomever you should see the spirit descend and rest upon him, he is the one baptizing with holy spirit" (1:33). For that reason, John says he knows that Jesus is the Son of God (v. 34), precisely the message of the divine voice in the Synoptics. John the baptist's testimony here has swallowed up any specific reference to the fact that Jesus was baptized; significance has overwhelmed narrative within the Johannine idiom. Yet there is a common theme in the Johannine discourse and the Synoptic story: Baptism in Jesus' name will alone give access to the Holy Spirit.

Paul presumes even more daringly upon the previous catechesis of his readers, as when he says (around 55 c.e.) to those in Corinth who styled themselves sophisticated Christians:

> I do not want you ignorant, brethren, that our fathers were all under the cloud and all passed through the sea, and all were baptized into Moses in the cloud and in the sea, and all ate the same spiritual food and all drank the same spiritual drink—for they drank from a spiritual rock that followed, which rock was Christ. (1 Cor. 10:1-4)

The confident assumption here is that the reader will know that the reference to "our fathers" will introduce a typology of the Exodus.

Within the typology, the Israelites' dwelling under the protection of the divine cloud in the wilderness (Exod. 13:21-22; 14:19-20, 24-25) and their passing through the sea (14:21-22) correspond to baptism by Spirit and water in the name of Jesus. The thought of baptism then triggers a reference to the Eucharist (which will take up our attention soon). The miraculous provision of food and drink in the wilderness (Exodus 16 and 17) relates to the underlying reality of the rock from which the water came,[7] which is Christ. Unless we know that baptism and Eucharist are standard practice among Corinthian Christians, and that they have appropriated the Scriptures of Israel as their own, we are at a loss to explain what Paul is talking about. Once we know what we need to know, it becomes clear that, for Paul, baptism is a matter of receiving the Spirit while being dipped in water in Jesus' name. As a consequence, each Christian is God's child, much as Israel was at the time of the Exodus (Exod. 4:21-23).

The use of Scripture as an instrument of analogy, in which texts of Israel in the past are applied to the church of the present, is no Pauline idiosyncrasy. 1 Peter, written for the churches in the northern portion of Asia Minor ca. 90 C.E. (that is, well after the apostle's death ca. 64), inherits the common habit of applying scriptural figures to the present.

In order to exhort its readers to patient suffering, the letter invokes the example of Jesus (3:18-22):

> For Christ also suffered for sins once for all, the righteous on behalf of the unrighteous, so that he might bring you to God. Put to death in flesh, he was made alive in spirit, in which also he went to preach to the spirits in prison, who were formerly disobedient, when God's patience waited in the days of Noah while the ark was prepared in which a few lives—that is, eight—were saved through water. The antitype of that, baptism, now saves you, not a removal of dirt from flesh but an appeal of clear conscience to God, through the resurrection of Jesus Christ, who having gone to heaven is at the right hand of God where angels and authorities and powers are subjected to him.

The flourish of the statement in the Greek text of 1 Peter is all the greater in that it stands as a single sentence in the original. Its elements, however, are fairly easily identified. It is Jesus' *resurrection* now that makes baptism efficacious; the roots of the practice in issues of ritual purity are no longer of concern.

Because Jesus was righteous and was raised from the dead, he becomes the spiritual basis of the commendation of clear consciences to God. Within that grounding logic, the statement in regard to Noah is a corollary. Made alive in spirit, Jesus was able to address the dead who had no opportunity to receive him when they were living. Those who were disobedient in Noah's day are examples of that group; the ark in the water is taken as a type of baptism, the foreshadowing of the more effective reality that is known as the antitype. (In classical terms, a "type" [*tupos*] is the impression something might make, while the "antitype" [*antitupos*] is the thing itself.) The salvation of eight lives, Noah with his three sons and the wives of all four, is asserted because the number is symbolic. It is evocative of the eighth day of one's life, when circumcision is to occur within Judaic practice (following Gen. 17:12). Baptism is the reality (the antitype) of the salvation for which the ark is a type, and the incorporation within God's people for which circumcision is a type.

An apparent indeterminacy at the catechetical level, then, intertwined Jesus' baptism and the baptism for which catechumens were trained. Baptism is located less within the life of Jesus than as a place where endowment with Spirit and identification as God's son are realized. That narrative representation by the Synoptic Gospels is confirmed by the discursive representation of Jesus as the source of Holy Spirit in John. The Johannine emphasis on the baptist's testimony to Jesus as he who baptizes in spirit as God's son is achieved without specific reference to the fact that Jesus was literally baptized. In their differing ways, 1 Corinthians and 1 Peter utterly submerge any ritual sense of baptism, its initial meaning, within an understanding that baptism into Jesus' name is fundamentally a quickening by the spirit of Christ, which is related to the Hebrew Scriptures as the reality of an antitype is related to the promise of a type.

Prayer

In his Letter to the Galatians (written around 53 C.E.), Paul subscribes to the commonly agreed sense of baptism, and goes on to demonstrate that a close connection between baptism and prayer was presupposed (4:4-6):

> When the fullness of time came, God sent forth his son, born of a woman, born under law, in order that he might redeem those under

law, in order that we might obtain sonship. And because you are
sons, God sent forth the spirit of his son into our hearts crying,
Abba, father!

Contrary to what is sometimes claimed, the Aramaic term *Abba,* a
direct form of address, would be at home within usages applied to God
within sources of Judaism prior to the New Testament.[8] In Paul's understanding, however, it is possible to refer to God as "Abba," although one
might be a Greek-speaking Gentile, because in baptism the spirit of
God's Son possesses one's heart. A similar conviction, expressed more
fulsomely, appears in Paul's Letter to the Romans (8:1-17), which was
written some four years after the Letter to the Galatians (ca. 57).
Accepting the spirit of God's Son puts one in a fresh relationship to
God, and one addresses God in a new way. "Abba" is the word of Aramaic that has best survived multiple translations during the history of
the church, because it has been accepted as the paradigm of how one
stands in relation to God through Christ.

To address God as Father initially in baptism implies that a continuing and intimate relationship has been established. In fact, in the same
chapter of Romans in which Paul refers to Christians' address of God as
"Abba," he also avers (Rom. 8:26):

> Similarly, the spirit also comes to the aid of our weakness; for we do
> not know just how we should pray, but the spirit itself intercedes in
> wordless sighs.

That is, a liturgical understanding of prayer is expressly set aside in favor
of an intimate, spontaneous, and even nonverbal conception of prayer.

It is consonant with Paul's claim that there are many imperatives to
pray within the New Testament (at every level), and several warnings
about the abuse to which formal prayer may lead, but only one actual
text of prayer. The single exception is what is commonly called the
Lord's Prayer, which is better considered a template or outline of prayer
than a liturgical form. The prayer is presented only by Matthew and
Luke. The omission in Mark does not appear deliberate; there are some
two hundred verses in Matthew and Luke (largely, examples of Jesus'
teaching) that are not found in Mark. They appear to reflect a source[9]
that no longer exists (and that may never have existed as a whole in writing). Originally a compendium of sayings such as the disciples of a rabbi
would treasure, a mishnah,[10] the collection of sayings was shaped by the

fervent expectation of final judgment within the churches in Syria where it was transmitted. It is notable that the nearest approach to a text of liturgical prayer within the New Testament is not included among the most basic of catechetical elements, but among those instructional materials teachers might refer to. Fundamentally, the Lord's Prayer is a guide to the sorts of intimacy that prayer in the spirit of Jesus might lead to, a model teachers might commend to catechumens who had already been instructed in the purpose of prayer.

Of the two versions of the Lord's Prayer in the New Testament (Matt. 6:9-15; Luke 11:2-4), Luke's is widely considered the earlier in form, and it seems plain that Matthew presents what is, in effect, a commentary woven together with the prayer:

Matthew	*Luke*
Our father in heaven	Father,
let your name be sanctified;	let your name be sanctified;
your kingdom come,	your kingdom come!
your will be done	
on earth as in heaven!	
Our daily bread	Our daily bread
give us today;	give us each day;
and forgive us our debts,	and forgive us our sins,
as we also	for we ourselves also
have forgiven our debtors;	forgive our every debtor;
and lead us not	and lead us not
into temptation,	into temptation.
but deliver us	
from the evil one.	

Certain uniquely Matthean elements appear to be expansions on the model. "Thy will be done" explicates "thy kingdom come." The late Philip Sigal identified texts of Rabbinic prayers that present similar phrases;[11] understood as a gloss in the Lord's Prayer, the phrase would nonetheless be quite early.

Similarly, the phrase "but deliver us from the evil one" only appears in Matthew's version of the prayer (6:13; cf. Luke 11:4); it explicates "do not lead us into temptation." Within Matthew the wording plainly refers to escaping the devil's wrath (as in 13:19, 38); English translations commonly obscure the point and give the impression that the petition is a general plea not to suffer from bad inclinations. Matthew's Greek (*ho poneros*, masculine and singular) refers to evil as personified ("the evil one"), not to evil in the abstract. The first Gospel casts the Lord's Prayer, as it casts many of Jesus' parables, into the key of a final judgment involving Jesus as the "Son of man," a figure understood by means of Daniel 7. Its final commentary on the prayer insures that the principal concerns of the Matthean community in Damascus are addressed and articulated. Apocalyptic formalism appears to be the characteristically Matthean tendency: to append "our" to "father" makes the model more liturgical (along with the addition of the phrases "in heaven," and "your will be done . . ."), as suits the Matthean setting, and also makes it accord with the Eighteen Benedictions and many other Judaic prayers.

The distinctiveness of the Lord's Prayer in Matthew as compared to Luke should make it plain beyond a doubt that one Gospel cannot be explained simply on the basis of scribal copying from another. Matthew gives us the received view of the prayer in Damascus, just as Luke provides us with the received view in Antioch. Both of them might have kept the silence of Mark, where the matter is not taken to be a part of initial catechesis. Had they followed suit, the version of the prayer in *The Didache* 8, which is comparable to Matthew's, would have been our only literary source of the Lord's Prayer from documents of primitive Christianity. There, the Lord's Prayer is to be said thrice daily, as is the Amidah in Judaism. An increasingly liturgical portrayal of the prayer, from Luke through Matthew, and on through *The Didache*, is obvious. In some ways, the version in *The Didache*, with its concluding doxology ("for yours is the power and glory, for ever and ever") is most like the traditional practice of Christianity.

The relative sparseness of Luke has won it virtually unanimous recognition among scholars as the nearest to the form of an outline that Jesus would have recommended. In view of the tendency we have seen toward an increasingly liturgical presentation, a filling out of the model, that verdict seems correct, but two cautions are in order.

First, scholars have persisted in confusing two categories, one literary and the other historical. When they reach what they believe is the earliest form of a passage, they frequently equate that with a dictum of Jesus. What falsifies that equation is that none of the Gospels (as they stand) could be called historical. A given Gospel might be catechetical, as in the case of the Synoptics (and even then, the catechesis involved is construed distinctively in each), or theologically discursive (as in John). There is no stemma of the relationship among them so that the "most primitive" is identifiable from the outset; even if there were, our experience of the texts to hand would make us suspicious of any claim that what was most primitive happened also to be the most historical. All of the texts are programmatic, and in that sense tendentious; none of them is historical in its governing intention, even to the extent that, say, Josephus' work is.

Yet the Gospels refer back to Jesus as their source. The literarily historical Jesus is a fact that any reading of the Gospels must take into account, even if the question of the historical Jesus remains problematic. That is to say, we cannot understand the documents at all unless we can identify what they believe they are referring to (whether or not we accept that they in fact do so). That reference constitutes the literarily historical Jesus for a particular document and the community that produced it. The disentanglement of the literarily historical Jesus from the historical figure we would call Jesus requires an investigation behind the texts to hand, and for the present purpose that is beside the point. If our concern is with the religious system that texts served and that produced those texts, the typically modern fixation with writing Jesus' biography must simply be put to one side. *The fundamental issue for the critical study of religion is not what Jesus said as the Lord's Prayer, but what generated the texts that are before us.*

That brings us to the second note of caution to be introduced into the conventional acceptance of the Lukan version as the more original. In terms of a generative exegesis (that is, an exegesis engaged with religious system first of all), Luke's version of the Lord's Prayer, as compared to Matthew's and *The Didache*'s, naturally strikes one's attention. It remains the most likely of the three to have produced the other two. But having identified lapses of logic in historical exegesis, we should avoid cognate errors in generative exegesis. Just because Luke's version is the simplest, that is no reason to suppose it actually generated the other two. There is no evidence of direct contact among the versions. All we can say is that the form of a model is better conveyed by Luke than by Matthew or *The Didache*. The possibility of secondary formations within Luke remains.

Indeed, although Matthew and Luke both explicate the forgiveness we ask in terms of the forgiveness we extend to others, there is evidence that suggests the latter element may be secondary. Matthew immediately follows the Lord's Prayer with an explanation of the necessity for forgiving others (6:14-15), although the prayer may well be held to include reference to many other elements in greater need of explanation (such as "kingdom," "daily," "temptation," and "evil"). The inference might be drawn that the transformation of the request for divine forgiveness into a demand for human forgiveness, although it is well established as an aspect of Jesus' teaching,[12] was interpolated into the prayer at the appropriate point in the model. Such an interpolation within the prayer would serve to encourage reconciliation within communities whose diversity occasioned tension and predisposed them toward factionalism.[13]

The generative model of the Lord's Prayer consists of calling God Father, confessing that God's name should be sanctified and that God's kingdom should come, and then asking for daily bread, forgiveness, and not to be led into temptation. Because a model is at issue rather than a liturgy, attempts to fix a precise form of words simply exceed the bounds of any achievable certainty. Luke 11:2b-4 appears to function as a paradigm in its brevity, and its terse petitions for elemental needs— bread, pardon, integrity—appear nearly anticlimactic in comparison with the sorts of appeals that were possible within the early Judaism of the period. The Lukan context (11:1-2a, 5-13) presents the prayer in a didactic manner, as something to be learned in contrast to other formulations. The Matthean context is the more liturgical, invoking as it does the issues of almsgiving (6:2-4), inappropriate and appropriate places of prayer (vv. 5-6), putting prayer into words (vv. 7-8), and fasting (vv. 16-18).[14]

The generative model permits us to specify the elements within the recommended outline of prayer under two major headings:

1. *an address* of God (a) as father, (b) with sanctification of God's name and (c) vigorous assent to the coming of God's kingdom;
2. *a petition* for (a) bread, (b) forgiveness, and (c) constancy.

The two major headings are clearly distinguished in grammatical terms. The address of God is as a third person, a father, and is followed by imperatives in the third person ("let your name be sanctified," "your kingdom come"), while the plea for bread is in the imperative of the second person ("give us"), as is the appeal for forgiveness ("forgive us") and constancy ("lead us not").

There is a symmetry between the two major divisions of the outline, which links the elements that constitute the divisions. In 1-a God is called father, an address that brings to mind God's merciful provision for Israel, as in Ps. 68:5:[15] "Father of orphans and judge of widows is God in his holy dwelling." That father is asked for the bread of the day in 2-a. The invocation of the sanctity of God in 1-b, commonly instanced in the Hebrew Scriptures (as in the same verse from Psalm 68), is then related to the petition for forgiveness in 2-b.

The link between sanctity and forgiveness is also straightforward, in that the forgiveness of sins is what may prepare one for fellowship with the Holy God. That connection is repeated many times in the book of Leviticus from 4:20 onward, when reference is made to forgiveness in order to describe people's fitness to engage in sacrifice again, once an offering has been made for sin. The fundamental conception is that God's appeasement by means of sacrifice leads to a forgiveness that makes continuing participation in worship and in the community possible.[16]

Finally, the prayer for God's kingdom in 1-c corresponds to the appeal for constancy in 2-c. The kingdom is a conception of systemic importance, to be investigated in chapter 4, but for the moment we may observe that by the time of Jesus and his followers, its sense within their Judaism was that God as king was extending himself to all peoples, and that they might either embrace or reject God. A typical expression of hope in God's royal judgment of the world is found in Ps. 96:10:

> Say among the Gentiles that the LORD reigns,
> that the world is established so as not to move:
> he will judge the peoples with equity.

God's extension into the world is to include judgment, so that loyalty to God's righteousness, the resistance of temptation that is the final plea of the prayer, becomes imperative.

Assessed by its individual elements, the Lord's Prayer may be characterized as a fairly typical instance of the Judaic piety of its period. To call God "Father" was, as such, nothing radical, and the association of

God's fatherly care with the actual provision for prayerful Israel is attested, as in Ps. 68:5.[17] The same passage shows that the connection of God's holiness to God's fatherhood was seen as natural, and the importance of sanctifying God's name within the earliest Rabbinic texts of prayer—such as the Kaddish, which means "Sanctified (be God's name)"—is well known. That God's holiness is consistent with people being forgiven and accepted by God is also unexceptionable. Finally, the idea that God's being king amounts to a "kingdom" that was about to be revealed is amply precedented within the Aramaic paraphrases of the Hebrew Bible known as the Targumim, and they insist on the loyal response of God's people to that revelation.

The frequently repeated remark, therefore, to the effect that the Lord's Prayer is essentially a prayer of early Judaism, is perfectly understandable and—from an atomistic point of view—justifiable. Indeed, the observation is consistent with the number of Aramaisms either present or implicit within the prayer.[18] Prominent among them are the reference to God as "Father" (ʾAbba in Aramaic, attested in early Judaism within nonliturgical prayers), the usage of the "kingdom" as a convention for divine self-disclosure, the assumption that the term "debt"—ḥovta in Aramaic, used routinely of sin within the Targumim—means "sin," and the understanding that nisyona ("temptation") is the ultimate test that might prove us disloyal.

By way of comparison, we might consider the development of the first nine of the Eighteen Benedictions, a standard prayer of Rabbinic Judaism:[19] "Blessed are you . . ."; "You are mighty . . ."; "You are holy . . ."; "Be gracious, our father . . ."; "Restore us . . ."; "Forgive us, our father . . ."; "Look upon our affliction . . ."; "Heal us . . ."; "Bring blessing upon us." The Eighteen Benedictions and the Lord's Prayer evince a comparable structure: invocations of the deity, in which the terms of reference identify God's power, are the first element and the presupposition of both prayers as they proceed to petitions, the second major element. In the Eighteen Benedictions, God is declared blessed, mighty, and holy, and the invocation of those attributes are the basis on which requests may be made to God. In the Lord's Prayer, petitions are only sensible after God's name as Father is sanctified and God's kingdom is called for.[20]

In the Eighteen Benedictions, each "benediction" takes many lines, while the units of the Lord's Prayer are indicated minimally. The brevity of the model of prayer given in the Gospels is as striking as the modesty of its petitions. Daily bread, forgiveness, and the avoidance of temptation are scarcely ambitious requests, as compared to the greater fulfillment (of Israel's election) that is the aim of the Eighteen Benedictions. Indeed, there is a curiously negative note in the final petition of the Lord's Prayer.

The deceptive simplicity of the generative model could cause one to overlook its significance. From the point of view of content and general structure, as we have noticed, claims of material originality–which are sometimes still made on behalf of the Lord's Prayer–seem to be wide of the mark. But it is apparent that the prayer must in some way be distinctive. After all, the tradition of prayer within the New Testament is not enthusiastic about formal texts, which is why the Lord's Prayer stands out in the first place. Matthew portrays Jesus as lampooning formal prayer (whether Judaic or Gentile) in the passage immediately preceding its presentation of the Lord's Prayer (6:5-8), and Luke conveys the prayer in didactic terms, as the equivalent of John the baptist's teaching (11:1-2a). Unless the outline had been understood to carry with it a distinctive characteristic of prayer for the church, it would not likely have been presented as it is in Matthew and Luke.

The initial point of the model is that God is to be approached as Father, God's name sanctified, and God's kingdom welcomed. The act of prayer along those lines, with great variety over time and from place to place and tradition to tradition, has been a hallmark of Christianity.

The claim of intimacy with God, of God's personal involvement with the one who prays as a divine child, is intrinsic within the first step of praying. It is in one sense odd, but in another sense profoundly revealing of our religion that Christians otherwise in dispute–even violently opposed to one another–can and do nonetheless pray together in the words their Savior taught them. Whatever the realities and the forces of division–institutional, theological, ethnic, social, economic, linguistic, and otherwise–the mutual, filial consciousness of Christians when they say "Our Father . . ." makes them family in a moment of time unconditioned by time. Unquestionably, those divisions remain. The scandal of Christians at violent odds with one another is not lost on Christians themselves. But because their unity is a unity in prayer, and often in prayer alone, the scandalous discrepancy is between earth and heaven, not just between theory and practice. What divides Christians from one another is not that they are Christians, but that they are human beings; their prayer, however, permits them to see humanity as one in the invocation of a single Father, intimately accessible to all.

The sanctity of God is not diminished by the approach to God as father. The intimacy between parent and child is not the intimacy of lovers or of friends on equal terms. Parents will usually know more, overlook more, care more, fret more, provide more, than anyone else of a person's acquaintance. It is precisely their greater love, however, that will predictably distance them from their children, and even at times alienate their children from them. God as father is altogether different from us and from what we know, as transcendent and unknowable as God's love knows no boundaries. What is holy is what stands apart from us and our usual relationships, a center of privilege but also of danger that is unlike all that we are familiar with, even as it permits us to exist.

To address God as Father, and yet to sanctify God's name, acknowledges the ambivalence that might permeate our attitude toward God. God approaches us freely and without restraint and yet is unapproachable, as holy as we are ordinary. The welcoming of God's kingdom, of God's comprehensive rule within the terms of reference of our world, wills away our ambivalence. God's intimate holiness is to invade the ordinary, so that any ambivalence is overcome by the force of God itself. The implications of a focus upon the kingdom will be developed in chapter 4, but the prayer makes it plain that the kingdom is to be seen as dynamically ingressive and as welcomed in the act of prayer, however others react to the kingdom.

The three elements that open the prayer, then, characterize a relationship and an attitude toward God which the one who prays makes his or her own. The distinctiveness of the prayer is nothing other than that consciousness of God and of one's relationship to God that is implied, and that is recapitulated whenever one prays in that way. Such an awareness of God and of oneself is what Christians kindle when they pray the Lord's Prayer. At the same time, the prayer is nothing other than the Lord's; whatever the merits of such a consciousness, it is only ours because it was Christ's first. That is why the filial consciousness of praying in this manner is as strong as it is: one is God's child, and Jesus' sister or brother in the same instant.

The conscious relationship to God conveyed and reinforced in the first three elements of the prayer, in which God is approached, is then extended into the last three elements, in which God is besought as a holy father and king. The apparent modesty of the requests is linked to the purpose of the prayer. Daily bread is asked for; its reception every day is to be taken as God's fatherly provision. Forgiveness is requested; one's need for it as a requirement of divine sanctity is therefore granted. And the dread of any apostasy from the hope of God's kingdom is presumed in the petition to be guarded from temptation. Precisely because the three elements one pleads for are ordinary, they mark the purpose of the prayer as the acquisition of the filial consciousness of Jesus, enacted daily as one eats, enjoys forgiveness, and remains loyal to God.

Much as baptism represents the narrative identification with Christ, so the Lord's Prayer (understood as the model of the sort of prayer in which one will engage) represents the appropriation of that consciousness of God that is initiated and made possible by Christ.

Ethical Performance

Jesus' consciousness of God as Father, such as is conveyed and promulgated in the Lord's Prayer, is the basis of the portrait of Jesus in the last moments before his arrest. The agreement of the Synoptic Gospels in presenting some version of Jesus' prayer to be spared the cup of his suffering attests its importance for ancient Christian catechesis. The highly schematic quality of the scene in Gethsemane suggests its usage as a model of Christian reflection in the midst of crisis.

Following Mark's version (14:32-42), we see Jesus and his disciples coming to the parcel of land called Gethsemane after his prediction of his betrayal (14:18-21), his final meal with the disciples (14:22-25), and his prediction of their denial of him (14:26-31). Within the scene itself, Jesus commands his disciples to sit while he prays on his own, but he takes Peter, James, and John with him some way further (14:32-33a). In deep distress, he asks them to remain and stay alert (vv. 33b-34). Only then does he start to pray; proceeding a little further, he falls to the earth, and asks that the "hour" which had come upon him might pass (v. 35). The words of his prayer are also given (14:36):

> Abba, father: everything is possible for you.
> Take this cup away from me.
> Yet not what I will, but what you will.

The reminiscence with the Lord's Prayer seems deliberate, because next, finding Peter and his companions sleeping, Jesus tells them to stay alert and pray, "so that you do not enter temptation" (14:37-38). The scene is repeated a second (vv. 39-40) and a third time (v. 41a), when Jesus announces that the hour has come; the Son of man is now betrayed (vv. 41b-42).

The passage is an example of the catechetical method followed in the Gospels. The text appears to be an incident concerning Jesus at prayer, but some care is taken to exclude the very witnesses whose presence would be required if the scene were to be historically credible in all its detail. At the crucial moment Jesus is alone, but for the presence of three sleeping disciples in his vicinity. Who was there to hear how he prayed? But the matter of his prayer turns out, in any case, to be predictable on the basis of the Lord's Prayer, whose paradigmatic importance is therefore confirmed.[21] The substance of the prayer is more a presupposition than the point of the passage; the scene in Gethsemane is more important for its setting than for Jesus' words and deeds there.

Those disciples who seem to be distanced from the action are in fact deeply implicated within it. After all, they are the group from which the betrayer comes; they are the ones who share a meal with Jesus as he tells them of his fate; their denial of Jesus (with Peter at their head) is openly predicted. And now, in Gethsemane, they cannot even watch and pray. Such prayerful attention is precisely the way of Jesus, his steeling for the hour that comes upon him, and the disciples are as yet no match for that "hour."

As in the case of the Lord's Prayer, what Jesus does is paradigmatic, but here the paradigm has more to do with the crisis he faces than with what he says in the midst of it. The sleep of the disciples, the repetition of the notice of their inattention as contrasted with Jesus' agonized struggle, are deliberately schematic, because the burden of the passage is how (and how not) to face the hour of trial without disloyalty (the "temptation" of which Jesus speaks in v. 38, as in the Lord's Prayer).

In that the principal concern of the scene is how followers of Jesus are to face crisis, the portrayal of Jesus' behavior (as well as that of his disciples) is deliberately unheroic. The catechesis is designed to identify catechumens with Jesus, and their fears are transferred to him within the narrative. He asks for what indeed seems impossible. The logic of his own action to that moment—a calculated visit to Jerusalem and a forceful, perhaps violent, controversy with the authorities of the temple—could only have led to the "hour" that indeed must come upon him. The single plausible alternative to arrest is flight, which is just the alternative the disciples will avail themselves of later in the narrative (see Mark 14:43-52). Yet Jesus asks for what any catechumen might desire: freedom from persecution, no matter how inevitable such persecution might be. He is shown praying after the manner of what the catechumen has learned as the model of prayer, and being as deeply conflicted as any recent convert might be.

Within the world of the Gospels, persecution is a likely result of baptism. Public identification with Jesus might bring with it a fate comparable to his. That reality casts its shadow on a principal motif of the New Testament, that of believers' call to what is usually termed the imitation of Christ.[22] The importance of 1 Peter as reflecting the place of baptism within the church has already been observed. It is consistent with that emphasis that the epistle addresses a plain word of advice to domestic servants who might suffer as a result of their faith (2:21): "for you were called to this, because Christ also suffered for you, leaving you an example in order that you might follow in his footsteps." The example of Christ comes at the close of a fairly well developed sequence of imperatives of a general nature (2:11-17), and is obviously a fitting conclusion; but the ease of the transition is predicated on the mention of domestic servants or slaves and their predicament from v. 18.

If one is baptized into Christ and practices the consciousness of Christ in prayer, how is one to be and behave in a world that has largely rejected Christ? The advice of 1 Peter to domestic slaves is to remain obedient to masters, good and bad, "for this is grace, if—on account of a consciousness of God—someone bears pain, suffering unjustly" (2:19). The position of oppression, provided it is combined with the will to do good (v. 20), enables one to walk in Jesus' footsteps. For that reason, a social status comparable with Jesus' vulnerability at the end of his life was commended. That commendation at the same time affirmed the position of the early Christians themselves, who were encouraged to see their position within underclasses as an indication of divine approval.

Jesus himself came to be seen principally as a servant, as in the famous passage from the Letter to the Philippians (2:5-8), which was probably composed after Paul's death, near the time of 1 Peter (that is, ca. 90):[23]

> Let this thought prevail among you, which was also in Christ Jesus: Who, being in God's form, did not consider the presumption of equality with God, but emptied himself, taking a servant's form; existing in men's likeness, and found as a man in shape, he humbled himself, becoming obedient unto death, death on a cross.

The impact of the text is to assign Jesus a role and status, that of servant or slave (*doulos*), quite unlike the relatively privileged standing of rabbis within early Judaism and Rabbinic Judaism. That transformation of Jesus' social identity is all the more startling in that Philippians carries practically no direct reference to Jesus in his own time.

Such transformations of Jesus within the tradition that concerns him are by no means aberrant. The framing of the Gospels, the epistles, and the other writings of the New Testament for those who were about to be or had been baptized resulted in appropriations of Jesus within environments quite unlike his own. The rabbi, as we have seen, became a slave in the epistles—and not only in the epistles. Within the Gospel according to John, the last meal of Jesus with his disciples in chapter 13 is a symposial gathering, complete with a discourse that continues for several chapters thereafter and consumes the bulk of Johannine attention. The introduction (13:1-12b) has Jesus perform the menial task of washing his disciples' feet, in order to exemplify the sort of mutual service he demands from his followers.

The Johannine point is driven home without symbolic embellishment (13:12c-17):

> He said to them, Do you know what I have done for you? You call me teacher and lord, and you say well; I am. If, then, I—lord and teacher—washed your feet, you also ought to wash one another's feet. For I have given you an example, so that just as I have done to you, so you also might do. Truly, truly I say to you, A servant is not greater than his lord, nor an apostle greater than the one who sent him. If you know these things, you are blessed if you do them.

John's placement of the scene, as the formal equivalent of the "last supper" in the Synoptics, suggests the importance of the model Jesus is held to convey. Serving others is the active equivalent of Jesus' ministry, the performance of his purpose.

The relative privilege of poverty within early Christianity is reflected in a pivotal catechetical section of the Synoptics (Matt. 19:16-30/Mark 10:17-31/Luke 18:18-30), beginning with the story of a would-be disciple with property. The enthusiastic catechumen is told, much to his dismay, to sell his possessions and give to the poor, in order to have treasure in heaven (Matt. 19:16-22/Mark 10:17-22/Luke 18:18-23). The normative value of the cautionary story is reinforced by Jesus' statement about rich people and the kingdom of God: A camel would have an easier time wriggling through the eye of a needle than the rich would have getting into the kingdom. Only God's capacity to overcome what is humanly impossible gives them any hope (Matt. 19:23-26/Mark 10:23-27/Luke 18:24-27). Peter, speaking for the body of Jesus' peripatetic followers, calls attention to their voluntary poverty and is promised rewards (Matt. 19:27-30/Mark 10:28-31/Luke 18:28-30).[24]

The message of the passage may appear mixed, but it is pointed. Those who are poor, simply because they belong to underclasses, enjoy relative proximity to the kingdom, and the rich may enter only by means of the exceptional grace of God. But Peter and his companions, by means of their voluntary poverty for the sake of the movement, are assured of life everlasting. The pericope reflects the stringent practice of Christianity in the circle of Peter; from that circle, the story of Ananias and Sapphira in Acts also derives. That couple claimed to have sold their property for the benefit of the apostles, but in fact retained some of the profit, and they died separately under Peter's interrogation (Acts 5:1-11). Within the Petrine group, there seems little question that voluntary poverty was a principal means of following Jesus, of enacting his ethos. The only evident alternative was the obvious alternative to eternal life.

Even the Petrine transformation of Jesus, from a rabbi with the resources of fishermen and artisans at his disposal into a peripatetic mendicant, allowed of the rich wriggling through the needle's eye. The analogy between Jesus' ministry and the voluntary acceptance of conditions typical of underclasses, however much it was recommended, was not taken by itself to be a fulfillment of the imperative to follow Jesus. That analogy was preferred, and even standard, and yet simply accepting poverty did not make one like Jesus and worthy of eternal life. There was an awareness within the Petrine circle, and—as we shall see shortly—within other communities of the New Testament, that the needle's eye was open for those with property, because voluntary poverty was at the service of a more basic means of enacting the ethos of the Christ, a principle that might be realized by programs other than voluntary poverty.

The purest form of the Petrine statement of the larger principle appears in Matthew and Mark (Matt. 22:34-40/Mark 12:28-34). In them both, Jesus is asked by someone outside his group (a Pharisee in Matthew, a scribe in Mark) what is the great (so Matthew) or first (so Mark) commandment. He replies by citing two commandments, to love God (drawing from Deut. 6:4, 5) and to love one's neighbor (drawing from Lev. 19:18). Jesus concludes in Matthew that all the law and the prophets hang from those two commandments, and in Mark that there is no other commandment greater than these.

Matthew and Mark construe the sense of the teaching distinctively. In Matthew, the organic connection among the commandments assures that they all hang together (with the teaching of the prophets) on the principle of love toward God and neighbor (22:40). Mark, on the other hand, has the scribe who initiated the scene conclude that to love is more important than all burnt offerings and sacrifices (12:32-33). The construal of Matthew is in the direction of claiming that Jesus represents the fulfillment of the law and the prophets, a thematic concern of the Gospel generally. The construal of Mark takes the tack that Jesus' principle establishes a noncultic means of approval by God. Both find their center of gravity, however, in the conviction that the commandment to love God and love one's neighbor is the action that unites one with Jesus in an approach to God. The emblem of that approach is fulfillment of the law and the prophets in Matthew (22:40), nearness to the kingdom of God in Mark (12:34). The differences between those construals are not to be minimized: They represent the substantive independence of the Gospels as catechetical instruments. But the systemic agreement between Matthew and Mark, that love is the means of access to God after the pattern of Jesus, is an equally striking attribute.

It is a commonplace of critical study to observe that Hillel, in a dictum comparable to Jesus', is said to have taught that the Torah is a commentary on the injunction not to do what is hateful to one's neighbor (Bavli, Shabbath 31a). The centrality of the commandment to love one's neighbor is also asserted by Aqiba, the famous rabbi of the second century (*Sifra* [the earliest Rabbinic commentary on Leviticus], Lev. 19:18). Differences of emphasis are detectable and important,[25] but the fact remains that Jesus does not appear to have been exceptional in locating love at the center of the divine commandments. Any rabbi, a teacher in a city or a local village, might have come up with some such principle, although the expressions of the principle attributed to Jesus are especially apt. The principle itself is little more than proverbial: Love, after all, is not easily dismissed as a bad idea or beside the point.

Precisely because Jesus' teaching is precedented in the early Judaism of his day, it becomes clear that the Petrine tradition presented in aggregate by Matthew and Mark is offering a transformation of that teaching. An example of such transformation is that Jesus' citation of the two biblical passages which demand and define love is no longer simply a matter of locating a coherent principle within the Torah, the stated terms of reference in the question of the Pharisee or scribe. Rather, the twin commandment of love is now held to be a transcendent principle, one that fulfills (so Matthew) or supersedes (so Mark) the Torah. Christ himself, by citing and enacting that principle, is held to offer the ethical key to communion with God.

The Lukan version of the teaching concerning love makes it especially apparent that the significance of Jesus' message lies at least as much in who is speaking as in what is said. There (Luke 10:25-28), an unidentified lawyer asks what to do in order to inherit eternal life; formally, the identity in Luke with the question of the rich man in 18:18 is striking. Clearly, a relationship between the latter question, which leads Jesus to commend poverty, and the question that leads Jesus to demand love is appreciated within the Lukan community at Antioch. Indeed, by reversing the order of the passages as compared to Matthew and Mark, poverty in Luke is presented as the subordinate virtue: The lawyer's question is the precedent of the rich man's question in Luke, while the discussion of love only appears after the praise of poverty in Matthew and Mark.

Yet in Luke it is not Jesus who cites the twin principle of love, but the lawyer (10:27). At first Jesus merely confirms what the lawyer already knows (10:28); Jesus' peculiar contribution comes in response to the lawyer's further question, Who is my neighbor? (10:29). The question and the response appear in uniquely Lukan material, the presentation of Jesus' teaching concerning love, which was characteristic of the church in Antioch (10:29-37). The Antiochene transformation of the principle, in distinction from the Petrine transformation, explicitly makes Jesus' *application* of the commandment, not its formulation, his systemic innovation.

The innovation is effected in the parable of the Good Samaritan

(Luke 10:29-37). Whether Jesus himself told the parable is beside the present point. What concerns us is that (1) the parable informs the commandment to love with a new gist, and that (2) the new gist is the systemic center of Lukan ethics, as distinct from Matthean and/or Markan ethics. Formally, the parable is designed to answer the question, Who is my neighbor? That formal issue is also addressed at the close of the parable, when Jesus tells his questioner to go and do what the Samaritan did, that is, show himself a neighbor to one in obvious need (10:36, 37). But the formal issue here is distinct from the systemic issue.

The systemic challenge is not the goodness of the Samaritan, but the fact that he *is* a Samaritan. The victim of the mugging is in no position to complain, but especially as a recent pilgrim to Jerusalem, he might well have objected to contact with a Samaritan, in that the religion that focused on Mount Gerizim was seen as antagonistic to and impure in respect of the religion that focused on Mount Zion. A priest and a Levite have already passed by, motivated by scruples concerning purity; after all, the victim is described as half dead (10:30), and he presumably would have been taken for dead—and therefore unclean—by any person who did not, out of pity, look more closely than an ordinary passerby would (see 10:33). In the parable, therefore, a victim who seemed impure is aided by a Samaritan who was actually impure, and that action nonetheless fulfills the commandment to love one's neighbor as oneself.

The parable of the Good Samaritan, then, is a story that formally conveys how to be a neighbor, and it is shaped systemically to insist that one viewed as "impure" may be a neighbor to one who is "pure." The commandment to love is such that, in its application, it creates a new sphere of purity that transcends any other notion of what is clean and unclean. The issue of purity was crucial to the church in Antioch. In Gal. 2:11-13, Paul describes factional fighting among three groups prior to 53 C.E., classed according to their leaders. On one extreme, Paul himself taught that Gentiles and Jews might freely eat with one another; on the other, James insisted on the separation of those who were circumcised. Peter and Barnabas were caught somewhere in between. Much later, around 90, Luke represents how the issue was resolved within Antiochene Christianity: The question of the boundaries established by purity was settled in terms of ethical engagement rather than dietary practice. It is no accident, then, that it is precisely Luke that conveys its unique parable and its peculiar perspective on how Jesus' teaching regarding love was distinctive.

Much as Jesus provides the model of a consciousness of God in prayer, so his performance of an ethos of love under duress provides a paradigm of loving service. The link with the social situation of catechumens is so strong that their lives are mirrored in Jesus' as much as his is in theirs, even when one might expect the texts to be straightforwardly historical. In both Jesus' case and believers', the ethos that goes by the name of love is transformed by distinctive conditions, so that love might be, for example, the integral principle of the Torah (Matthew), or a principle beyond cultic Judaism (Mark), or the single term of reference that determines the purity of one person for another (Luke).

Eucharist

An awareness of how Jesus' teaching concerning love, apparently of a proverbial nature, was transformed in a signally different way in Luke as compared to Matthew and Mark, provides the point of departure for our consideration of the next medium of communion with God in Christianity. Eucharist has been the object of even more dramatic transformations. In one understanding or another, it is claimed as a hallmark of identity—along with baptism, prayer, and ethics—by nearly every group of Christians, and yet how Eucharist is understood has been a greater and more frequent cause of division than any other single issue. Division, of course, has proved to be a regular feature of Christendom (for reasons that will be discussed in chapter 6), but the regularity with which Eucharist has been cited as a matter of contention between and among groups over the centuries is striking. A principal cause of the contention can now be identified: There are already, within the New Testament, multiple transformations of the meaning of Eucharist, which in aggregate are both variant and conflicting. A systematic assessment of Christianity is impossible without an appreciation of those sacramental transformations.

Six types of Eucharist in early Christian tradition may be distinguished within the text of the New Testament. Each type represents the meaning of the Eucharist, with attendant words and gestures, for particular circles of Christians. In a longer study,[26] I have isolated each type according to a generative exegesis designed to analyze the meanings that produced particular texts, but here we may follow through the types in their chronological order in a summary way.

The types were generated within distinct circles of the movement during its formative stages. The first two types were produced by Jesus, the first during the larger part of his ministry, the second after his abortive attempt to occupy the temple and influence sacrificial worship there. The third type is that of Peter and his network in Judah, Galilee, and beyond, while the fourth bears the imprint of James's group, the prestigious church headquartered in Jerusalem. The fifth type represents an attempt to rationalize the variant views of Eucharist that had emerged by the mid-first century. The Pauline group attempted a radical appropriation of the type of Peter and a rejection of the type of James, while the group around Barnabas at Antioch (the wellspring of the Synoptic Gospels) practiced a symbolic reconciliation of elements included in previous types. Especially at that stage, "This is my body" and "This is my blood" came to mean that bread and wine become for the believer a direct communion with Christ in his death. The Gospel according to John, an example of the sixth type, demonstrates the extent to which the understanding of the Eucharist as a consumption of Christ's body and blood dominated the movement by the end of the first century.

Six Types of Eucharist in the New Testament

1. The Purity of the Kingdom

Jesus' frequent meals with his disciples throughout his ministry represent the practice of purity in anticipation of the kingdom. Each meal is a pledge that the kingdom is to come. As Jesus says in a famous dictum: "I shall not again drink of the fruit of the vine until I drink it new in the kingdom of God" (Matt. 26:29/Mark 14:25/Luke 22:18). The intention of the saying within its originating context was to assure Jesus' followers that every meal taken in his fellowship was a warrant of the festal kingdom that was shortly to come, and Jesus himself undertook to consume wine in no other way. Meals within the first type were often repeated, and inclusive of those in Israel generally: Jesus held that the fellowship created by mutual forgiveness and common offering was pure by definition, and he opposed exclusive practices of dietary purity.

2. The Surrogate of Sacrifice

After Jesus' occupation of the temple, and his failure to change arrangements in the cult,[27] he presented his "blood" and "body "—his meals in anticipation of the kingdom—as a replacement of conventional sacrifice. The sense of the gesture is straightforward: Pure wine and bread, shared in a community created by mutual forgiveness, is a better sacrifice than the priesthood of the temple is willing to permit.[28] The gesture is confrontative, but does not involve the formal blasphemy that a later interpretation of the saying would require. Jesus did not in history refer to himself as "blood" and "body"; he referred to his meals with followers under those terms, in order to designate them as a surrogate of sacrifice within the temple.

3. The Covenantal Sacrifice

Jesus' practice at the end of his life ran the risk, if simply repeated by his followers, of being taken as a challenge to the regular practice of sacrificial offering. That was how the authorities in the Temple had understood Jesus' own meals after his occupation of the outer court. The Petrine circle saw Jesus' meals after the manner of Moses' sacrifice with his followers in Exodus 24, where the Mosaic covenant had been inaugurated. That transformation enabled those around Peter to proceed with regular worship in the temple, while insisting on the normative value of what Jesus had done. The portrayal of Jesus in Mosaic terms, which was a feature of the Petrine cycle (see the transfiguration),[29] was advanced by the new wording in its explicit reference to *covenant*:[30] Jesus' inclusive definition of purity, a principal feature of his teaching, was accepted by his followers for ordinary worship in the temple, which could proceed without interruption while communal meals were arranged in their homes.

4. The Passover

Passover became the paradigmatic association within the circle of James. However emphatic the association,[31] it is also artificial: the Gospels admit that the authorities wished (with good reason) to execute Jesus prior to the feast.[32] The paschal connection of the meal was an effective means of incorporating Jesus' movement fully within cultic worship, which was the program of James. In a stroke, the meal was more tightly linked to the liturgical year than it ever had been before, and Jerusalem—the hub of Jacobean influence—was accorded irreducible importance as the single place where Passover/Eucharist could be observed fully. The dominical and Petrine meals were repeatable anywhere and frequently. The Jacobean transformation of what was a last Passover could truly be enacted only "between the evenings" of 14 and 15 Nisan, and in the vicinity of the temple, where the paschal lambs were slain.

Once Jesus' movement included Gentiles, the matter of their participation in a truly paschal supper became problematic. After the destruction of the temple, Jews generally celebrated a modified Seder, without a lamb. Still, the implications of James's position are evident: An extension of the Torah to the "last supper," as to a paschal meal, would carry with it the consequence that "no uncircumcised person shall eat of it" (Exod. 12:48). In other words, it would constitute a logical development of the exclusionary policy of James, as reflected in Galatians 2.

5. The Heroic Sacrifice for Sin: Pauline and Synoptic Symposia

Hellenistic Christians most naturally associated the dominical meal with a philosophical symposium, the sober version of gatherings that for other purposes could be uproarious. Paul stresses the importance of order and moderation at meals in the Lord's name (see 1 Cor. 11:17-34). In resistance to Jacobean hegemony, he also insists that the primitive tradition (1 Cor. 11:23) made no tight connection with the Passover, but simply with the night in which Jesus was betrayed. Paul so emphasizes the connection with Jesus' death (1 Cor. 11:26) that the older, Petrine understanding of the meal in terms of covenantal purity is lost on non-Jewish readers. The understanding that Jesus offered himself in connection with the meal as a sacrifice for sin was current in the emerging consensus of Hellenistic Christianity,[33] and is assumed by Paul elsewhere (Gal. 1:4; Rom. 3:21-26). The association with Jesus' death becomes so fundamental in his thought, he believes that anyone who does not discern the Lord's body and blood in the proceedings is condemned (1 Cor. 11:27-30).

The Synoptic Gospels reflect the conception of Jesus as a heroic sacrifice for sin (*ḥaṭa'at*, see Leviticus 4) which characterized the Hellenistic catechesis invoked by Paul. The blood of the covenant is "poured out" in the Synoptic tradition in the manner of the blood of the sacrifice for sin, in the interest of the communities for which the Gospels were written (Matt. 26:28/Mark 14:24/Luke 22:20). That same basic thought is spelled out differently in each Gospel.[34]

The Synoptic Gospels relate more closely to one another than to Paul, and yet they are not simple copies of one another. At the Synoptic stage, as earlier, the tradition was protean, subject to local variation, shifts of perspective, and structural evolution, as well as changes of wording. Nonetheless, the agreement in the substance and method of presentation suggests that the transformation of Jesus' Eucharist into a heroic sacrifice at the stage of the Synoptics was definitive for each of them, and that the distinctions of each Gospel from the others are a function of distinctive construals of that transformation. They agree in a systematic emphasis on Jesus' voluntary decision to pour out his blood as a sacrifice for sin. Because that image dominates the picture within the Synoptics, the Jacobean material regarding Passover can be accepted as symbolic, without its regulating actual practice. Jesus' decision to die for all who will join him is effective for those who are willing to see that, in bread and wine, his offer to them stands.

6. Miraculous Food

The Johannine Gospel identifies the story of the feeding of the five thousand with Passover (6:1-15, v. 4) and then develops fully a quasi-magical exposition of the Eucharistic bread as manna, the miraculous bread of Exodus 16 (John 6:26-71).[35] Conceptually, John marks a daring advance beyond the Hellenistic catechesis represented in the Synoptics. Jesus no longer merely offers solidarity in martyrdom by means of his symbolic body and blood: Jesus now claims that he is what is consumed, the true bread of heaven (John 6:35). The fact that the new identification is developed within the complex of the feeding, rather than within a narrative of the "last supper," may be an indication of the self-consciousness of creativity at this point.[36]

**

By now it should be clear that Christianity as a movement was fated to define itself along differing lines in eucharistic terms. The ministry of Jesus set in motion a process of transformation, in which an initial practice of purity by means of forgiveness at meals was transformed into a surrogate of sacrifice after Jesus' occupation of the outer court of the temple. Peter's circle changed that type into a new sort of covenantal sacrifice, not a permanent replacement but a foundational act that permitted Jesus' followers in the Petrine circle to go on worshiping in the Temple while they accepted Jesus' view of purity. If the Petrine transformation of the meal may be regarded as a domestication of dominical types, what happened at the next stage was even more emphatically so. James's circle restricted Eucharist to Jewish followers of Jesus, in the manner of Passover. The Jacobean definition of the movement, in stark contrast to the Pauline definition, was as a version of ethnic Judaism centered in Jerusalem; only the revolt that resulted in the Roman arson of the Temple in 70 C.E. eclipsed what may have emerged as the dominant form of Christianity.

The fifth type of Eucharist, however, became normative in the history of the church. The Synoptic reading, derived from Barnabas, the great compromiser at Antioch with whom Paul had disagreed, proved to have the resilience to reconcile the stark alternatives represented by the Petrine and Jacobean circles. The Synoptic reference to the "body" and "blood" within a biographical context permitted the association with Jesus himself at the point of martyrdom. Solidarity with him could be regarded as being as literal as eating bread and drinking wine. Although the Synoptic tradition did not impose that understanding, it was open to such a reading. A notion that would have been unthinkable at earlier stages—eating a person's flesh and drinking his blood—became the ordinary paradigm of Christian worship.

The compromise of Barnabas was successful, but not simply because it offered an amalgam of what had gone before. It is rather a case of a transformation that manages to express and enhance the systemic drive of a religious movement. Before and after Jesus' occupation of the temple, and within the Petrine and the Jacobean types of Eucharist, the central focus was always what Jesus had done, whether it was to celebrate purity, to offer a replacement of sacrifice, to validate a covenant, or to keep Passover. All of that imagery could be taken up within eucharistic theology and leave room for further developments, because the common denominator was also the common detonator: The same rabbi said and did things to fill a meal with meaning. But to say we consume his "flesh" and his "blood"—as is plainly asserted by the time of John—is to say that the very means of our communion with

Christ are alternative to any reasonable construction of purity within Judaism. It is no longer Jesus' practice but his very self that is the substance of Eucharist. At just the moment Eucharist discloses its systemic force, the divergence of Christianity from Judaism is accomplished. Communion in Christ's body and blood is separation from classic constructions of purity within Judaism, even as it is held to be communion with God.

A Judaic Response to a Christian's Community with God

Jacob Neusner

⁓

S ETTING SIDE BY SIDE my companion's account of community with God and mine, I am struck by the incongruity. I talk about communion with God through intellect and forthwith open the Talmud, the ultimate statement of the Torah, wherein and by which God is made manifest to humanity. There I find myself weighing the claims of conflicting parties—joint tenants to a property, for instance. What has God to do with such a conflict between persons? Have I not glided silently away from issues of theology altogether when, by way of introducing God as I find God (which means, in the Torah), I take up so secular a program as the one on which I concentrate in chapter 1? Here we really do address a religious alternative not only to Christianity but to all other religions, a religion different from all others by reason of its claim to know God through God's self-manifestation in words of a very particular order.

So far as my examples have made the point that in the Torah we learn how to use our minds in service to, and in the quest for, God, they accomplish their goal. But so far as they suggest that what is at stake is only, or mainly, affairs of this world, so that the Torah (also known as "Judaism") addresses secular concerns in a this-worldly way, I have not accomplished the purpose I set for myself. For the Torah covers a vast range of impractical, as much as practical, topics. Any claim that the Torah focuses on the secular misconstrues the character of the documents. Two facts point to a very different view.

91

First, the basic document of the oral Torah, the Mishnah, covers a vast number of topics that bear no practical consequences. In volume nearly one-half of the laws address the conduct of the temple cult and the upkeep of its buildings, on the one side, and the laws of cultic anti-sepsis ("purity"), on the other; none of these matters bore practical consequence at the time the Mishnah reached closure. Time and again the Talmud points to the utter impracticality of issues and defends its commitment to pure theory with the phrase, "It is Torah, expound the matter for its own sake and gain a reward thereby."

Second, and still more to the point, our sages of blessed memory receive the written Torah as not only the Word of God in the Protestant sense, but as the actual words of God. This is a most important distinction. We know precisely how God speaks, and from the language God uses when addressing Moses and the prophets, we enter into the intellect of God, as much as through the analysis of language we gain access to the thought of the other. We know not only the Word but the words, the wording, the grammar of thought and the syntax of cognition that the Creator of the world has found self-evidently reasonable. There is a shared rationality that links us to God, and the study of the Torah exposes to our minds the main structures of that rationality. As much as contemplation of nature manifests God's glory, so contemplation of the Torah opens up to us a glimpse into the glories of the universe of God's construction. The Torah's conception is only now finding comparable human efforts in the works of contemporary cosmology. But then physics will have to meet the competition of this ancient and enduring conception of cosmology: God's conception of creation, conveyed in the Torah; and then the mathematics of physics and the analysis of language—the Torah's, that is, God's language, in particular.

Difficult though such a conception of the encounter with God may prove for Christians, that conception cannot pose for holy Israel, the Judaist of the here and now, more intractable problems of understanding than does the engagement with God through Christ that Christianity offers for its counterpart. Let us move through the concrete points at which the Christian meets God and ask ourselves what the Torah offers in context. Baptism defines matters in such a way that a line is to be drawn between what one was and what one becomes. There was a time at which one was not in communion with God, then there came a time at which one entered communion—and that applies as much to Jesus, who required baptism, as to anyone else. But for those born into holy Israel, the supernatural entity, there never is a time at which one stands outside of the Torah. Circumcision is no counterindication; the uncircumcised Israelite remains an Israelite, beginning, after all, with Abraham for most of his life. True, the Gentile becomes Israel upon baptism (for the woman) or baptism and circumcision (for the man). But the Gentile really had been outside the Torah, and enters under the wings of God's presence with that act of entry marked by baptism and circumcision, as the case requires. There never is a moment at which holy Israel is not what it is, which makes the conception of baptism into communion with God exceedingly difficult to grasp. For us, we are Israel by reason of genealogy of a supernatural order, deriving from Abraham and Sarah and the other patriarchs and matriarchs; and the Gentile enters into that same supernatural genealogy by becoming a child of Abraham and Sarah too. But what enduring communion comes to the Christian, who generation by generation must regain the faith?

The same difference pertains to prayer. We know exactly how we should pray, because the Torah has ordained our prayers, the patriarchs being assigned authorship of the principal parts, the Torah itself supplying other important components of liturgy. To us, liturgy involves obligation; these are the words we are supposed to say; whether we wish to say them or not, they form part of our duty to heaven. True, prayer transcends the obligatory, but it always begins with what is assigned to us by heaven. Prayer is a form of service, as much as—and now, instead of—the offerings of the temple. The Lord's Prayer, which corresponds to our Kaddish ("Magnified and sanctified be the great Name in the world that He has created in accord with his will"/"Our father in heaven, hallowed be thy name"; "and may his kingdom come, in your lifetime and in the lifetime of all Israel"/"thy kingdom come, thy will be done. . . ."), forms the bridge. That obligatory prayer can convey to Christians how prayer lives for the holy Israel set forth by the Torah.

For us, much prayer is devoted to a rehearsal of the world's existence, a reprise of creation, revelation, and redemption. We not only address God and sanctify God's name, we not only ask God for what we want—bread, forgiveness, constancy. Prayer proclaims, as much as petitions; and first comes the proclamation. I find the Christian counterpart to our Shema—the Creed—to border on the perfunctory. We celebrate the faith; it is the centerpiece. All else comes later and subordinates itself to that. Let me dwell on this point, for those Christian readers who may not have ready at hand a copy of the liturgy of Judaism.

The Shema constitutes the credo of the Judaic tradition. It is "what the Jews believe." The three elements of the creed cover (1) creation, (2) revelation, then the proclamation of God's uniqueness and unity, and (3) redemption, that is to say, God as Creator of the world, God as revealer of the Torah, God as redeemer of Israel. To make the divisions of the prayer clear, I give headings in boldface type; these are not part of the liturgy but serve as signals to enable you to follow the propositional outline as it unfolds.

The Blessings Recited before the Shema

1. Creation of the World, attested by sunrise, sunset
Praised are You, O Lord our God, King of the universe.
You fix the cycles of light and darkness;
You ordain the order of all creation.
You cause light to shine over the earth;
Your radiant mercy is upon its inhabitants.
In Your goodness the work of creation
Is continually renewed day by day. . . .
O cause a new light to shine on Zion;
May we all soon be worthy to behold its radiance.
Praised are You, O Lord, Creator of the heavenly bodies.[1]

The corresponding prayer in the evening refers to the setting of the sun:

Praised are You. . . .
Your command brings on the dusk of evening.
Your wisdom opens the gates of heaven to a new day.
With understanding You order the cycles of time;
Your will determines the succession of seasons;
You order the stars in their heavenly courses.
You create day, and You create night,
Rolling away light before darkness. . . .
Praised are You, O Lord, for the evening dusk.

Morning and evening, Israel responds to the natural order of the world with thanks and praise of God, who created the world and who actively guides the daily events of nature. Whatever happens in nature gives testimony to the sovereignty of the Creator. And that testimony is not in unnatural disasters, but in the most ordinary events: sunrise and sunset.

These, especially, evoke the religious response to set the stage for what follows.

For Israel God is not merely Creator, but purposeful Creator. The works of creation serve to justify and to testify to Torah, the revelation of Sinai. Torah is the mark not merely of divine sovereignty, but of divine grace and love, source of life here and now and in eternity. So goes the second blessing:

2. Revelation of the Torah as the expression of God's love for Israel

Deep is Your love for us, O Lord our God;
Bounteous is Your compassion and tenderness.
You taught our fathers the laws of life,
And they trusted in You, Father and king,
For their sake be gracious to us, and teach us,
That we may learn Your laws and trust in You.
Father, merciful Father, have compassion upon us:
Endow us with discernment and understanding.
Grant us the will to study Your Torah,
To heed its words and to teach its precepts. . . .
Enlighten our eyes in Your Torah,
Open our hearts to Your commandments. . . .
Unite our thoughts with singleness of purpose
To hold You in reverence and in love. . . .
You have drawn us close to You;
We praise You and thank You in truth.
With love do we thankfully proclaim Your unity.
And praise You who chose Your people Israel in love.

Here is the way in which revelation takes concrete and specific form in the Judaic tradition: God the Creator reveals God's will for creation through the Torah, given to Israel, God's people. That Torah contains the "laws of life."

Moved to worship by the daily miracle of sunrise and sunset, corporate Israel responds with the prayer that Israel, like nature, may enjoy divine compassion. But what does that compassion consist of? The ability to understand and the will to study Torah. This is the point at which the classics we have now reviewed enter into the living faith: The words we have studied form the substance of the oral part of that same Torah to which, at prayer, Israel refers. Now comes the proclamation of the faith:

The Recitation of the Shema ("Hear . . .")

Hear, O Israel, the Lord Our God, the Lord is One.

This proclamation of the Shema is followed by three scriptural passages. The first is Deut. 6:5-9: "You shall love the LORD your God with all your heart, with all your soul, with all your might."

Further, the passage from Deuteronomy says that one must diligently teach one's children these words and talk of them everywhere and always, and place them on one's forehead, doorposts, and gates. The second Scripture is Deut. 11:13-21, which emphasizes that if Jews keep the commandments, they will enjoy worldly blessings; but that if they do not, they will be punished and disappear from the good land God gives them. The third is Num. 15:37-41, the commandment to wear fringes on the corners of one's garments. The theme of God, not as Creator or Revealer, but as Redeemer, concludes the twice-daily drama:

The Blessing Recited after the Shema

3. Redemption of Israel then and in the future
You are our King and our father's King,
Our redeemer and our father's redeemer.
You are our creator. . . .
You have ever been our redeemer and deliverer.
There can be no God but You. . . .
You, O Lord our God, rescued us from Egypt;
You redeemed us from the house of bondage. . . .
You split apart the waters of the Red Sea,
The faithful you rescued, the wicked drowned. . . .
Then Your beloved sang hymns of thanksgiving. . . .
They acclaimed the King, God on high,
Great and awesome source of all blessings,
The everliving God, exalted in his majesty.
He humbles the proud and raises the lowly;
He helps the needy and answers His people's call. . . .
Then Moses and all the children of Israel
Sang with great joy this song to the Lord:
Who is like You O Lord among the mighty?
Who is like You, so glorious in holiness?

So wondrous your deeds, so worthy of praise!
The redeemed sang a new song to You;
They sang in chorus at the shore of the sea,
Acclaiming Your sovereignty with thanksgiving:
The Lord shall reign for ever and ever.
Rock of Israel, arise to Israel's defense!
Fulfill Your promise to deliver Judah and Israel.
Our redeemer is the Holy One of Israel,
The Lord of hosts is His name.
Praised are You, O Lord, redeemer of Israel.

Just as creation takes place not only in the beginning, but every day, morning and night, so redemption occurs not only at the Red Sea, but every day, in humble events. Just as revelation occurred not at Sinai alone, but takes place whenever people study Torah, whenever God opens their hearts to the commandments, so redemption and creation are daily events. We note once more that while the individual may recite these prayers, the affirmation concerns the entire social entity, holy Israel.

With these prayers in mind, the gap between Christian and Judaic communion with God emerges with striking clarity. While a "You" figures in these prayers, the prayers focus on the proclamation of faith, taking up a central position in worship morning and evening. The conception of liturgy as a form of labor, an act of service to the divinity that consists of repeating words that God wishes us to repeat, becomes vivid in the Shema, encompassing its blessings fore and aft. To the religion of love for God expressed through obedience to the Torah and service to God that Judaism comprises, how we feel, what we are thinking, right attitude, and correct conscience—these perfectly natural considerations take a subordinate position. The issue here is not intimacy, it is dignity. We know who we are because God knows who we are, and we know what God wants us to say to God in prayer because the Torah has told us. So when I say, God is made manifest in the Torah—that is the whole of Judaism—the implications for prayer prove compelling.

At what point do we of supernatural Israel find the earthly instruction that, for Christians, the figure of Jesus Christ conveys? The Torah encompasses the prophets, and the prophets, with their stress on the priority of right over rite, teach Israel in simple images and powerful words, as much as the Gospels' Jesus Christ embodies and instructs concerning the right way to live. But, for the prophets, the transcendent principle cannot be identified as love. Prophecy is explicit, repeating itself from one prophet to the next, beginning with Moses' insistence on the priority of justice, reaching its climax in Amos' invidious contrast between sacrifice and righteousness. I wonder how much Christianity has lost in its insistence on the uniqueness of Jesus Christ to the exclusion of the heritage of Israelite prophecy. That is not to suggest for one minute that important teachings of Jesus do not cohere with the Torah's and the prophets' re-presentations of God's instruction; they do. It is only to point out how much more we have received in the Torah than Christians, claiming to revere "the Old Testament" too, have found therein. If I had to identify a single reason for Christianity to complete its mission as preparation for humanity to come to Sinai and receive the Torah, it would be this: God has taught us more, about more things, than even the empty tomb conveys. Victory over death is one thing, but not the main thing. For this world the Torah bears a far broader range of messages, and because of its demonstration of how we in our own intellects may listen for some of those messages, the Torah calls upon all humanity to exercise its rightful option.

Part Two

≈

THE KINGDOM OF GOD

≈

3

Living under the Yoke of the Kingdom of Heaven

JACOB NEUSNER

ONLY A FEW STUDY the Torah, but every Judaist is commanded to live in the kingdom of heaven and according to its laws. And life in God's kingdom is another way in which eternal Israel knows God. Accepting the "yoke of the kingdom of heaven"—which is to say, the dominion of God—and the "yoke of the Torah" by reciting the Shema ("Hear, Israel, the LORD our God, the LORD is one"), the Judaist day by day formulates his or her existence as a life of covenanted loyalty to the Torah. While only a few Judaists master the Talmud in such a way as to commune through the compelling perfection of right thinking, all of them accept the discipline of the Torah. To live in the kingdom of heaven means to live in accord with the revealed laws of the Torah, as these are explained and applied by the sages of Judaism.

When people think of law, they often imagine a religion for book-keepers, who tote up the good deeds and debit the bad and call the result salvation or damnation, depending on the outcome. And the Judaic religious way of life has been described by Christian "scholars" as a life of guilt for sin, a life in which people make trades with God—I give, you give—and a life utterly lacking in true piety. That of course represents a malicious caricature, contrasting the covenant of law with the gospel of love. Such a caricature has no bearing upon the realities of the holy way of life of Judaism. Life under the Torah brings the joy of expressing love of God through a cycle of celebration. In fact, the Judaic way of life joins three separate cycles, one in the rhythm of the year, the second in the rhythm of the week, the third in the rhythm of a person's life. Let us survey these three cycles.

Three Cycles in Judaic Life

The Judaic year follows the lunar calendar, so the appearance of the new moon marks the beginning of a month, and that beginning is celebrated. There are two critical moments in the unfolding of the year: the first full moon after the autumnal equinox, and the first full moon after the vernal equinox. These mark times of heightened celebration. To understand how the rhythm of the year unfolds, however, we begin with the new moon of the month of Tishri, corresponding to September. That marks the New Year, Rosh Hashanah. Ten days later comes the Day of Atonement, Yom Kippur, commemorating the rite described in Leviticus 16, and marking God's judgment and forgiveness of humanity. Five days afterward is the full moon, which is the beginning of the festival of Tabernacles, in Hebrew, Sukkot; that festival lasts for eight days and ends with a day of solemn assembly, Shemini Aseret, and of rejoicing of the Torah, Simhat Torah. So nearly the whole month of Tishri is spent in celebration: eating, drinking, praying, studying, enjoying, and celebrating God's sovereignty, creation, revelation, redemption, as the themes of the festivals and solemn celebrations of the season work themselves out.

The next major sequence of celebration follows the first new moon after the vernal equinox, which begins the month of Nisan and culminates, at its full moon, with Passover (in Hebrew, Pessah), which commemorates the Exodus of Israel from Egypt and celebrates Israel's freedom, bestowed by God. Fifty days thereafter comes the festival of Pentecost or Feast of Weeks (in Hebrew, Shavuot), which commemorates the giving of the Torah at Mount Sinai. Other occasions for celebration exist, but (apart from the Sabbath) the New Year, Day of Atonement, Tabernacles, Passover, and Pentecost are the main holy days.

The three historical-agricultural festivals pertain, in varying ways and combinations, to the themes we have already considered. Passover is the festival of redemption and points toward the Torah-revelation of the Feast of Weeks; the harvest festival in the autumn celebrates not only creation, but especially redemption.

Sabbath: Kingdom of Heaven on Earth

Let us consider the Sabbath first, since it is the single most important moment at which the kingdom of heaven is realized on earth: the fore-taste of the messianic era. The great theologian Abraham Joshua Heschel spells out the human transformation accomplished by the Sab-bath, showing what changes:

> Judaism is a religion of time aiming at the sanctification of time. Unlike the space-minded man to whom time is unvaried, iterative, homogeneous, to whom all hours are alike . . . , the Bible senses the diversified character of time. There are no two hours alike. Every hour is unique and the only one given at the moment, exclusive and endlessly precious. Judaism teaches us to be attached to holiness in time, to be attached to sacred events, to learn how to consecrate sanctuaries that emerge from the magnificent stream of a year. The Sabbaths are our great cathedrals, and our Holy of Holies is a shrine that neither the Romans nor the Germans were able to burn. . . . Jewish ritual may be characterized as the art of significant forms in time, as architecture of time. Most of its observances . . . depend on a certain hour of the day or season of the year. . . . The main themes of faith lie in the realm of time. We remember the day of the exodus from Egypt, the day when Israel stood at Sinai; and our Messianic hope is the expectation of a day, of the end of days.[1]

The Sabbath lays down a judgment on the fundamental issues of civiliza-tion. Specifically, it demands restraint, dignity, reticence, and silent rest—not commonplace virtues. If, therefore, the transformation of time, the centerpiece of the life of Judaism, takes place for only a few, the reason is not obsolescence but the opposite: excessive relevance. The Sabbath calls into question the foundations of the life of one dimension only, asking how people can imagine that what they see just now is all there is. The Sabbath celebrates the completion and perfec-tion of creation, that is, of nature:

> When the heaven and earth were done, and all their array, when God had finished the work that he had been doing, then he rested on the seventh day from all the work that he had done. Then God blessed the seventh day and made it holy, because on it God

desisted from all of the work of creating in which he had been engaged. (Gen. 2:1-3)

That account of the first Sabbath stands in judgment on those who, like God, create, but, unlike God, never rest. They deny themselves occasion to admire and enjoy. I can find no more penetrating judgment upon the human condition than the position of the Sabbath: One can have too much, enjoy too little, and so care about things that do not count:

> Inner liberty depends upon being exempt from domination of things as well as from domination of people. There are many who have acquired a high degree of political and social liberty, but only very few are not enslaved to things. This is our constant problem—how to live with people and remain free, how to live with things and remain independent.[2]

The Sabbath speaks of transcendent things, of life with God and in God, in ways in which the more concrete celebration of freedom does not. For the Sabbath penetrates into the heart of commonplace being, while Passover addresses the merely social and political. Societies do well with that kind of problem. In a world that celebrates deed, not deliberation, reckoning value in what is weighed and measured, what words can create a world so intangible as one of time?

> We cannot solve the problem of time through the conquest of space, through either pyramids or fame. We can only solve the problem of time through sanctification of time. To men alone time is elusive; to men with God time is eternity in disguise. This is the task of men: to conquer space and sanctify time. We must conquer space in order to sanctify time. All week long we are called upon to sanctify life through employing things of space. On the Sabbath it is given us to share in the holiness that is in the heart of time.[3]

The words that precipitate the world of the Sabbath invoke the day both as a memorial of creation and as a remembrance of the redemption from Egypt. The primary liturgy of the Sabbath is the reading of the Scripture lesson from the Torah in the synagogue service. So the three chief themes of the Judaic system—creation, revelation, and redemption—are combined in the weekly observance of the seventh day. The Sabbath works more than through words. It is the creation also of one's actions and omissions in making of time a different world. The Sabbath is protected by negative rules: One must not work; one must not pursue mundane concerns. But the Sabbath is also adorned with less concrete but affirmative laws: One must rejoice; one must rest.

How to make and keep the Sabbath? All week long Judaists look forward to it, and the anticipation enhances the ordinary days. By Friday afternoon in general those who keep the Sabbath will have bathed, put on their Sabbath garments, and set aside the affairs of the week. At home, the family—husband, wife, children, or whoever stands for family—will have cleaned, cooked, and arranged the finest table. It is common to invite guests for the Sabbath meals. The Sabbath comes at sunset Friday and leaves when three stars appear Saturday night. After a brief service the family comes together to enjoy its best meal of the week, a meal at which particular Sabbath foods are served. In the morning comes the Sabbath service, including a public reading from the Torah, the Five Books of Moses, and prophetic writings, and an additional service in memory of the temple sacrifices on Sabbaths of old. Then the faithful return home for lunch and commonly a Sabbath nap, the sweetest part of the day. As the day wanes, the synagogue calls for a late afternoon service, followed by Torah study and a third meal. Then comes a ceremony, havdalah (separation)—effected with spices, wine, and candlelight—between the holy time of the Sabbath and the ordinary time of weekday.

I do not mean to suggest that this idyllic picture characterizes all Sabbath observance, nor do I believe (though many do) that the only way to sanctify the Sabbath is in the received way I have described. Reform Judaism has displayed the wisdom to honor a variety of abstinences and actions as acts of sanctification of the time of the Sabbath. But, in the main, the Sabbath works its wonder when people retreat into family—however they understand their family—and take leave of work and the workaday world.

This simple, regular observance has elicited endless praise. To the Sabbath-observing Jew, the Sabbath is the chief sign of God's grace:

> For thou hast chosen us and sanctified us above all nations, in love and favor has given us thy holy Sabbath as an inheritance.

So states the Sanctification of the Sabbath wine. Likewise in the Sabbath morning liturgy:

> You did not give it [Sabbath] to the nations of the earth, nor did you make it the heritage of idolators, nor in its rest will unrighteous men find a place.
>
> But to Israel your people you have given it in love, to the seed of Jacob whom you have chosen, to that people who sanctify the Sabbath day. All of them find fulfillment and joy from your bounty.
>
> For the seventh day did you choose and sanctify as the most pleasant of days and you called it a memorial to the works of creation.[4]

Here again we find a profusion of themes, this time centered on the Sabbath. The Sabbath is a sign of the covenant. It is a gift of grace, which neither idolators nor evil people may enjoy. It is the testimony of the chosenness of Israel. And it is the most pleasant of days. Keeping the Sabbath *is* living in God's kingdom:

> Those who keep the Sabbath and call it a delight will rejoice in your kingdom.

So states the additional Sabbath prayer. Keeping the Sabbath now is a foretaste of the redemption: "This day is for Israel light and rejoicing." The rest of the Sabbath is, as the afternoon prayer affirms, "a rest granted in generous love, a true and faithful rest."

> . . . Let your children realize that their rest is from you, and by their rest may they sanctify your name.

That people need respite from the routine of work is no discovery of the Judaic tradition. That the way in which they accomplish such a routine change of pace may be made the very heart and soul of their spiritual existence is the single unique element in Judaic tradition. The word *Sabbath* simply renders the Hebrew *Shabbat;* it does not translate it, for there is no translation. In no other tradition or culture can an equivalent word be found. Certainly those who compare the Sabbath of Judaism to the somber, supposedly joyless Sunday of the Calvinists know nothing of what the Sabbath has meant and continues to mean to Jews.

From this brief description of what the Jew does on the seventh day, we can hardly derive understanding of how the Sabbath can have meant so much as to elicit words such as those of the Jewish prayer book and of Rabbi Heschel. Those words, like the negative laws of the Sabbath—not to mourn, not to confess sins, not to repent, not to do anything that might lead to unhappiness—describe something only the participant can truly comprehend and feel. Only a family whose life focuses upon the Sabbath week by week, year by year, from birth to death, can know the sanctity of which the theologian speaks, the sacred rest to which the prayers refer. The heart and soul of the Judaic tradition, the Sabbath cannot be described, only experienced. For the student of religions, it stands as that element of Judaism that is absolutely unique and therefore a mystery. It therefore forms the heart of the enchanted life of Judaism: where and how and why Judaism is a religion, not merely a social entity or a politics or a culture or a way of life. For transformation speaks not of external things but of a change at the very core of being: there is religion; there, in the language of Judaism, is the Torah; there we meet God; there we become like God, "in our image, after our likeness."

Cycles of the Season: Sukkot, Pessah, Shavuot

The festivals mark the passage of time, not of the week but of the seasons. Those seasons of sanctification and celebration are three: Sukkot, the week following the first full moon after the autumnal equinox, called in the classical sources The Festival par excellence; Pessah, or Passover, the week following the first full moon after the vernal equinox; and Shavuot, or Weeks, seven weeks later. Each festival both celebrates and commemorates, celebrating an event in nature, commemorating an event in Israel's sacred history.

Sukkot, Feast of Tabernacles
Sukkot, the Feast of Tabernacles, marks the end of agricultural toil. The fall crops by then are gathered in from the fields, orchards, and vineyards. The rainy season in the Holy Land of Israel (and in North America) is about to begin. It is time both to give thanks for what has been granted and to pray for abundant rains in the coming months. Called a festival of the in-gathering, it was the celebration of nature. But the mode of celebration also after the fact commemorates a moment in Israel's history, specifically, the wandering in the wilderness. Then the Israelites lived not in permanent houses but in huts or booths. At a time of bounty it is good to be reminded of humankind's travail and dependence on heavenly succor, which underlies the message of the Sabbath. The principal observance of the festival is the construction of a frail hut,

or booth, for temporary use during Sukkot. In warmer climates Jews eat their meals outdoors in the booths. The huts are covered with branches, leaves, fruit, and flowers, but light shows through, and at night, the stars.

Passover and the Seder

This brings us to Passover, the Jewish spring festival. The symbols of the Passover Seder—hard-boiled eggs and greens, lying on a plate on the Seder table, curiously neglected in the Passover narrative—are not unfamiliar in other spring rites. But here the spring rite has been transformed into a historical commemoration. The natural course of the year, while important, is subordinated to the historical events remembered and relived during the festival. Called the Feast of Unleavened Bread and the season of our freedom, Passover preserves ancient rites in a new framework.

It is, for example, absolutely prohibited to make use of leaven, fermented dough, and the like. The agricultural calendar of ancient Canaan was marked by the grain harvest, beginning in the spring with the cutting of barley and ending with the reaping of wheat approximately seven weeks later. The farmers would get rid of all their sour dough, which they used as leavening, and discard old bread as well as any leaven from last year's crop. The origins of the practice are not clear, but that the Passover taboo against leaven was connected with the agricultural calendar is beyond doubt. Just as the agricultural festivals were historicized, likewise much of the detailed observance connected with them was supplied with historical "reasons" or explanations. In the case of the taboo against leaven, widely observed today even among otherwise nonobservant Jews, the "reason" was that the Israelites had to leave Egypt in haste and therefore had to take with them unleavened bread, for they had no time to permit the bread to rise properly and be baked. Therefore we eat the matzoh, unleavened bread.

The most important rite of Passover is the Seder, a festival banquet at which the Haggadah, or narrative of the Exodus to freedom, is recited. Jewish families gather around their tables for a holy meal. There, speaking in very general terms, they retell the story of the Exodus from Egypt in times long past. With unleavened bread and sanctified wine, they celebrate the liberation of slaves from Pharaoh's bondage. During the rite, a single formula captures the moment in words; to understand how the "we" of the family becomes the "we" of Israel, how the eternal and perpetual coming of spring is made to mark a singular moment, a one-time act on the stage in the unfolding of linear time, we begin here:

> For ever after, in every generation, *every Israelite must think of himself or herself as having gone forth from Egypt* [italics added].

One theme stands out: We, here and now, are really living then and there. So, for example:

> *We* were slaves of Pharaoh in Egypt and the Lord our God brought us forth from there with a mighty hand and an outstretched arm. And if the Holy One, blessed be He, had not brought our fathers forth from Egypt, then we and our descendants would still be slaves to Pharaoh in Egypt. And so, even if all of us were full of wisdom, understanding, sages and well informed in the Torah, we should still be obligated to repeat again the story of the Exodus from Egypt; and whoever treats as an important matter the story of the Exodus from Egypt is praiseworthy.

And again:

> This is the bread of affliction which our ancestors ate in the land of Egypt. Let all who are hungry come and eat with us, let all who are needy come and celebrate the Passover with us. This year here, next year in the land of Israel; this year slave, next year free people.

And yet a third statement:

> This is the promise which has stood by our forefathers and stands by us. For neither once, nor twice, nor three times was our destruction planned; in every generation they rise against us, and in every generation God delivers us from their hands into freedom, out of anguish into joy, out of mourning into festivity, out of darkness into light, out of bondage into redemption.

Enchantment is not subtle. As though the implicit premise were not clear, let us revert to the point at which we began and hear how it is stated in so many words:

> For ever after, in every generation, *every Israelite must think of himself or herself as having gone forth from Egypt* [italics added]. For we read in the Torah: "In that day thou shalt teach thy son, saying: All this is because of what God did for me when I went forth from

Egypt." It was not only our forefathers that the Holy One, blessed be He, redeemed; us too, the living, He redeemed together with them, as we learn from the verse in the Torah: "And He brought us out from thence, so that He might bring us home, and give us the land which He pledged to our forefathers."

Passover celebrates the family of Israel and is celebrated by the families of Israel. So Passover, with its rhetoric of rejoicing for freedom, plays out in a minor key the song of liberation: today slaves, next year free; today here, next year in "Jerusalem" (that is, not the real Jerusalem but the imagined, heavenly one):

> We were slaves in Egypt . . . and if the Holy One . . . had not . . . , we would still be slaves . . .
> This year here slaves here, next year free in Jerusalem . . .
> In every generation they rise against us, and in every generation God delivers us . . .
> For ever after, in every generation every Israelite must think of himself or herself as having gone forth from Egypt. . . .

Passover speaks not to history alone but to personal biography; it joins together history with the experience of the individual, because the individual as a minority finds self-evident—relevant, true, urgent—a rite that reaches into the everyday and the here and now and turns that common world into a metaphor for the reality of Israel, enslaved but also redeemed. The Seder effects its enchantment by showing the individual that the everyday stands for something beyond, the here and now represent the everywhere and all times: "In every generation they rise against us." True, but also, God saves. Who would not be glad to have supper to celebrate that truth, if only through commemoration?

The word Seder means "order," and the sense is that a sequence of actions takes place as prescribed. Here is the order of the Seder. The word *matzoh* refers to unleavened bread. I have divided the order into the gestures, on the one side, the recitation of words, indented and in italics on the other:

Deeds
>   *Words*
First washing of the hands
Eating of the parsley
Breaking of the middle cake of matzoh

Recital of the narrative
Second washing of the hands
Grace for bread
Breaking and dividing up of topmost piece of matzoh
Eating of bitter herb dipped in charoset (chopped apple, nuts, wine)
Eating of bitter herb with matzoh
Meal
Eating of the afikomon (a piece of matzoh eaten to mark the end of the meal)
Grace after the meal
Hallel (recitation of Psalms 113–118)
Closing prayer

The curious picture emerges of two quite separate occasions, running side by side but not meeting. Were we to describe the banquet on the basis of this catalog, we should expect a recitation much engaged by attention to hand-washing, the eating of parsley, the breaking and disposition of pieces of unleavened bread (the raising and lowering, breaking, hiding, and eating of pieces of matzoh). We would then be unprepared for the reality of the Seder rite, which involves an enormous flow of words. Not only so, but the introit of the rite focuses on the ritual aspect of the meal, not on the narrative:

> Why has this night been made different from all other nights? On all other nights we eat bread whether leavened or unleavened, on this night only unleavened; on all other nights we eat all kinds of herbs, on this night only bitter ones; on all other nights we do not dip herbs even once; on this night, twice; on all other nights we sit at the table either sitting or reclining, on this night we all recline.

In point of fact, none of these questions, addressed by the youngest person present to the one presiding, is ever answered. Instead we get the following (I italicize the operative words):

> We were the slaves of Pharaoh in Egypt; and the Lord our God brought us forth from there with a mightily hand and an outstretched arm. And if the Holy One, blessed be He, had not brought our fathers forth from Egypt, then surely we, and our children, and our children's children, would be enslaved to Pharaoh in Egypt. *And so, even if all of us were full of wisdom and understand-*

ing, well along in years and deeply versed in the tradition, we should still be bidden to repeat once more the story of the Exodus from Egypt; and he who delights to dwell on the liberation is one to be praised.

Now we shift from the symbols present to the occasion commemorated and celebrated, and, until the completion of a considerable "narrative," we forget the pillow and the parsley and the matzoh and remember Pharaoh and Egypt. This narrative is composed of bits and pieces that do not flow together at all, a citation and exegesis of some verses of Scripture, some games, prayers, snatches of stories, hymns. Made up of incoherent liturgies, joining together varieties of essentially unrelated materials, the so-called narrative tells this story, and I take it to form the centerpiece of the Seder:

> Long ago our ancestors were idol-worshippers but now the Holy One has drawn us to his service. So we read in the Torah: And Joshua said to all the people, "Thus says the Lord, God of Israel: From time immemorial your fathers lived beyond the river Euphrates, even to Terah, father of Abraham and of Nahor, and they worshipped idols. And I took your father Abraham from beyond the river and guided his footsteps throughout the land of Canaan. I multiplied his offspring and gave him Isaac. To Isaac I gave Jacob and Esau. And I set apart Mount Seir as the inheritance of Esau, while Jacob and his sons went down to Egypt."

The first part of the narrative is deeply relevant to those present, for it says who they (really) are and for whom they (really) stand. In the here and now they stand for "our ancestors," Abraham, Isaac, and Jacob. Here is the second, and more important part (I italicize the key words):

> Blessed is *he who keeps his promise to Israel . . . for the Holy One, set a term to our bondage,* fulfilling the word which He gave our father Abraham in the covenant made between the divided sacrifice: Know beyond a doubt that your offspring will be *strangers in a land that is not theirs,* four hundred years they shall serve and suffer. But in the end I shall pronounce judgment on the oppressor people and your offspring shall go forth with great wealth.

Herein lies the power of the Passover banquet rite to transform ordinary existence into an account of something beyond. The ordinary existence imposes its tensions. Jews are different from Gentiles. That difference is what defines them as Jews. But now, in the transformation at hand, to be a Jew means to be a slave who has been liberated by God. To be Israel means to give eternal thanks for God's deliverance. And that deliverance does not occur at a single moment in historical time. Transformed into a permanent feature of reality, it is made myth, a story of deep truth that comes true in every generation and is always celebrated. Here again, events of natural, ordinary life are transformed through myth into paradigmatic, eternal, and ever-recurrent sacred moments. In terms we have used before, the everyday is treated as a paradigm and a metaphor. Jews think of themselves as having gone forth from Egypt, and Scripture so instructs them. God did not redeem the dead generation of the Exodus alone, but the living too—especially the living. Thus the family states:

> Again and again, in double and redoubled measure, are we beholden to God the All-Present: that He freed us from the Egyptians and wrought His judgment on them; that He sentenced all their idols and slaughtered all their first-born; that He gave their treasure to us and split the Red Sea for us; that He led us through it dry-shod and drowned the tyrants in it; that He helped us through the desert and fed us with the manna; that He gave the Sabbath to us and brought us to Mount Sinai; that He gave the Torah to us and brought us to our homeland—there to build the Temple for us, for atonement of our sins.

Israel was born in historical times. Historians, biblical scholars, and archaeologists have much to say about that event. But to the classical Jew their findings, while interesting, have little bearing on the meaning of reality. The redemptive promise that stood by the forefathers and "stands by us" is not a mundane historical event but a mythic interpretation of historical, natural events. Oppression, homelessness, extermination—like salvation, homecoming, renaissance—are this-worldly and profane events, supplying headlines for newspapers. The myth that a Jew must think of himself or herself as having gone forth from Egypt and as being redeemed by God renders ordinary experience into a moment of celebration. If "us, too, the living, He [has] redeemed," then the observer no longer witnesses only historical persons in historical time, but an eternal return to sacred time: The kingdom of heaven takes place in the here and now, but nowhere in particular.

Shavuot, Feast of Weeks

The Feast of Weeks, Shavuot or Pentecost, comes seven weeks after Passover. In the ancient Palestinian agricultural calendar, it marked the end of the grain harvest and was called the feast of harvest. In temple times, two loaves of bread were baked from the wheat of the new crop and offered as a sacrifice, the firstfruits of wheat harvest. So Shavuot came to be called the day of the firstfruits. Judaism added a historical explanation to the natural ones derived from the land and its life. The rabbis held that the Torah was revealed on Mount Sinai on that day and celebrated it as "the time of the giving of our Torah." Passover is the festival of redemption and points toward the Torah-revelation of the Feast of Weeks; the harvest festival in the autumn celebrates not only creation, but especially redemption. Like the Sabbath, these festivals take ordinary people and turn them into Israel; they take profane time and sanctify it.

Days of Awe: New Year and Day of Atonement

The Days of Awe—the New Year and the Day of Atonement—concern life and death, which take mythic form in affirmations of God's rule and judgment. The words create a world aborning, the old world gone, the new just now arriving.

Rosh Hashanah

The New Year, Rosh Hashanah, celebrates the creation of the world: *Today the world was born.* The time of new beginnings also marks endings: *On the New Year the decree is issued: Who will live and who will die?* At the New Year, so the words state, humanity is inscribed for life or death in the heavenly books for the coming year, and on the Day of Atonement the books are sealed. The world comes out to hear these words. The season is rich in celebration. The synagogues on that day are filled—whether with penitents or with people who merely wish to be there hardly matters. The New Year is a day of remembrance on which the deeds of all creatures are reviewed. The principal themes of the words invoke creation and God's rule over creation, revelation, God's rule in the Torah for the created world, and redemption, God's ultimate plan for the world.

On the birthday of the world God made, God asserts sovereignty, as in the New Year prayer:

> Our God and God of our Fathers, rule over the whole world in Your honor . . . and appear in Your glorious might to all those who dwell in the civilization of Your world, so that everything made will know that You made it, and every creature discern that You have created him, so that all in whose nostrils is breath may say, "The Lord, the God of Israel is king, and His kingdom extends over all."

Liturgical words concerning divine sovereignty, divine memory, and divine disclosure correspond to creation, revelation, and redemption. Sovereignty is established by creation of the world. Judgment depends upon law: "From the beginning You made this, Your purpose known. . . ." And therefore, since people have been told what God requires of them, they are judged:

> On this day sentence is passed upon countries, which to the sword and which to peace, which to famine and which to plenty, and each creature is judged today for life or death. Who is not judged on this day? For the remembrance of every creature comes before You, each man's deeds and destiny, words and way. . . .

The theme of revelation is further combined with redemption; the ram's horn, or shofar, which is sounded in the synagogue during daily worship for a month before the Rosh Hashanah festival, serves to unite the two:

> You did reveal yourself in a cloud of glory. . . . Out of heaven you made them [Israel] hear Your voice. . . . Amid thunder and lightning You revealed yourself to them, and while the shofar sounded You shined forth upon them. . . . Our God and God of our fathers, sound the great shofar for our freedom. Lift up the ensign to gather our exiles. . . . Lead us happily to Zion Your city, Jerusalem the place of Your sanctuary.

The complex themes of the New Year, the most "theological" of Jewish holy occasions, thus weave together the tapestry of a highly charged moment in a world subject to the personal scrutiny of a most active God.

Yom Kippur

What of the Day of Atonement? Here too we hear the same answers, see the unfolding of a single process of transformation of secular into sacred time. The most personal, solemn, and moving of the Days of Awe is the Day of Atonement, Yom Kippur, the Sabbath of Sabbaths. It is marked by fasting and continuous prayer. On it, the Jew makes confession:

> Our God and God of our fathers, may our prayer come before You. Do not hide yourself from our supplication, for we are not so arrogant or stiff-necked as to say before You. . . . We are righteous and have not sinned. But we have sinned.
> We are guilt laden, we have been faithless, we have robbed. . . .
> We have committed iniquity, caused unrighteousness, have been presumptuous. . . .
> We have counseled evil, scoffed, revolted, blasphemed. . . .

The Hebrew confession is built upon an alphabetical acrostic, as if by making certain every letter is represented, God, who knows human secrets, will combine them into appropriate words. The very alphabet bears witness against us before God. Then:

> What shall we say before You who dwell on high? What shall we tell You who live in heaven? Do You not know all things, both the hidden and the revealed? You know the secrets of eternity, the most hidden mysteries of life. You search the innermost recesses, testing men's feelings and heart. Nothing is concealed from You or hidden from Your eyes. May it therefore be Your will to forgive us our sins, to pardon us for our iniquities, to grant remission for our transgressions.

A further list of sins follows, built on alphabetical lines. Prayers to be spoken by the congregation are all in the plural: "For the sin which we have sinned against You with the utterance of the lips. . . . For the sin which we have sinned before You openly and secretly. . . ." The community takes upon itself responsibility for what is done in it. All Israel is part of one community, one body, and all are responsible for the acts of each. The sins confessed are mostly against society, against one's fellows; few pertain to ritual laws. At the end comes a final word:

> O my God, before I was formed, I was nothing. Now that I have been formed, it is as though I had not been formed, for I am dust in my life, more so after death. Behold I am before You like a vessel filled with shame and confusion. May it be Your will. . . . that I may no more sin, and forgive the sins I have already committed in Your abundant compassion.

While much of the liturgy speaks of "we," the individual focus dominates from beginning to end. The Days of Awe speak to the heart of the individual, telling a story of judgment and atonement. So the individual Jew stands before God, possessing no merits yet hopeful of God's love and compassion. Any relationship between the Judaic view of the human situation and "a religion of accountants and shopkeepers" is to be seen only in the imagination of the enemies of Judaism in Protestant theological circles, past and present.

Rites of Passage in the Individual's Life

Now we turn to the life cycle and its celebrations: The passage of the individual's life, from birth to death, marks out the third of the three cycles in the way of Torah, the cycles that convey the spirit of the Torah, or "law" as the word is translated. The principal points are birth, puberty, marriage, and death. Birth in the case of males is marked by circumcision on the eighth day. Nowadays in the synagogue the birth of both sons and daughters is celebrated by a rite of naming of the child. A simple rite in the synagogue celebrates a child's becoming responsible to carry out the religious duties that are called mitzvot, or commandments; the child enters the status known as bar mitzvah for the boy and bat mitzvah for the girl. The young woman or man is called to the Torah, which she or he reads, and the newly responsible young adult also reads the prophetic passage of the day. Marriage forms yet another rite of passage, with its own distinctive liturgy. The liturgy invokes Adam and Eve as the new family begins a new creation. Rites of death involve a clear recognition that God rules and is the true and just authority over all humanity. The memorial prayer, or Kaddish for mourners, expresses the worshiper's recognition of God's holiness and dominion and states the hope for the coming of the Messiah. In a few words these celebrations, which one might call "life-cycle events," define life in the kingdom of heaven and explain how Judaists seek to live in accord with God's will, which is that Israel live the holy life in the here and now and await salvation at the end of time.

Life in Accord with Halakhah: The Way

The word for concrete instruction of one's duty, of the proper way of doing things, is halakhah, and when we speak of life in the kingdom of heaven, we mean life in accord with the halakhah, the rules and regulations of the holy life. The mythic structure built upon the themes of creation, revelation, and redemption finds expression, not only in synagogue liturgy, but especially in concrete, everyday actions or action-symbols—that is, deeds that embody and express the fundamental mythic life of the classical Judaic tradition.

These action-symbols are set forth in halakhah. This word is normally translated as "law," for the halakhah is full of normative, prescriptive rules about what one must do and refrain from doing in every situation of life and at every moment of the day. But halakhah derives from the root *halakh,* which means "go," and a better translation would be "way." The halakhah is "the way": The way man lives his life; the way man shapes his daily routine into a pattern of sanctity; the way man follows the revelation of the Torah and attains redemption.

For the Judaic tradition, this *way* is absolutely central. Belief without the expression of belief in the workaday world is of limited consequence. The purpose of revelation is to create a kingdom of priests and a holy people. The foundation of that kingdom, or sovereignty, is the rule of God over the lives of humanity. For the Judaic tradition, God rules much as people do, by guiding others on the path of life, not by removing them from the land of living. Creation lies behind; redemption, in the future; Torah is for here and now. To the classical Jew, Torah means revealed law or commandment, accepted by Israel and obeyed from Sinai to the end of days.

The spirit of the Jewish way (halakhah) is conveyed in many modes, for law is not divorced from values, but rather embodies human beliefs and ideals. The purpose of the commandments is to show the road to sanctity, the way to God. In a more mundane sense, the following provides a valuable insight:

> Rava [a fourth-century rabbi] said, "When a man is brought in for judgment in the world to come, he is asked, 'Did you deal in good faith? Did you set aside time for study of Torah? Did you engage in procreation? Did you look forward to salvation? Did you engage in the dialectics of wisdom? Did you look deeply into matters?'"
> *Babylonian Talmud Tractate Shabbat,* p. 31(A)

Rava's interpretation of the Scripture "and there shall be faith in thy times, strength, salvation, wisdom and knowledge" (Isa. 33:6) provides one glimpse into the life of the classical Jew who followed the way of

Torah. The first consideration was ethical: Did the man conduct himself faithfully? The second was study of Torah, not at random but every day, systematically, as a discipline of life. Third came the raising of a family, for celibacy and abstinence from sexual life were regarded as sinful; the full use of the human's creative powers for the procreation of life was a commandment. Nothing God made was evil. Wholesome conjugal life was a blessing. But, fourth, merely living day-by-day according to an upright ethic was not sufficient. It is true that people must live by a holy discipline, but the discipline itself was only a means. The end was salvation. Hence the pious people were asked to look forward to salvation, aiming their deeds and directing their hearts toward a higher goal. Wisdom and insight completed the list, for without them, the way of Torah was a life of mere routine, rather than a constant search for deeper understanding.

If in this context we have not referred also to women, it is not because they were wholly excluded from the system, but because in this setting the principal activities—study of Torah, for example—were done by men only. The halakhah, in fact, clearly recognized that there were religious duties incumbent on both men and women, but some were required only of men. Women were excluded, in particular, from the requirement to perform those religious acts that had to be done at a particular time. The reason was that their responsibilities to their families overrode their responsibilities to heaven. If a woman had to perform a particular commandment and at the same time take care of her child, she could not do the former with a whole heart. Therefore from the very beginning the law excluded her—but not anymore.

Prayer in Judaic Piety

Life in the kingdom of heaven means praying—morning, noon, night, and at meals—both routinely and when something unusual happens. To be a Jew in the classical tradition, one lives his or her life constantly aware of the presence of God and always ready to praise and bless God. The way of Torah is the way of perpetual devotion to God. What is the substance of that devotion? For what do pious Jews ask when they pray?

The answers to these questions tell us about more than the shape and substance of Judaic piety. They tell us, too, what manner of person would take shape, for the constant repetition of the sacred words and moral and ethical maxims in the setting of everyday life is bound to affect the personality and character of the individual and the quality of communal life as well. Prayer expresses the most solemn aspirations of the praying community; it is what gives that community a sense of one-ness and of shared hopes; it embodies the values of the community. But if it is the community in its single most idiomatic hour, it also presents the community at its least particular and self-aware, for in praying, peo-ple stand before God without the mediation of culture and ethnic con-sciousness. But, as we shall see, that does not mean that we do not find in Judaic prayer an acute awareness of history and collective destiny. These are very present.

In the morning, noon, and evening prayers are found the Eighteen Benedictions. Some of these, in particular those at the beginning and the end, recur in Sabbath and festival prayers. They are said silently. Each individual prays by and for himself or herself, but together with other silent, praying individuals. The Eighteen Benedictions are then repeated aloud by the prayer leader, for prayer is both private and pub-lic, individual and collective. To contemplate the meaning of these prayers, one should imagine a room full of people, all standing by them-selves yet in close proximity, some swaying this way and that, all address-ing themselves directly and intimately to God in a whisper or in a low tone. They do not move their feet, for they are now standing before the King of kings, and it is not meet to shift and shuffle. If spoken to, they will not answer. Their attention is fixed on the words of supplication, praise, and gratitude. When they begin, they bend their knees—so too toward the end—and at the conclusion they step back and withdraw from the Holy Presence. These, on ordinary days, are the words they say; the italicized words are the translator's summary of the theme of the benediction that follows:

> *Wisdom-Repentance*
> You graciously endow man with intelligence;
> You teach him knowledge and understanding.
> Grant us knowledge, discernment, and wisdom.
> Praised are You O Lord, for the gift of knowledge.
> *Our Father, bring us back to Your Torah*
> Our King, draw us near to Your service;
> Lead us back to you truly repentant.

Praised are You, O Lord who welcomes repentance.
Forgiveness-Redemption
Our Father, forgive us, for we have sinned;
Our King, pardon us, for we have transgressed;
You forgive sin and pardon transgression.
Praised are You, gracious and forgiving Lord.
Behold our affliction and deliver us
Redeem us soon for the sake of Your name,
For You are the mighty Redeemer.
Praised are You, O Lord, Redeemer of Israel.
Heal Us, Bless Our Years
Heal us, O Lord, and we shall be healed;
Help us and save us, for You are our glory.
Grant perfect healing for all our afflictions,
O faithful and merciful God of healing.
Praised are You, O Lord, Healer of His people.
O Lord our God! Make this a blessed year;
May its varied produce bring us happiness.
Bring blessing upon the whole earth.
Bless the year with Your abounding goodness.
Praised are You, O Lord, who blesses our years.
Gather Our Exiles; Reign Over Us
Sound the great shofar to herald [our] freedom;
Raise high the banner to gather all exiles;
Gather the dispersed from the corners of the earth.
Praised are You, O Lord, who gathers our exiles.
Restore our judges as in days of old;
Restore our counselors as in former times;
Remove from us sorrow and anguish.
Reign over us alone with loving kindness;
With justice and mercy sustain our cause
Praised are You, O Lord, King who loves justice.
Humble the Arrogant—Sustain the Righteous
Frustrate the hopes of those who malign us;
Let all evil very soon disappear;
Let all Your enemies be speedily destroyed.
May You quickly uproot and crush the arrogant;
May You subdue and humble them in our time.
Praised are You, O Lord, who humbles the arrogant.
Let Your tender mercies, O Lord God, be stirred
For the righteous, the pious, the leaders of Israel,
Toward devoted scholars and faithful proselytes.
Be merciful to us of the house of Israel;

Reward all who trust in You;
Cast our lot with those who are faithful to You.
May we never come to despair, for our trust is in You.
Praised are You, O Lord, who sustains the righteous.
Favor Your City and Your People
Have mercy, O Lord, and return to Jerusalem, Your city;
May Your Presence dwell there as You promised.
Rebuild it now, in our days and for all time;
Re-establish there the majesty of David, Your servant.
Praised are You, O Lord, who rebuilds Jerusalem.
Bring to flower the shoot of Your servant David
Hasten the advent of the Messianic redemption;
Each and every day we hope for Your deliverance.
Praised are You, O Lord, who assures our deliverance.
O Lord, our God, hear our cry
Have compassion upon us and pity us;
Accept our prayer with loving favor.
You, O God, listen to entreaty and prayer.
O King, do not turn us away unanswered,
For You mercifully heed Your people's supplication.
Praised are You, O Lord, who is attentive to prayer.
O Lord, Our God, favor Your people Israel
Accept with love Israel's offering of prayer;
May our worship be ever acceptable to You.
May our eyes witness Your return in mercy to Zion.
Praised are You, O Lord, whose Presence returns to Zion.
Our Thankfulness
We thank You, O Lord our God and God of our fathers,
Defender of our lives, Shield of our safety;
Through all generations we thank You and praise You.
Our lives are in Your hands, our souls in Your charge.
We thank You for the miracles which daily attend us,
For Your wonders and favor morning, noon, and night.
You are beneficent with boundless mercy and love.
From of old we have always placed our hope in You.
For all these blessings, O our King,
We shall ever praise and exalt You.
Every living creature thanks You, and praises You in truth.
O God, You are our deliverance and our help. Selah!
Praised are You, O Lord, for Your Goodness and Your glory.
Peace and Well-Being
Grant peace and well-being to the whole house of Israel;
Give us of Your grace, Your love, and Your mercy.

Bless us all, O our Father, with the light of Your Presence.
It is Your light that revealed to us Your life-giving Torah,
And taught us love and tenderness, justice, mercy, and peace.
May it please You to bless Your people in every season,
To bless them at all times with Your fight of peace.
Praised are You, O Lord, who blesses Israel with peace.

The first two petitions pertain to intelligence. The Jew thanks God for mind: knowledge, wisdom, discernment. But knowledge is for a purpose, and the purpose is knowledge of Torah. Such discernment leads to the service of God and produces a spirit of repentance. We cannot pray without setting ourselves right with God, and that means repenting for what has separated us from God. Torah is the way to repentance and to return. So knowledge leads to Torah, Torah to repentance, and repentance to God. The logical next step is the prayer for forgiveness. That is the sign of return. God forgives sin; God is gracious and forgiving. Once we discern what we have done wrong through the guidance of Torah, we therefore seek to be forgiven. It is sin that leads to affliction. Affliction stands at the beginning of the way to God; once we have taken that way, we ask for our suffering to end; we beg redemption. This is then specified. We ask for healing, salvation, a blessed year. Healing without prosperity means we may suffer in good health or starve in a robust body. So along with the prayer for healing goes the supplication for worldly comfort.

The individual's task is done. But what of the community? Health and comfort are not enough. The world is unredeemed. Jews are enslaved, in exile, and alien. At the end of days a great shofar, or ram's horn, will sound to herald the Messiah's coming. This is now besought. The Jewish people at prayer ask first for the proclamation of freedom, then for the in-gathering of the exiles to the Promised Land. Establishing the messianic kingdom, God needs also to restore a wise and benevolent government, good judges, good counselors, and loving justice.

Meanwhile Israel, the Jewish people, finds itself maligned. As the prayer sees things, the arrogant who hate Israel hate God as well. They should be humbled. And the pious and righteous—the scholars, the faithful proselytes, the whole house of Israel that trusts in God—should be rewarded and sustained. Above all, God is beseeched to remember Jerusalem. Rebuild the city and dwell there. Set up Jerusalem's messianic king, David, and make him prosper. These are the themes of the daily prayer: personal atonement, good health, and good fortune; collective redemption, freedom, the end of alienation, good government, and true justice; the final and complete salvation of the land and of Jerusalem by the Messiah. At the end comes a prayer that prayer may be heard and found acceptable; then an expression of thanksgiving, not for what may come, but for the miracles and mercies already enjoyed morning, noon, and night. At the end comes a prayer for peace, a peace that consists of wholeness for the sacred community.

People who say such prayers do not wholly devote themselves to this world. True, they ask for peace, health, and prosperity, but these things are transient. At the same moment they ask, in many different ways, for eternity. They arise in the morning and speak of Jerusalem. At noon they make mention of the Messiah. In the evening they end the day with talk of the shofar to herald freedom and the in-gathering of the exiles. Living here in the profane, alien world, they constantly talk of going to the Holy Land and its perfect society. They address themselves to the end of days and the Messiah's time. The praying community above all seeks the fulfillment and end of its—and humanity's—travail.

Transfiguring Commonplaces: The Kingdom in Christianity

BRUCE CHILTON

T HE RABBINIC IDEA that the kingdom of heaven is to be equated with the Torah, such that reciting the Shema amounts to accepting the yoke of God's dominion, has exerted a powerful influence in recent Christian theology. In his classic work, *The Teaching of Jesus*, T. W. Manson wrote, "In all that has so far been sketched of our Lord's teaching about the Kingdom on earth there is nothing which might not have been uttered by an enlightened Rabbi of a liberal turn of mind, and very little to which the most orthodox could take exception."[1] Insofar as Jesus represents a departure, it is because he claims alone to be "the Son of Man, the incarnation of the Kingdom of God on earth."[2]

For two reasons, Manson's line of analysis has proved attractive. First, by accepting the Rabbinic equation of the kingdom and the Torah as the starting point of Jesus' preaching, the importance of eschatology may be qualified. Because he begins with an identification with Torah, and discusses eschatology as derivative from it, Manson can conclude "that the important question is not whether Jesus was correct in his dating of the Parousia [that is, his appearance on earth as the Son of man in glory], but whether he was right in his description of its nature."[3] Second, the initial definition permits Manson to return to "Religion and Morals" as the theme of Jesus' message in the final chapter of his book.

The alacrity of Christian scholars to accept Rabbinic definitions of the kingdom, as if they were to be equated with the understanding of the kingdom in early Judaic pluralism, betrays a desire to deny that the kingdom for Jesus was principally in the future and to affirm that he endorsed traditional constructions of morality. Neither point can be sustained easily. One does not announce as near something that has actually arrived, nor is it appropriate to pray for something to come that is already present. And parables such as the wedding feast (Matt. 22:1-14/Luke 14:16-24), the demanding owner (Matt. 25:14-30/Luke 19:12-27), the unforgiving servant (Matt. 18:23-35), the rich fool (Luke 12:16-21), and the clever steward (Luke 16:1-9) make the ethics of the kingdom seem anything but straightforward.[4]

The discipline of studying the New Testament has recently emerged from a period of some thirty years in which it has come to grips with the fact that passages such as those used by Manson represent Rabbinic Judaism after the destruction of the Temple, and therefore may not be assumed to describe Judaism in the time of Jesus. Most of the discussion has been conducted as if the issue at stake were chronological, but a framing concern has been whether Jesus' picture of the kingdom was fundamentally eschatological and morally unconventional. A simple reading of the Synoptics, whether at face value or critically, would have suggested that the answer was yes to both questions, whatever one made of the development of early Judaism.

Now, however, there is a common realization that the sources of Rabbinic Judaism achieved written form after the New Testament did. One might have hoped that such an acknowledgment would have brought interpretive progress in its wake, but the hope would have been somewhat disappointed. Graduate schools, especially in the United States, have reacted to recent discussion by deemphasizing the importance of any study of Judaism for students of the New Testament generally. Increasingly, what passes for advanced theological study is pursued without competence in Hebrew or Aramaic, and with familiarity with only selected sources of Judaism in translation. The study of Judaism, inclusive of the Rabbinic Judaism that was the outcome of early Judaism and whose texts sometimes reflect the early Judaism of the first century, has been pushed aside. The result is predictable: We have Jesus the Gnostic, Jesus the Victim, Jesus the Nonviolent, Jesus the Feminist, Jesus the Cynic, Jesus the Charismatic, above all Jesus the Universalist. If all these fashionable Jesuses were being sold in drugstores, that would be a sign of the intellectual and spiritual health of our culture. Instead, people are awarded doctorates for such caricatures, and what is sold in drugstores is even less plausible. It has come to the point where observing that Jesus might have had something to do with Judaism is regarded as an argument rather than a truism.

Before we leave the topic of the disenchantment with Judaism in graduate courses of theology, two common features of the diverse Jesuses of fashion need to be identified. For all that the range might seem bewildering, every one of them accomplishes just what Manson's Jesus did: Each speaks of a kingdom that is not fundamentally eschatological but is symbolic and/or political, and each comes complete with an agenda of how we ought to behave. The program of assimilating Jesus within a view of how our world should be, in other words, is still haunted by a sense of scandal that Jesus' world might not be ours at all, and that he might not tell us what to do in terms we would approve of.

Manson concluded his book by saying, "for Christians the sum of all morality is to have the same mind which was also in Christ Jesus."[5] As the description of a system of religion, his statement (as we have seen in chapter 2) is literally and precisely true. His confusion lies in equating the "Christ Jesus" of Philippians with the literarily historical Jesus of the Synoptics, and both of them with what Jesus of Nazareth did and said. Manson reified the mind of Christ with a particular reconstruction of Jesus within Rabbinic Judaism; some of his successors in North America reify that mind by means of a programmatic avoidance of Judaism. There is not much to choose between the two forms of reification. Neither of them offers a cogent construction of history; neither elucidates the sources well; neither offers an accounting of the emergence of Christianity from Judaism.

Christianity developed its view of God's kingdom first within the matrix of early Judaism, and then in growing antipathy to Rabbinic Judaism; similarly, by the time the Rabbinic definition of the kingdom became dominant within Judaism, as distinct (for example) from apocalyptic or political definitions, Christianity had established itself as a significant movement within the Greco-Roman world. Here is a case, then, when comparative analysis of systems of religion not only can but must be pursued, since each generated its meaning with at least some awareness of the other.

The equation between the kingdom and accepting the Torah (pp. 101, 118) implies that the human act of obedience creates a space, the realm in which the rule of God prevails. The focus on the periodicity of time, regulation by Sabbath and by feast, follows cogently from the establishment of just that space: "But, in the main, the Sabbath works its wonder when people retreat into family—however they understand their family—and take leave of work and the workaday world" (p. 105). What is described is the creation of a space out of time, in which the family on the seventh day is the territory of God's rule: "Keeping the Sabbath *is* living in God's kingdom" (p. 106).

The account of the principal feasts (the complex of Sukkot with the New Year and the Day of Atonement, Pessah, and Shavuot) reveals a deliberate disruption of ordinary time. Not only does an ancient agricultural calendar break in on what has long been ordinary urban life within Judaism; that calendar itself is then associated with events that are out of their historical sequence. Israel is in booths before it has left Egypt or received the Torah. It might be argued that the cycle once commenced at Passover, and that the New Year was later associated with Sukkot, but the programmatic disruption of the present calendar remains. The odd dislocation of words and gestures within the Seder (see pp. 108–13) achieves a similar result: ordinary time, sequence, and causality are subverted in order to make existence in time "into a metaphor for the reality of Israel" (p. 110).

The "something beyond" toward which the disruption points is the myth that is a permanent reality, unconditioned by time (p. 110). The calendar that frames Israel's obedience and creates the space of God's kingdom is the matrix of sacred moments that are timeless and therefore without sequence. There is no before or after in Talmud, nor in any vehicle of Israel's myth of eternity.

The calendar involves "an eternal return" to a place where "the kingdom of heaven takes place in the here and now, but nowhere in particular" (p. 113). What never seems to be far from view, however, is that ordinary time is experienced in tension with the sacred moment. Family is the bulwark of Sabbath, but any bulwark must appear provisional in light of the memory that other institutions which also once appeared reliable—prophecy, monarchy, temple—have failed. At the Seder one is freed from Egypt, and yet longs to be truly in the land of Israel (p. 110). Where Mircea Eliade referred to "the myth of the eternal return" in order to refer to rituals which, he held, dissolved all time within their unconditioned terms of reference, Judaic mythology insists on the confrontation of ordinary time with sacred eternity. That confrontation highlights the fragility of the present and the fulfillment of the eternal.

The insistence that God made and makes the world—the ordinary, recalcitrant world—is the basis on which God's sovereignty is claimed (p. 114), and that claim makes the confrontation between ordinary time and the sacred moment inevitable. The "way," the halakhah, which joins the creation that is primordial and the redemption that is final, leads through a Torah for here and now (p. 118). That Torah, instantiated in the halakhah, is the road to eternal sanctity. For that reason, halakhic concerns may not rest with the regulation of feast and calendar, but touch on the whole of social relations: Everything that is done or might be done might articulate (or might resist) the eternal kingdom in ordinary time. The specificity of the halakhah is as inexorable as the punctuality of the Sabbath. When one performs a deed commanded, that person accepts the yoke of the kingdom; if the person refuses, the yoke has been shunned. When the sun sets on Friday, the Sabbath is either greeted as God's, or an opportunity for eternal praise has been lost. Eternity comes in definable moments, occasions, and gestures.

Christianity can boast a variety of liturgical years, the nearest approximation to the calendar of Judaism. Some of those schedules of prayer, fasting, celebration, and meditative reading were devised in monastic settings and manifest aspirations for an ordered cycle of life. The patterns and particulars of events and practices are to some extent comparable with those of Judaism. But any attempt to provide as clear an analysis of the liturgical year as can be offered for the calendar of Judaism is thwarted by the simple fact that no single liturgical year, even in its major outlines, is common to the church generally.

Eastern and Western traditions continue to differ in the method by which the Sunday of the resurrection is reckoned, and Orthodox Epiphany does not bear the same meaning as Catholic and Protestant Christmas. Significant numbers of Protestants continue a long-established tradition of objection to keeping any special days. So while one might say that something about the incarnation generally features near the turn of the solar year, and that the Sunday of the resurrection is usually placed after the vernal equinox (in deliberate proximity to Passover), even that generality is not beyond contradiction. Moreover, there is variety among and within traditions concerning what to do before the major feasts of Easter and Christmas. Lent and Advent, respectively, might be observed as periods of fasting prior to the two feasts, but even liturgical churches might eschew public expressions of penitence. Disagreements among churches make a single cycle of Christianity impossible to specify, and even churches with such cycles commonly display a certain reserve about them.

When all the varieties of what to do (if anything) about observing the resurrection and the incarnation within a liturgical cycle are taken into account, the question of the rest of the year emerges. It is not surprising that national holidays (such as Independence Day and Thanksgiving in the United States), days of public recognition for personal duty (such as Memorial Day and Mother's Day), and commemorations of heroes (from Saint Patrick to Martin Luther King, Jr.) are typically folded into the liturgical year. The simple fact is that there is a great deal of space to fill. Liturgy abhors a vacuum, although that natural abhorrence has not been sufficient to cause Christianity to agree on a calendar.

The practice of Sunday as the day of Jesus' resurrection itself raises the issue of whether a cyclical view of time can be expressive of Christianity. Sunday, like the event of the resurrection, is dated on the basis of what follows the Sabbath within Judaism. Their rest finished, some women who had followed Jesus went to his tomb and found it empty (Matt. 28:1-8/Mark 16:1-8/Luke 24:1-12/John 20:1-13). That narrative was cognate with the practice among Christians of meeting following the observance of the Judaic Sabbath. But Sunday boasts no intrinsic meaning that is not summed up in the claim of the resurrection itself. The preaching that God raised Jesus from the dead asserts in a radically noncyclical fashion that human nature has been changed. The crucial distinction in time is not what day of the week we might remember the resurrection on, but: What is to happen now that resurrection has occurred?

It is frequently stated that "Western" or "Christian" views of time are linear, while "Eastern," "Asian," or "Judaic" views of time are cyclical. More accurately, the Judaic calendar might be described as dialectical, in its juxtaposition of eternal Israel and everyday life as it is lived, but the eternity envisaged is that to which a return is possible, as we have seen. The resurrection of Jesus changes for Christians the terms of reference of both ordinary time and eternity. Eternity is held to have been subjected to temporality, such that the truth of God's nature in its relation to humanity was only revealed at the appointed time, in the case of Jesus. And from that moment, ordinary time—defined by the interplay of human beings now understood to be called to be God's children—is characterized by success or failure to live up to the stature of eternity.

The radical change in the conception of time is but the abstract edge of a different attitude toward the significance of human institutions generally. Although conservative Christians at present often put forth "the family" as the bulwark of their values, the fact is that the critique of the family within the church is as old as Jesus' recorded preference for those who listened to him over his own family (see Matt. 12:46-50/Mark 3:31-35/Luke 8:19-21). Thomas Aquinas owes his magnificent career to the willingness of the Dominicans to take him from his family in Naples and see to his education in Paris, while an emblem of Martin Luther's piety is his willingness to give up the wife he had married with such difficulty for the sake of the cross of Christ. As compared to the qualification of such fundamental loyalties as family and marriage, it is hardly surprising that Christianity and the cultures it has influenced will commit themselves to no single cycle of worship. After all, even the agricultural year belongs to the form of a world that is passing away in the light of the resurrection. When Christians join in their creeds, postbiblical résumés of faith, they are not praising God or praying, but taking their bearings. Creeds specify those things in which we can put our trust, where the cycle of the old world has given way to the world that is to come.

Paul wrote trenchantly and prophetically to the Galatians, "As many of you as were baptized into Christ, put on Christ: there is neither Jew nor Greek, there is neither slave nor free, there is neither male nor female, for you are all one in Christ Jesus" (3:27-28). The denial of such obvious distinctions involved the destruction of what many saw as fundamental institutions, and Christian history may be viewed as the struggle to discover and defy whatever makes ordinary time less than the eternal moment it was created and redeemed to be. Commitment to social revolution is not simply an optional attitude among politically motivated Christians: Once time has become the vehicle of the eternal, the holy passion to challenge this temporal world and its powers becomes inexorable. No matter how basic institutions and their distinctions—religious, racial, sexual, and/or social— may seem to be, they will be questioned and sometimes denied by the claims of the gospel. Whatever the force behind such structures, even the force of nature itself, it will pale in the imagination of Christians as compared to the power of God in the resurrection of Christ Jesus.

The redemption that occurs in commonplace, daily events from the dialectical perspective of Judaism may be realized in equally humble circumstances from the perspective of Christianity. But the perspective of transformed time demands that even the commonplace be unconventional: When we pray "Your kingdom come," we give up the sovereignty of our own aspirations. The ancient power of a motif of the Psalms is invoked (see chapter 4), because the kingdom is held to press the created order toward the all-embracing feast that is its seal. An infinite variety of circumstances are to be transformed. The case of Jesus establishes that the transformation has begun; there is no question of his uniqueness limiting what may happen and is happening as the kingdom revolutionizes our lives. Christians expect God to be all in all (1 Cor. 15:28) in a way that transfigures everything that has been God's from the beginning. That is the hope of the kingdom that Jesus preached; the church in every time celebrates that kingdom with him, anticipates it with him, and walks the way of self-denial with him in order to attain it.

4

The Reign of Forceful Grace

BRUCE CHILTON

Wisdom guided the righteous refugee from his brother's wrath in direct ways, showed him God's kingdom, and gave him knowledge of holy things. . . . —Wisd. of Sol. 10:10

THE CONCEPT OF THE KINGDOM of God within the New Testament is foundational, and yet elusive. There is agreement among the Gospels and among scholars that the kingdom lay at the heart of the preaching of Jesus. Focus on the kingdom also persisted as the movement centered on Jesus survived his crucifixion and reached out to new followers, even Gentiles, with the claim of his victory over death. But by the end of the first century, as we shall see, the emphasis on the kingdom in its initial form had disappeared and had been replaced by a fresh understanding.

The approach to the kingdom of God in the New Testament along the lines of a generative exegesis—as described in chapter 2—seems appropriate. After all, the underlying issue is how the sense of the concept was transformed as it passed through circles of Jesus' followers and different stages of the movement itself. Initially, we shall be concerned with the stages of evangelization and of catechesis, as represented chiefly by the Synoptic Gospels. The study of the Synoptics is complicated by the need to distinguish within the texts as they stand diverse circles of tradition that differ over questions of meaning—sometimes sharply, as we have seen in the matter of the Eucharist. But the Synoptics will be treated very selectively here,[1] in order to permit consideration of theological reflection on catechesis (the third stage) as represented in John, the Pauline controversy concerning the kingdom (the fourth stage), and the attempted synthesis in the last of the Epistles (the fifth stage). As we observe the transformations of meaning as the movement proceeded through circles of tradition and stages of development, the kingdom will emerge as a consistent term of reference in the claim that God makes himself available through Christ in the form of ultimate and radical intervention on behalf of God's people.

The Gospel of the Kingdom

No person who has read the relevant sources attentively will deny that Jesus' preaching of the kingdom of God was rooted in the conception of the kingdom within early Judaism. That has been a matter of consensus since the end of the nineteenth century. The discovery of the importance of early Judaic theology as the foundation of Jesus' theology was nothing short of revolutionary in its impact.[2]

What most struck scholars at the end of the nineteenth century was that the kingdom of God within early Judaism was a reference neither to an individual's life after death in heaven nor to a movement of social improvement on the earth. Those had been dominant understandings, deeply embedded in the theology and preaching of the period, prior to the brilliant and incontrovertible assertions of Johannes Weiss and Albert Schweitzer. They demonstrated that the kingdom of God in early Judaism and the preaching of Jesus referred to God's final judgment of the world; the concept was part and parcel of the anticipation of the last things (*eskhata*, whence the term eschatology). Christian thought has been in some confusion ever since Weiss and Schweitzer made their point. Some scholars (such as T. W. Manson, as we have already seen) attempt to deny that Jesus' focus was eschatological, although they can offer no convincing alternative. Others (see note 4) accept that Jesus' thought was indeed eschatological, but then try to find a way around the difficulty that the world has continued on its less than cheerful way for some two millennia since it was supposed to be about to end. What sort of Messiah can have been so mistaken? Once the challenge of eschatology has been appreciated, it is easy to understand why much Christian thought has been in a retreat from its own Scriptures for most of the twentieth century. Typically, the retreat has taken one of two directions.

The less orderly withdrawal is that of what is usually called liberal Christianity. Rather than face what the Scriptures say, many liberal theologians have simply taken the vocabulary of the Bible and inflated it with a meaning of their own. So, just when Weiss and Schweitzer were proving that the kingdom of God can only be understood as God's own intervention in human affairs, a school of thought in liberal Christianity called "the Social Gospel" tried to convince Americans that legislation and social action would bring about their understanding of society's perfection, which they called the kingdom of God.[3] Instead of perfection, of course, what they got was Prohibition, and insofar as there has been confidence in the benign influence of government since that time, its basis has been pragmatic rather than theological. The Social Gospel is no longer a coherent agenda, although it has survived in the shape of engagement with issues of poverty, racism, and liberation. Whatever shape such engagement takes and however effective it might be, the liberal inattention to Scripture has become as obvious as liberals' widespread ignorance of the Bible.

The retreat of conservative Christians from the Scripture has been more strategic. They cite the Bible and instruct themselves in its contents, but they also restrict the number of meanings they will accept from Scripture. The heart of fundamentalism is a small body of "fundamentals" that the Bible is claimed to convey infallibly. Popularly, it is claimed that fundamentalists are literalists, but that is a confusion that serves the conservatives' aims. The fact is that fundamentalists ignore meanings that do not suit their theology. In the case of Jesus' preaching of the kingdom, conservatives commonly assert that, although his understanding was eschatological, Jesus' teaching was nonetheless timeless, because it illustrated his personal hope in God as his father.[4] An oxymoron such as timeless eschatology is an interesting theological construction, but it is not a scriptural oxymoron.

A generative exegesis can be bound by neither a conservative nor a liberal agenda. The New Testament, as the canon of the system that is Christianity, may be neither ignored nor tamed. In the matter of the kingdom of God, moreover, cognizance must be taken especially of the milieu within early Judaism—represented by the Hebrew Bible, the Apocrypha, the Pseudepigrapha, and Rabbinic sources inclusive of the Targumim—which framed the conception that Jesus developed and preached. Weiss and Schweitzer correctly focused on the kingdom as a systemic category of early Judaism, rather than as a moral doctrine for modern Christians. But they assigned disproportionate importance to eschatology, the issue of the time of the kingdom.[5] The insistence of early Judaism that the kingdom represents the end of things as we know them is, no doubt, the most striking departure from most modern ways of conceiving of God and the world, but the eschatological aspect is only one among several distinct emphases in the overall conception of the kingdom.

In order to facilitate consideration, five emphatic aspects of the kingdom of God will be cited here, and then related to Jesus' conception of the kingdom. Each of the aspects will be illustrated by means of a key passage from the Book of Psalms, because psalmic usage was foundational for the early Judaism that was Jesus' milieu. In Psalms we must reckon with a much more nuanced application of a language of kingship to God than the modern fixation on eschatology would allow. The assertion of God as king refers normally to God's rule on behalf of God's people, as present and to come, intervening and yet all-pervasive, demanding righteousness and anticipating perfection, requiring a purity cognate with God's sanctity, and extending from Israel to be inclusive of all peoples.

Five dimensions of the kingdom, then, play a paradigmatic role within the Psalms:

(1) The eschatological dimension. The kingdom is so near in time as to be present, and yet ultimate from the point of view of full disclosure (96:10):

> Say among the nations that the LORD reigns.
> The world is established, so as not to move:
>   he shall judge the peoples with equity.

(2) The dimension of transcendence. The kingdom is forceful in its impact, but will permeate all things (145:10-12):

> All your creatures will give you thanks, LORD,
>   and your faithful will bless you;
>   they shall speak of the glory of your kingdom,
>   and tell of your might,

> to make your mighty deeds known to the sons of men,
>   and the glorious splendor of his kingdom.

(3) The dimension of judgment. The kingdom is ever righteous, but attains to consummation (10:15-16):

> Break the arm of the wicked, and evil;
>   search out his wickedness until it cannot be found!
> The LORD is king forever and ever;
>   the nations perish from his earth!

(4) The dimension of purity. The kingdom is only consistent with what is clean, until all things are holy (24:3-4, relevant here in view of the reference to God as king in vv. 7-10):

> Who will ascend the mount of the LORD,
>   and who will stand in his holy place?
> The innocent of hands and pure of heart,
>   who has not lifted up his soul to vanity,
>   and has not sworn deceitfully.

(5) The dimension of inclusivity. Although the kingdom is local (in Zion and in heaven), it is to include all peoples (47:8-9):

> God reigns over the nations;
> God sits upon his holy throne.
> The nobles of the peoples are gathered,
>   the people of the God of Abraham;
>   for the shields of the earth are God's.
> He is highly exalted!

Because the five dimensions are so closely related within the language of the kingdom, one example from the Psalms might illustrate more than one aspect.[6] That tends to confirm that we have here identified dimensions of meaning for the kingdom that are systemic, although a given speaker or circle of usage would develop a particular significance appropriate to the historical conditions involved.[7]

Within each dimension, the first pole designates the kingdom as it impinges on those who might respond to it; for them, the kingdom appears: (1) near, (2) powerful, (3) demanding, (4) pure, and (5) associated with Zion in particular. The second pole of each dimension designates the goal implicit within the kingdom: (1) the final, (2) immanent,

(3) faultless, (4) holy, (5) and inclusive reality it promises to be. The kingdom of God, in other words, is not only a scandal for modern thinking because it purports to be final. It is indeed eschatological in respect of time, as Weiss and Schweitzer maintained, but also transcendent in respect of place (in Zion, heaven, everywhere), perfect in respect of action, sacred in its purity, and all-embracing in its choice of Israel.

Jesus' gospel of the kingdom represented a distinctive development of dimensions of usage that had already been established for the meaning of God's kingdom. Perhaps his most signal innovation was the very act of announcing the kingdom: What was generally known as a promise of the Scripture was claimed by Jesus to be breaking in on the people he addressed in disparate towns and villages in Galilee. Within the résumé of the Petrine gospel from Acts 10, which has already been cited in chapter 2, in the house of Cornelius Peter speaks of the word of God that "he sent to the sons of Israel, triumphantly preaching peace through Jesus Christ" (Acts 10:36). Here is an example of a replacement of the concept of the kingdom, in this case by "peace." But the catechesis of the Petrine circle was unequivocal that the central focus of Jesus' preaching was the kingdom of God. Matthew (4:17), Mark (1:15), and Luke (4:43) differ from one another in the wording with which they introduce the kingdom as the theme of Jesus' message, but that is only to be expected, since the Gospels are not simply literary copies, but portraits of Christian catechesis in churches of distinct places and times. Their typical variety, however, makes all the more significant their consensus that the kingdom was the theme of Jesus' message.

To promulgate the kingdom as a message was, at least implicitly, to claim God's forceful intervention along the lines of time, place, judgment, purity, and people. Those dimensions in fact become explicit in Jesus' gospel, as when he states in the Mishnaic source known as Q (Matt. 8:11/Luke 13:28, 29):[8]

> Many shall come from east and west
> and recline in feasting
> with Abraham and Isaac and Jacob. . . .

There can be no doubt of the emphasis on a future consummation here, involving a particular but unnamed place, the actions and material of festivity (including the luxurious custom of reclining, not sitting, at a banquet), and the incorporation of the many who shall rejoice in the company of the patriarchs.

Jesus' use of the imagery of feasting in order to refer to the kingdom, a characteristic of his message, is resonant both with early Judaic language of the kingdom and his own ministry. The picture of God offering a feast on Mount Zion "for all peoples," where death itself is swallowed up, becomes an influential image from the time of Isa. 25:6-8. Notably, the Targum of Isaiah refers to the divine disclosure on Mount Zion that includes the image of the feast as "the kingdom of the LORD of hosts" (24:23).[9] Sayings such as the one cited from Q invoke that imagery, and Jesus' practice of fellowship at meals with his disciples and many others amounts to a claim that the ultimate festivity has already begun.

The dynamic of inclusion is not without its dark side, both in Isaiah and in Jesus' preaching. The Isaian feast on Mount Zion is to be accompanied by the destruction of Moab (25:10-12);[10] the feast with the patriarchs includes the threat of exclusion for some (Matt. 8:12/Luke 13:28). The ethics of the imagery, which at first may seem to be little more than an ethos of festivity, turn out to involve the dimension of judgment, as is natural within an expectation of the kingdom. The kingdom of God in the saying from Q is a feast for the future whose invitation is issued now by Jesus, so that response to the invitation is implicitly a condition of entry. The feast's location is related to Mount Zion, upon which Isaiah predicted a feast for all peoples. The judgment of the kingdom will exclude the wicked, and what is enjoyed in luxurious fashion will be pure. Finally, the kingdom's radiant power will include those from far away, all of whom are to be joined with the patriarchs. No wonder Jesus himself had to face the question, among those who responded to his gospel, What is the way into this kingdom?

The Catechesis of the Kingdom

The movement of Jesus may be regarded as having started from the moment his preaching of the kingdom was accepted. Accepting his theme that the kingdom was dawning naturally involved a desire to enjoy the kingdom's light. How could one be among the many who were to feast in the kingdom, and not among those who were to be cast out? Jesus' own response to such issues within the movement is largely contained in the instruction for his disciples known as Q. In respect of social function, Jesus' instruction of his closest followers is to be distinguished from the catechetical program for beginners of which the Synoptic Gospels are example, but the agenda of preparing adherents of the movement is shared by Q and the Synoptics.

The image of a feast that appears in Matt. 8:11, 12 and Luke 13:28, 29 is developed along narrative lines in what is commonly known as the parable of the wedding feast, after the version in Matt. 22:1-10 (cf. Luke 14:16-24). Within the parable, Jesus engages in the rabbinic method of using narrative in order to recommend a certain ethical performance.[11] The feast is prepared, but invitations must be accepted in order to be effective, and God is ready to drag outsiders in, rather than permit the festivity to go unattended. Within the festal imagery we have just considered, the parable is an interesting development. Who would conceive of the Isaian feast being passed up by those invited? The Jesus of this tradition, however, conceives of the kingdom as sufficiently elusive as to occasion a willful ignorance of it. That is to say, the parable's narrative conveys the kingdom within a fresh perspective. The narrative is designed as performance, to speak without words of what the kingdom means for us.

The performance of meaning effected by the parable is not entirely a matter of reference to the imaginary. Precisely because the parable concerns God's activity as king, it makes a claim within the experience of anyone who knows what a king is. God, the parable claims, has been brought to act sovereignly but surprisingly. God's present offer is out of the ordinary. The extraordinarily bad, even violent, behavior of those who should have been guests provides the impetus for a radical expansion in scope of an increasingly insistent invitation: Leave your cares (however legitimate) and join the feast, take the opportunity of an invitation you could never have anticipated. The parabolic motif portrays divine action as begun, but not as perfected. The parabolic actions point toward the future as the locus of the kingdom's ultimate disclosure. Similarly, the ethical theme of the parable frames and encourages a wary, clever—even opportunistic—response to the disclosure that is under way but not complete.

The Petrine circle of tradition came increasingly to portray itself as a group apart from other sorts of Judaism (a self-portrait that is also readily apparent in the development of the parable of the wedding feast). We have already observed in chapter 2 how Jesus' saying regarding wealth and the kingdom of God was transformed into a commendation of the peripatetic disciples whose support derived from those they taught (Matt. 19:16-30/Mark 10:17-31/Luke 18:18-30). Another, more subtle example of the Petrine transformation of the kingdom is the way in which an obscure saying of Jesus is presented. Some version of the statement, "There are some standing here who will not taste death until they see the kingdom of God," is presented in each of the Synoptics (Matt. 16:28/Mark 9:1/Luke 9:27) and has been variously interpreted.[12] An exegesis of the dictum will not be pursued here; the relevant concern is rather the context of the saying within the Petrine tradition.

The statement occurs just after Jesus promises that all those who deny themselves, take up their cross, and follow Jesus—even to the point of losing their lives—will save their lives (Matt. 16:24-27/Mark 8:34-38/Luke 9:23-26). So presented, the saying regarding those "standing here" would seem to be a promise of life until the *eskhaton*. Then, however, the transfiguration follows (Matt. 17:1-9/Mark 9:2-10/Luke 9:28-36), when Peter, James, and John are taken up a mountain by Jesus, whose own appearance changes prior to the arrival of Moses and Elijah. The three privileged disciples, Peter at their head, have seen the promise of the kingdom in terms reminiscent of Moses' ascent of Sinai with three privileged followers (Exod. 24:1-11). Here are the emblems of the Petrine catechesis: Jesus is related to God as Moses once was, and Peter is his Aaron, a witness that the kingdom has been covenanted.[13]

The signature of the Jacobean circle, by contrast, is detectable in Matt. 13:10-15, Mark 4:10-12, and Luke 8:9-10, where it is claimed that Jesus conveys the secret(s) of the kingdom to the larger group of twelve disciples, the precursor of what has come to be called the apostolic college in Jerusalem.[14] The group concerned is not the select company around Peter, but those of Jesus' disciples who devote themselves to the authoritative interpretation of his teaching. Indeed, the passage occurs immediately prior to Jesus' explanation of the parable of the sower, which is the foundation of the collection of parables in all three Synoptics. The message of the Jacobean group is that the company of James enjoys particular insight into the kingdom, and that the kingdom is essentially a didactic matter, into which Jesus' disciples offer initiation.

The circles of Peter and of James were able to control and transform the meaning of the kingdom by mastering the context of its presentation in sayings of and stories about Jesus. In each, a principle of privilege was claimed, for either the Petrine or the Jacobean circle. But at the same time, the meaning of the kingdom shifted in each case. What for Jesus was a divine intervention in the world (of time, space, judgment, purity, and humanity) became for the Petrine group the assurance of a particular, visionary experience (the transfiguration), and for the Jacobean group a method of authoritative interpretation (the explanation of parables).

Transformation by means of context is also evident in the other circles that fed the Synoptic Gospels, although the impact of their changes appears less dramatic. Reference has already been made to Jesus' promise of the inclusion of many from east and west in the patriarchal feast of the kingdom (Matt. 8:11-12/Luke 13:28-29). The Mishnaic source (Q) of which that saying was part is marked by a tendency to be pointed against the Jewish opponents of the movement. In the Matthean version, the saying appears as an addendum to the healing of the servant of the Roman centurion, and with an explicit warning against "the sons of the kingdom" (v. 12). In the Lukan version, the saying is presented as part of a discourse concerning salvation, in which hearers are warned that merely having enjoyed Jesus' company during his lifetime is no guarantee of fellowship with the patriarchs in the eschatological feast (13:22-30). The differences between the two versions make the supposition of a fixed, written Q appear implausible at this point, and commend the model of an instructional source that was susceptible of local variation.

Even at a later stage, context could result in variegated portrayals of the kingdom. Before we proceed to discuss what is achieved by contextualization in each Synoptic Gospel, however, it is necessary to explain that there is a commonly Synoptic transformation of the kingdom, a transformation that is plausibly associated with the circle of Barnabas in Antioch. The transformation is sufficiently general so that the construal of each Synoptic Gospel may be described as a variation on a theme, while it is so distinctive that no other ancient document may be described as sharing it. The transformation introduces the kingdom as preached by Jesus.[15] This obvious feature of the Gospels' narratives is no less influential for being evident: The kingdom from this point onward is established as the burden of Jesus' message and no other's. Moreover, an acceptance of him involves embracing the characteristic understanding of the kingdom that unfolds.

The next major phase in the Synoptic transformation of the kingdom is pedagogical. The Jesus who is the kingdom's herald is also its advocate, who explains its features to those who hear and yet are puzzled (or even scandalized). The extent of the material each Gospel devotes to this phase varies greatly, but in every case it is the largest phase.[16] The distribution of this material also varies, but it is striking that none of the Synoptic Gospels invokes the term "kingdom" as a link to include all statements on the subject in a single complex of material. Such an association by catchword is indeed detectable over short runs of material, so that isolated sayings are the exception, not the rule, but in no case is subject matter or wording the sole determinative influence on context. Rather, there is a narrative contextualization, in which Jesus' activity in preaching, teaching, and disputing becomes the governing framework for a given run of sayings. Those frameworks vary from Gospel to Gospel, as do the logia presented; the distribution of sayings cannot be explained by reference to some fixed, historical ordering. The point is rather that the typically Synoptic transformation of Jesus' preaching embeds the kingdom within his ministry, so that he and the kingdom approximate to being interchangeable. The particular textual moves that achieve this identification vary; the fact that it is achieved does not.

The last phase of the Synoptic transformation of the kingdom pursues the logic of the identification: Jesus' death and the kingdom are presented as mutually explicating. "I shall not drink of the fruit of the vine again, until I drink it with you new in God's kingdom" (cf. Matt. 26:29/Mark 14:25/Luke 22:18). Whatever the sense of that saying was within the ministry of Jesus, within the Synoptics it serves to insist that the same Jesus who announced and taught the kingdom is also the sole guarantor of its glorious coming.

The Synoptic transformation of the kingdom essentially involves a unique pattern of the distribution of sayings and of their narrative contextualization within Jesus' ministry. The result is to focus on Jesus as the herald, advocate, and guarantor of the kingdom in an innovative fashion. Arguably, the transformation explicates what is implicit within the sayings' tradition: an awareness that Jesus' ministry is a seal of the kingdom. The most obvious instance of such a claim within his sayings is Jesus' observation concerning his exorcisms and the kingdom (Matt. 12:28/Luke 11:20). But the emphasis even there falls more on the kingdom than on Jesus, so that the saying only heightens by contrast the Synoptic transformation, in which Jesus' preaching of the kingdom becomes the seal of his divine mission, not the principal point at issue. He who witnessed the kingdom is, within the Synoptics, attested as God's Son by virtue of his own message. Precisely because a signal adjustment of precedence between Jesus and the kingdom has taken place, the language of "transformation" is appropriate.

In view of its distinctiveness from the sense of the kingdom in other documents of early Judaism and Christianity, the Synoptic transformation is a particular framing of Jesus' sayings, not merely a loose characterization of similar material in three Gospels. How the transformation was effected, whether by literary borrowing from one document to another, or the sharing of a now lost antecedent, is a matter of conjecture.[17]

Although each of the Synoptic Gospels substantially conveys the Barnaban transformation of the kingdom, each construes it distinctively. That is perhaps most easily appreciated by considering how Jesus' initial preaching is presented. In Matthew, Jesus says, "Repent, for the kingdom of heaven is at hand" (4:17), but he is not the first to do so. John the baptist is portrayed as delivering the same message (3:2). Part of the authority of the Matthean Jesus is that he is the climax of the prophetic witness that went before him; in Matthew alone, Jesus consciously decides to preach in Galilee, and his decision is held to fulfill a passage from the book of Isaiah (4:12-16). Mark has no such reference, but it does uniquely have Jesus say, "Repent, and believe in the gospel" (1:15c). That is an effective way to link Jesus' preaching to the preaching about him, and Mark's Gospel alone commences, "The beginning of the gospel . . ." (1:1). As if to underline the point, Jesus' announcement of the kingdom is itself called "the gospel of God" (1:14). The most confident equation between the kingdom and the one who preaches it is offered in Luke. Although it is assumed that Jesus preaches the kingdom (4:43), the instance of initial preaching which precedes that notice has Jesus quoting Scripture to the effect that he is God's anointed (4:16-21).

The narrative identification between the progress of the kingdom and Jesus' own ministry is of the essence of the transformation of traditions that the Synoptic Gospels reflect. Part of that transformation is the unequivocal belief that Jesus is to be the agent, along with God, in the final judgment of the kingdom. Much as the book of Isaiah provided the principal image of the festivity of the kingdom, the book of Daniel provided the principal image of Jesus' role in that judgment. In the book, four beasts represent the great empires that were to rule from Daniel's time (Assyria, Babylonia, Persia, and Greece). After the beasts are described, God appears on a throne (7:9-10); "one like a son of man," a human being, is presented to God and receives total dominion (7:13-14). Within Daniel itself, the figure is essentially an agent of redemption and disclosure within the heavenly court. The faith of early Christians identified Jesus with that angelic vision.[18] At the moment when Jesus is interrogated by the authorities of the Temple, in the absence of any witness from the company of disciples, he replies without equivocation to the question whether he is the Messiah, by citing Daniel 7 (see Matt. 26:63-64/Mark 14:61-62/Luke 22:66-69). Jesus, as that Son of man of whom Daniel spoke, was not merely an angelic figure, but was to return to earth to claim and vindicate his own. A complex of material within the Synoptics develops an apocalyptic scenario in which the most important elements are the destruction of the Temple and Jesus' coming as the triumphant Son of man of Daniel 7 (see Matt. 24–25/Mark 13/Luke 21:5-36). The Synoptic identification of Jesus with the kingdom is therefore coherent with the eschatological expectation of early Christians.

Reflection and Controversy

Even our brief consideration of the catechetical stage reveals its formative influence on the meaning of the kingdom within the New Testament. Transformations of the meaning of the kingdom at that stage—particularly in the Barnaban phase, when the kingdom was integrated biographically with the preaching concerning Jesus—permitted the next developments to take place. Unless the catechetical transformations are appreciated, the paradox of the apparent disappearance of the kingdom of God as an emphasis within early Christianity will remain.

The Gospel according to John effects a radical reduction in focus on the kingdom: Only one statement, about seeing (3:3) or entering

(3:5) the kingdom, is ever made. Such explanation as is offered explicates the requirement for this experience: being born "from above" (*anothen*) or "from water and spirit."[19] The assumption is that no explanation of the kingdom itself is required. The passage is rather designed to insist that baptism in Jesus' name—birth from above by water and spirit—alone permits of participation in the kingdom. The distinctively Johannine fashioning of traditions concerning Jesus does not center on the kingdom, and that is a mark of its singularity. The focus now is on receiving Jesus in such a manner as one might become a child of God (1:12). The Gospel is so consumed with the discursive and narrative issue of attaining eternal life (cf. 3:16) that the kingdom, the vision of what is actually achieved at the point where the eternal meets the temporal, is taken as a matter of course. The issue for John is means, not ends, because the Fourth Gospel is composed for those whose baptism is taken for granted.

Paul also communicates with those who have already been catechized, but he is notoriously less sanguine in regard to his readers' conceptions of their own faith. His frequently controversial purposes comport well with his manner of reference to the kingdom, which is typically by way of correction. His insistence that the kingdom of God is not to be confused with food and drink (Rom. 14:17) is not the truism it may at first appear to be. Paul makes his statement in the midst of an argument that he mounts against both maintaining regulations of purity in diet and blatantly flouting customs of purity (14:13-23). Writing to the congregation in Romans near the end of his career (ca. 57 C.E.), Paul makes his assertion that the kingdom is available as "righteousness and peace and joy in the Holy Spirit" to humanity as a whole (14:17), whatever their views of purity. The primitive association of the kingdom and Eucharist, rooted in the practice of Jesus, here becomes the point of departure for insistence upon the inclusive reach of the kingdom. That theme is of such importance, Paul claims, it would be better not to eat at all than to risk contravening it (14:21).

Because the kingdom for Paul is effective for those who attain to the promises of God through baptism into Christ, he views it as something that those who follow Christian ethics may "inherit." Even within the idiom of inheritance, however, Paul's formulation is typically negative; it lists those who will not inherit the kingdom of God (so in Gal. 5:19-21, ca. 53 C.E.; 1 Cor. 6:9, 10, ca. 56). The foundational metaphor of inheritance is not an obvious development from earlier usage.[20] Why should the kingdom now be inherited, rather than entered? The transformation obviously has implications for eschatology, in that Paul's construction of the kingdom is more consistently future than Jesus'. He ridicules those in Corinth who fancy themselves already regnant (1 Cor. 4:8), and explicitly portrays the kingdom as beyond the inheritance of flesh and blood (1 Cor. 15:50). But that moment of inheritance may be attained, according to Paul, because Jesus as life-giving spirit (15:45) has prepared a spiritual people, fit for the resurrection of the dead (15:42-58).

By the reflective and controversial stages of John and Paul, then, the increasing focus of interest is preparation for the kingdom by means of baptism into Christ and the ethical performance of the baptismal spirit. There are evident differences in regard to the temporal emphasis of eschatology. The ultimacy of the kingdom may be expressed as "above" any concern for time or sequence (as in John 3:3, 5), or as keyed to that future moment when (as Paul puts it) Christ hands over the kingdom to God (1 Cor. 15:24). In either case, the issue of systemic importance is that Christ effects the transfer of the believer (at baptism, and thereafter) from his or her previous condition into the realm of God.

Royal Synthesis: The Kingdom of Christ

The stages of catechesis, reflection, and controversy added nothing, for all the variations of emphasis they involved, to the dimensions implicit in the gospel of the kingdom. At the end of a generation of development, the kingdom remained God's realm: ultimate, transcendent, perfect, holy, inclusive. But he who had at first preached the kingdom was now at the forefront, explicitly and without compromise, as the means—and the only means—of access to the kingdom.

The stark character of that development is measurable by the phrase, "kingdom of Christ," used interchangeably with "kingdom of God." The earliest usage appears in Col. 1:13, one of the letters attributed to Paul, but emanating from the circle of Timothy ca. 90. The putative authors, Paul and Timothy together (1:1), give thanks to the Father for making believers worthy "of a share of the portion of saints in the light, who delivered us from the authority of the darkness and transferred us into the kingdom of the son of his love . . ." (1:12, 13). The continuity with Pauline emphases is obvious here, as is the statement from approximately five years later in Eph. 5:5, where the putative Paul speaks of those who do not have "an inheritance in the kingdom of Christ and of God."[21]

The latest documents of the New Testament in the present case simply identify a systemic principle that had been active since at least the period of catechesis. Because baptism into Christ, prayer in the manner of Christ, the ethical imitation of Christ, and Eucharist in remembrance of Christ were the means of access into God's kingdom, functionally God's reign was also Christ's. All that could be said, then, of the kingdom of God in all its dimensions could also be said of what believers enjoyed as a result of their identification with Christ.

We spoke in chapter 2 of a deeply filial consciousness that was associated with prayer in the manner of Jesus. Awareness in prayer as a child of God may focus upon the divine parent, upon Jesus as brother, upon one's many sisters and brothers in the act of praying. That relational corollary of prayer to God as Father becomes paramount in the systemic force of the kingdom. Now our inclusion with the patriarchs as God's children, a gracious act that God undertakes by having Jesus proclaim it, is an aspect of God's disclosure of God's kingdom. God has determined to include us with all those who have attended and will attend to the gospel at one and the same moment as God has determined to dissolve time, ignore space, perfect righteousness, and manifest sanctity.

The same mercy that would include us with the patriarchs would also destroy the world in a conflagration of all that is not consistent with God's integrity, God's demand for ethical perfection and holiness. The kingdom of God and of Christ is experienced by Christians as a power more elemental than the elements, because with its coming God is unmaking and remaking what God alone created. The kingdom takes us out of the world, because the world in the light of God's judgment appears to be an empty shell, collapsing upon its hollow center. Time and space have no constraint that we will recognize, because we are joined with those who went before, and those to come, in the single, ultimate disclosure of God's primordial rule.

A Judaic Response
to Forceful Grace

Jacob Neusner

T HE KINGDOM OF GOD, so central to the message of Jesus, gave way to the worldly government of emperors, as Christianity took the easy way to worldly effect. The conversion of persons and the formation of fragile communities consume centuries of effort and may in the end yield an ephemeral moment, not an enduring society. So we have found, so we find today, in Judaism. No wonder then that many Jews follow the Christian reasoning in the aftermath of the remarkable event of Constantine's conversion and the Christian conquest of pagan Rome. From that moment Christianity made its way not one by one but all at once, through the monarch. And it is hardly surprising that people seek security in a state that empowers the faith—the State of Israel for Judaism—rather than pursuing eternity through a faith that conveys a different kind of power.

The kingdom of God for the Torah encompasses not the end time only but also the here and now. What changes in the age to come, so insisted the great authority Samuel, in the third century C.E., is only politics. Now Israel is unempowered, subject to the will of others; then Israel will be unempowered, but subject to the will of heaven. The kingdom of heaven will remain then what it now is. And everyone will have a share, except for those who deny the very foundations of God's rule:

Mishnah-tractate Sanhedrin 10:1

10:1 A.   All Israelites have a share in the world to come,

B.   as it is said, Your people also shall be all righteous,

they shall inherit the land forever; the branch of my planting,
the work of my hands, that I may be glorified (Isa. 60:21).

    C.   And these are the ones who have no portion in the
world to come:

    D.   (1) He who says, the resurrection of the dead is a
teaching which does not derive from the Torah, (2) and the
Torah does not come from Heaven; and (3) an Epicurean.

Here we have a clear statement that the people of Israel—that is, the
supernatural people called into being at Sinai through the Torah—
wholly share in the world to come, unless they exclude themselves by
denying the resurrection of the dead, or denying that the Torah comes
from God. Putting that fact together with Samuel's judgment, we come
to the clear conclusion that the kingdom of God is here among us, when
we declare ourselves its citizens, and this we do by how we live our lives
in community. Community is the key, since "kingdom" is a political
metaphor, an account of what people do together—indeed, what they
legitimately may insist all among them do.

Where does holy Israel part company from other heirs of Israel's
Torah? The paths meet at the grave. For Christianity, the kingdom
comes with resurrection beyond death. For the Torah of holy Israel, the
kingdom comes in holy time, which comes in its own rhythm, with the
Sabbath's advent at sunset on Friday evening, for example. We do not
have to die to enter God's kingdom; we have to live. That is why we concern ourselves with the conditions of the nations and the world in the
here and now, not because of a secular meliorism, but because of our
different sense for where God's rule must matter. That accounts for the
language of prayer recited when we go forth from the synagogue's holy
community meeting in an enchanted moment of prayer and study of
Torah.

When Jews complete their service of worship, they mark the conclusion by making a statement concerning themselves in the world: the
corporate community looking outward. Synagogue service concludes
with a prayer prior to going forth, called *Alenu,* from its first word in
Hebrew: "It is incumbent on us. . . ." Like the Exodus, the moment of
the congregation's departure becomes a celebration of Israel's God, a
self-conscious, articulated rehearsal of Israel's peoplehood, that is to
say, Israel's forming a community under, and by reason of the act of,
God's rule:

Alenu: The Community Takes Leave

It is incumbent on us to praise Him, Lord over all the world;
Let us acclaim Him, Author of all creation.
He made our lot unlike that of other peoples;
He assigned to us a unique destiny.
We bend the knee, worship, and acknowledge
The King of kings, the Holy One, praised is He.
He unrolled the heavens and established the earth;
His throne of glory is in the heavens above;
His majestic Presence is in the loftiest heights.
He and no other is God and faithful King,
Even as we are told in His Torah:
Remember now and always, that the Lord is God;
Remember, no other is Lord of heaven and earth.

The first part of the prayer identifies Israel as the people called into being, set apart, by God. The second part turns to the matter of the kingdom, that is, God's dominion, and asks that all the peoples come under God's rule too:

We, therefore, hope in You, O Lord our God,
That we shall soon see the triumph of Your might,
That idolatry shall be removed from the earth,
And false gods shall be utterly destroyed.
Then will the world be a true kingdom of God,
When all mankind will invoke Your name,
And all the earth's wicked will return to You.
Then all the inhabitants of the world will surely know
That to You every knee must bend,
Every tongue must pledge loyalty.
Before You, O Lord, let them bow in worship,
Let them give honor to Your glory.
May they all accept the rule of Your kingdom.
May You reign over them soon through all time.
Sovereignty is Yours in glory, now and forever.
So it is written in Your Torah:
The Lord shall reign for ever and ever.

Israel thanks God that it enjoys a unique destiny. But the community asks that God, who made their lot unlike that of all others, will soon rule as sovereign over *all*. The secular difference, which stands for the unique destiny, is for the time being only. When the destiny is fulfilled, there will be no further difference. The kingdom of God in the here and now is not the place where Israel, the holy people, is; it is the time when that holy people comes together: enchanted time.

In that context, we find a holy people—the counterpart to Christianity's "mystical body of Christ," not to be confused with a this-worldly social entity—defined not in space but in time; not in permanent, ongoing forms such as institutions, but in occasions and moments. And that is how life is with God, I think: not in some one circumstance, but under any conditions God calls; not for some permanent purpose but for a variety of vocations God summons; and never predictably, never by reason of empowerment, but always in the moment, for the moment. The kingdom of God, a metaphor, after all, embodies the occasion of God's summons and God's rule; that is what we mean by so anachronistic a formulation as "kingdom." By using a political metaphor, referring then to the media of legitimate violence, we invoke the conception that God intervenes, God works God's will upon us, with us, through us. In that sense, for the Torah, God's kingdom comes about through the commandments, and through deeds that transcend the commandments and give to God what God cannot command but greatly values: the gift that is voluntary and uncoerced.

This brings us back to the kingdom of Christ, the counterpart, for Christianity, of God's kingdom for the religion of the Torah that the world calls Judaism. "All that could be said, then, of the kingdom of God in all its dimensions could also be said of what believers enjoyed as a result of their identification with Christ." So far as this means imitation of Christ, prayer in the manner of Christ, Eucharist in remembrance of Christ, baptism into Christ, I find a focus upon not the regeneration of the holy community but the transformation of the individual. For what has this to do with the history of peoples and nations, the condition of the world of conflict and contention, that the kingdom of God supersedes? Ethical perfection and personal holiness, the kingdom that takes us out of the world, a world beyond time and space— these dimensions take the measure of everything but the main thing. If God's rule is to make a difference, it must take place in the here and now of real, ordinary time and space. And what must change in the here and now are not private feelings or attitudes, but policies and programs that govern the public interest and shape the public good.

Judaism speaks of God's rule in this world, not because Judaism is

a this-worldly religion, but because Judaism has taken the measure of
this world. To put matters in the language of the Torah, we revert to
God's judgment of the world. The first kingdom of God was Eden.
There man and woman put their will above God's. Eden was over in an
hour. The second kingdom of God commenced at Sinai. Here is how
our sages of blessed memory tell the story of the first kingdom; the passage is found in *The Fathers according to Rabbi Nathan:*

I:XII.1.   A. What was the order of the creation of the first Man
[just how did things unfold]? [The entire sequence of events of the
creation and fall of Man and Woman took place on a single day,
illustrating a series of verses of Psalms that are liturgically utilized on
the several days of the week.]

B.   In the first hour [of the sixth day, on which Man was
made] the dirt for making him was gathered, in the second, his form
was shaped, in the third, he was turned into a mass of dough, in the
fourth, his limbs were made, in the fifth, his various apertures were
opened up, in the sixth, breath was put into him, in the seventh, he
stood on his feet, in the eighth, Eve was made as his match, in the
ninth, he was put into the Garden of Eden, in the tenth, he was
given the commandment, in the eleventh, he turned rotten, in the
twelfth, he was driven out and went his way.

C.   This carries out the verse: "But Man does not lodge
overnight in honor" (Ps. 49:13).

D.   On the first day of the week [with reference to the acts of
creation done on that day], what Psalm is to be recited? "The earth
is the LORD's and the fullness thereof, the world and they who dwell
in it" (Ps. 24:1). For [God] is the one who owns it and transfers ownership of it, and He is the one who will judge the world.

E.   On the second day? "Great is the LORD and greatly to be
praised in the city of our God" (Ps. 48:2). He divided everything He
had made [between sea and dry land] and was made king over His
world.

F.   On the third day? "God is standing in the congregation
of the mighty, in the midst of the mighty He will judge" (Ps. 82:1).
He created the sea and the dry land and folded up the land to its
place, leaving a place for His congregation.

G.   On the fourth day? "God of vengeance, O LORD, God of
vengeance, appear" (Ps. 94:1). He created the sun, moon, stars, and
planets, which give light to the world but He is going to exact
vengeance from those who serve them.

H.   On the fifth? "Sing aloud to God our strength, shout to the God of Jacob" (Ps. 81:2). He created the fowl, fish, mammals of the sea, who sing aloud in the world [praises of God].

I.   On the sixth? "The LORD reigns, clothed in majesty, the LORD is clothed, girded in strength, yes, the world is established and cannot be moved" (Ps. 93:1). On that day He completed all His work and arose and took His seat on the heights of the world.

J.   On the seventh? "A Psalm, a song for the Sabbath day" (Ps. 92:1). It is a day that is wholly a Sabbath, on which there is no eating, drinking, or conducting of business, but the righteous are seated in retinue with their crowns on their heads and derive sustenance from the splendor of God's presence, as it is said, "And they beheld God and ate and drank" (Exod. 24:11), like the ministering angels.

K.   And [reverting back to B] why [was man created last]?

L.   So that [immediately upon creation on the sixth day] he might forthwith take up his Sabbath meal.

I:XIV.1   A.   On the very same day Man was formed, on the very same day Man was made, on the very same day his form was shaped, on the very same day he was turned into a mass of dough, on the very same day his limbs were made and his various apertures were opened up, on the very same day breath was put into him, on the very same day he stood on his feet, on the very same day Eve was matched for him, on the very same day he was put into the Garden of Eden, on the very same day he was given the commandment, on the very same day he went bad, on the very same day he was driven out and went his way,

B.   thereby illustrating the verse, "Man does not lodge overnight in honor" (Ps. 49:13).[1]

Here is what is at stake in God's kingdom. The first kingdom, at Eden, lasted but a moment and was lost. The second began at Sinai and endures to this time. If you want to know where, come to the synagogue on the eve of the Sabbath and hear the memory of creation; visit the home of holy Israel, and enjoy the world to come in the here and now; come to the synagogue on the Sabbath morning and hear declaimed the Torah that came forth at Sinai, when Israel said, "We shall do and we shall obey." God's kingdom takes place wherever, whenever, Israel does and obeys. And Israel, the transcendent, holy, supernatural social entity that God brought into being, takes place where and when Israel accepts the yoke of heaven and the yoke of the commandments, with its "Hear

O Israel" and its ". . . who has sanctified us by the commandments and commanded us to. . . ."

In this context, I wonder where and how our kingdom of heaven and the Christian kingdom of God or kingdom of Christ correspond at all. The difference strikes me as formidable. Christianity's kingdom of God and kingdom of Christ concern personal obedience in the private life; the Torah's kingdom of Heaven speaks to the formation of a kingdom of priests and a holy people, a light to the nations, a community that embodies the Torah and realizes God's will not in some one place but in every circumstance subject to God's plan and will. We speak of Eden and Sinai, we aspire to the world to come because it is here, when we will it; that is, when our will accepts the priority of God's will. That is why we invoke that deeply political metaphor of "kingdom" when we want to explain how we have recovered from the calamity of Eden and risen to the height of Sinai.

Part Three

~

THE MYSTERY OF THE MESSIAH

~

5

Bringing the Messiah:
The Torah and
Responsive Grace

JACOB NEUSNER

L IVING IN THE KINGDOM OF GOD, eternal Israel does not constitute a
democracy or even imagine sharing with God the call to judgment.
God rules, humanity obeys—except when sin intervenes; and sin is the
act of rebellion. Humanity, represented by Eve and Adam, is created
with the freedom to choose and the power to accept; that is its glory,
contained in the commandment to love God, iterated in the adolescent
yearning and even jealousy of God for humanity's concurrence. The
kingdom of God, the joy of a life shaped by the commandments of the
Torah—these signify willing and freely given affirmation.

Keeping the commandments as a mark of submission, loyalty, and
humility before God is the Judaic system of salvation. So Israel does not
"save itself." Israel never controls its own destiny, either on earth or in
heaven. Only God can send the Messiah, savior of Israel and humanity
at the end of time. Nothing Israel can do in a worldly sense matters, but
Israel nonetheless makes its choice. The only choice is whether to cast
one's fate into the hands of cruel, deceitful humans, or to trust in the living God of mercy and love. Israel's arrogance alienates God; Israel's
humility and submission win God's favor. We shall now see how this
position is spelled out in the setting of discourse about the Messiah in
the Talmud of the Land of Israel.

Bar Kokhba: Arrogance against God

The failed Messiah of the second century, Bar Kokhba, who led a brave but suicidal war against Rome at the height of its power, above all exemplifies arrogance against God. He lost the war because of that arrogance. His emotions, attitudes, sentiments, and feelings form the (negative) model of how the virtuous Israelite is not to conceive of matters. In particular, he ignored the authority of sages:

Yerushalmi Taanit 4:5

[XJ] Said R. Yohanan, "Upon orders of Caesar Hadrian, they killed eight hundred thousand in Betar."

[K] Said R. Yohanan, "There were eighty thousand pairs of trumpeters surrounding Betar. Each one was in charge of a number of troops. Ben Kozeba was there and he had two hundred thousand troops who, as a sign of loyalty, had cut off their little fingers.

[L] "Sages sent word to him, 'How long are you going to turn Israel into a maimed people?'

[M] "He said to them, 'How otherwise is it possible to test them?'

[N] "They replied to him, 'Whoever cannot uproot a cedar of Lebanon while riding on his horse will not be inscribed on your military rolls.'

[O] "So there were two hundred thousand who qualified in one way, and another two hundred thousand who qualified in another way."

[P] When he would go forth to battle, he would say, "Lord of the world! Do not help and do not hinder us! 'Hast thou not rejected us, O God? Thou dost not go forth, O God, with our armies'"[Ps. 60:10].

[Q] Three and a half years did Hadrian besiege Betar.

[R] R. Eleazar of Modiin would sit on sackcloth and ashes and pray every day, saying "Lord of the ages! Do not judge in accord with strict judgment this day! Do not judge in accord with strict judgment this day!"

[S] Hadrian wanted to go to him. A Samaritan said to him, "Do not go to him until I see what he is doing, and so hand over the city [of Betar] to you. [Make peace . . . for you.]"

[T] He got into the city through a drain pipe. He went and found R. Eleazar of Modiin standing and praying. He pretended to whisper something in his ear.

[U]   The townspeople saw [the Samaritan] do this and brought him to Ben Kozeba. They told him, "We saw this man having dealings with your friend."

[V]   [Bar Kokhba] said to him, "What did you say to him, and what did he say to you?"

[W]   He said to [the Samaritan], "If I tell you, then the king will kill me, and if I do not tell you, then you will kill me. It is better that the king kill me, and not you.

[X]   "[Eleazar] said to me, 'I should hand over my city.' ['I shall make peace. . . .']"

[Y]   He turned to R. Eleazar of Modiin. He said to him, "What did this Samaritan say to you?"

[Z]   He replied, "Nothing."

[AA]   He said to him, "What did you say to him?"

[BB]   He said to him, "Nothing."

[CC]   [Ben Kozeba] gave [Eleazar] one good kick and killed him.

[DD]   Forthwith an echo came forth and proclaimed the following verse:

[EE]   "Woe to my worthless shepherd, who deserts the flock! May the sword smite his arm and his right eye! Let his arm be wholly withered, his right eye utterly blinded! [Zech. 11:17].

[FF]   "You have murdered R. Eleazar of Modiin, the right arm of all Israel, and their right eye. Therefore may the right arm of that man wither, may his right eye be utterly blinded!"

[GG]   Forthwith Betar was taken, and Ben Kozeba was killed.

That kick—an act of temper, a demonstration of untamed emotions—tells the whole story. We notice two complementary themes. First, Bar Kokhba treats heaven with arrogance, asking God merely to keep out of the way. Second, he treats an especially revered sage with a parallel arrogance. The sage had the power to preserve Israel. Bar Kokhba destroyed Israel's one protection. The result was inevitable.

The Messiah, the centerpiece of salvation history and hero of the tale, emerged as a critical figure. The historical theory of this Yerushalmi passage is stated very simply. In their view Israel had to choose between wars, either the war fought by Bar Kokhba or the "war for Torah." "Why had they been punished? It was because of the weight of the war, for they had not wanted to engage in the struggles over the meaning of the Torah" (Yerushalmi Taanit 3:9 XVII). Those struggles, which were ritual arguments about ritual matters, promised the only victory worth winning. Then Israel's history would be written in terms of wars over the meaning of the Torah and the decision of the law.

The Talmud of Babylonia maintains that the principal result of Israel's loyal adherence to the Torah and its religious duties will be Israel's humble acceptance of God's rule. The humility, under all conditions, makes God love Israel.

Babli Hullin 89A

"It was not because you were greater than any people that the Lord set his love upon you and chose you" [Deut. 7:7]. The Holy One, blessed be He, said to Israel, "I love you because even when I bestow greatness upon you, you humble yourselves before me. I bestowed greatness upon Abraham, yet he said to me, 'I am but dust and ashes' [Gen. 18:27]; upon Moses and Aaron, yet they said, 'But I am a worm and no man' [Ps. 22:7]. But with the heathens it is not so. I bestowed greatness upon Nimrod, and he said, 'Come, let us build us a city' [Gen. 11:4]; upon Pharaoh, and he said, 'Who are they among all the gods of the countries?' [2 Kings 18:35]; upon Nebuchadnezzar, and he said, 'I will ascend above the heights of the clouds' [Isa. 14:14]; upon Hiram, king of Tyre, and he said, 'I sit in the seat of God, in the heart of the seas' [Ezek. 28:2]."

The issue of the Messiah and the meaning of Israel's history framed through the Messiah myth convey in their terms precisely the same position that we find everywhere else in all other symbolic components of the Judaic system and canon.

The heart of the matter then is Israel's subservience to God's will, as expressed in the Torah and embodied in the teachings and lives of the great sages. When Israel fully accepts God's rule, then the Messiah will come. Until Israel subjects itself to God's rule, the Jews will be subjugated to pagan domination. Since the condition of Israel governs, Israel holds the key to its own redemption. But this it can achieve only by throwing away the key! The paradox must be crystal clear: Israel acts to redeem itself through the opposite of self-determination, namely, by subjugating itself to God. Israel's power lies in its negation of power. Its destiny lies in giving up all pretense at deciding its own destiny. So weakness is the ultimate strength, forbearance the final act of self-assertion, passive resignation the sure step toward liberation. (The Christian parallel is the crucified Christ.) Israel's freedom is engraved on the tablets of the commandments of God: To be free is freely to obey. That is not the meaning associated with these words in the minds of others who, like the sages of the Judaic canon, declared their view of what Israel must do to secure the coming of the Messiah.

The passage, praising Israel for its humility, completes the circle begun with the description of Bar Kokhba as arrogant and boastful. Gentile kings are boastful; Israelite kings are humble. So, in all, the Messiah story deals with a concrete and limited consideration of the national life and character. That conception stands at the center of the Judaic system; it shapes and is shaped by that system. In context, the Messiah expresses the system's meaning and so makes it work. The Judaic system, then, transformed the Messiah myth in its totality into an essentially ahistorical force. If people wanted to reach the end of time, they had to rise above time (that is, history) and stand at the side of great movements of political and military character. That is the message of the Messiah theme as it reaches full exposure in the Judaic system of the two Talmuds. Israel must turn away from time and change, submit to whatever happens, so as to win for itself the only government worth having: God's rule, accomplished through God's anointed agent, the Messiah.

The Messiah's Place in History: Sage against Emperor

In the Talmud of the Land of Israel and in associated writings, therefore, we find a fully exposed doctrine of not only *a* Messiah (for example, a kind of priest or general), but *the* Messiah, the one who will save Israel: who the Messiah is, how we will know him, what we must do to bring him. It follows that the Talmud of the Land of Israel presents clear evidence that the Messiah myth had entered into the larger Torah myth that characterized Judaism in its later formative literature. A clear effort to identify the person of the Messiah and to confront the claim that a specific, named individual had been, or would be, the Messiah—these come to the fore. This means that the issue had reached the center of lively discourse at least in some Judaic circles. The disposition of the issue proves distinctive to sages: the Messiah will be a sage, the Messiah will come when Israel has attained that condition of sanctification, marked also by profound humility and complete acceptance of God's will, that signify sanctification.

These two conditions say the same thing twice: the Judaism of sages will identify the Messiah and teach how to bring him nearer. In Christian terms, it was: Jesus is Christ, proved by the triumph of Christianity in the politics of the Roman Empire, the conversion of the emperors, the Christianization of the state. This the Judaic sages maintain was not only irrelevant, it was contrary to God's plan; the Messiah stands not for worldly power but otherworldly patience. The Messiah will be a sage, coming when Israel fully accepts, in all humility, God's sole rule. The Messiah will come in the form of a sage, and therefore no one who now claims to be the Messiah is in fact the savior.

Issues are joined in a confrontation of ideas. There is a clear fit between one side's framing of the Messiah theme and the other party's framing of the same theme. And we cannot forget that larger context in which the theme worked itself out: Messiah joined to the doctrine of history and of Israel, fore and after, forms a large and integrated picture. If Jesus is Christ, then history has come to its fulfillment and Israel is no longer God's people. The sages' counterpart system: The Messiah has not yet come, history as the sequence of empires has in store yet one more age, the age of Israel, and, of course, Israel remains the family, the children of Abraham, Isaac, and Jacob. So Christianity, so Judaism; both confronted precisely the same issues defined in the same way.

In the Talmud of the Land of Israel, two historical contexts framed discussion of the Messiah: the destruction of the Temple and the messianic claim of Bar Kokhba. Rome played a role in both, and the authors of the materials gathered in the Talmud made a place for Rome in the history of Israel. This they did in conformity to their larger theory of who is Israel, specifically by assigning to Rome a place in the family. As to the destruction of the Temple, we find a statement that the Messiah was born on the day that the Temple was destroyed. The Talmud's doctrine of the Messiah therefore finds its place in its encompassing doctrine of history. What is fresh in the Talmud is the perception of Rome as an autonomous actor, as an entity with a point of origin (just as Israel has a point of origin) and a tradition of wisdom (just as Israel has such a tradition). As Rome is Esau, so Esau is part of the family—a point to which we shall return—and therefore plays a role in history. And yet another point of considerable importance: Since Rome does play a role in history, Rome also finds a position in the eschatological drama. This sense of poised opposites, Israel and Rome, comes to expression in two ways. First, Israel's own history calls into being its counterpoint, the antihistory of Rome. Without Israel there would be no Rome—a wonderful consolation to the defeated nation. If Israel's sin created Rome's power, then Israel's repentance would bring Rome's downfall. Here is the way in which the Talmud presents the match:

The concept of two histories, balanced opposite each other, comes to particular expression, within the Talmud of the Land of Israel, in the balance of Israelite sage and Roman emperor. Just as Israel and Rome, God and no-gods, compete (with a foreordained conclusion), so do sage and emperor. In this age, it appears that the emperor has the power. God's Temple, by contrast to the great churches of the age, lies in ruins. But just as sages can overcome the emperor through their inherent supernatural power, so too will Israel and Israel's God in the coming age control the course of events. In the doctrine at hand, we see the true balance: sage against emperor. In the age of the Christian emperors, the polemic acquires power.

The sage, in his small claims court, weighs in the balance against the emperor in Constantinople—a rather considerable claim. So two stunning positions are set forth: First, the notion of emperor and sage in mortal struggle; second, the idea of an age of idolatry and an age beyond idolatry. The world had to move into a new orbit indeed for Rome to enter into the historical context formerly defined wholly by what happened to Israel. How does all this relate to the messianic crisis at hand? The doctrine of sages, directly pertinent to the issue of the coming of the Messiah, holds that Israel can free itself of control by other nations only by humbly agreeing to accept God's rule. The nations—Rome, in the present instance—rest on one side of the balance, while God rests on the other. Israel must choose between them. There is no such thing for Israel as freedom from both God and the nations, total autonomy and independence. There is only a choice of masters, a ruler on earth or a ruler in heaven. Then the choice was easy to make: God's burden is easy, God's yoke is light; life of sanctification by the commandments in time yields salvation at the end of days.

Once the figure of the Messiah has come on stage, discussion arises as to who, among the living, the Messiah might be. The identification of the Messiah begins with the person of David himself: "If the

Messiah-King comes from among the living, his name will be David. If he comes from among the dead, it will be King David himself" (Yerushalmi Berakhot 2:3 VP). A variety of evidence announced the advent of the Messiah as a Rabbinic sage in particular, a master of the Torah:

Yerushalmi Berakhot 2:4
(Translated by T. Zahavy)

[A]   Once a Jew was plowing and his ox snorted once before him. An Arab who was passing and heard the sound said to him, "Jew, loosen your ox and loosen the plow and stop plowing. For today your Temple was destroyed."

[B]   The ox snorted again. He [the Arab] said to him, "Jew, bind your ox and bind your plow, for today the Messiah-King was born."

[C]   He said to him, "What is his name?"

[D]   "Menahem."

[E]   He said to him, "And what is his father's name?"

[F]   The Arab said to him, "Hezekiah."

[G]   He said to him, "Where is he from?"

[H]   He said to him, "From the royal capital of Bethlehem in Judea."

[I]   The Jew went and sold his ox and sold his plow. And he became a peddler of infant's felt-cloths [diapers]. And he went from place to place until he came to that very city. All of the women bought from him. But Menahem's mother did not buy from him.

[J]   He heard the women saying, "Menahem's mother, Menahem's mother, come buy for your child."

[K]   She said, "I want to bring him up to hate Israel. For on the day he was born, the Temple was destroyed."

[L]   They said to her, "We are sure that on this day it was destroyed, and on this day of the year it will be rebuilt."

[M]   She said to the peddler, "I have no money."

[N]   He said to her, "It is of no matter to me. Come and buy for him and pay me when I return."

[O]   A while later he returned to that city. He said to her, "How is the infant doing?"

[P]   She said to him, "Since the time you saw him a spirit came and carried him away from me."

[Q]   Said R. Bun, "Why do we learn this from [a story about] an Arab? Do we not have explicit scriptural evidence for it? 'Lebanon with its majestic trees will fall' [Isa. 10:34]. And what follows this? 'There shall come forth a shoot from the stump of Jesse' [Isa. 11:1]. [Right after an allusion to the destruction of the Temple the prophet speaks of the messianic age.]"[1]

This is a set-piece story, adduced to prove that the Messiah was born on the day the Temple was destroyed. Hence, God prepared for Israel a better fate than had come about that day.

A more concrete matter, the identification of the Messiah with a known historical personality, was associated with the name of Aqiba. He is said to have claimed that Bar Kokhba, leader of the second-century revolt, was the Messiah. The important aspect of the story, however, is the rejection of Aqiba's view. The discredited Messiah figure (if Bar Kokhba actually was such in his own day) finds no apologists in the later Judaic canon. What is striking in what follows, moreover, is that we really have two stories. At G, Aqiba is said to have believed that Bar Kokhba was a disappointment. At H–I, he is said to have identified Bar Kokhba with the King-Messiah. Both cannot be true, so what we have is simply two separate opinions of Aqiba's judgment of Bar Kokhba/Bar Kozebah.

Yerushalmi Taanit 4:5

[X G] R. Simeon b. Yohai taught, "Aqiba, my master, would interpret the following verse: 'A star (*kokhab*) shall come forth out of Jacob' [Num. 24:17] 'A disappointment (*Kozeba*) shall come forth out of Jacob.'"

[H]   R. Aqiba, when he saw Bar Kozeba, said, "This is the King Messiah."

[I]   R. Yohanan ben Toreta said to him, "Aqiba! Grass will grow on your cheeks before the Messiah will come!"

The important point is not only that Aqiba had been proved wrong. It is that the very verse of Scripture adduced in behalf of his viewpoint could be treated more generally and made to refer to righteous people in general, not to the Messiah in particular. And that leads us to the issue of the age, as sages had to face it: What makes a Messiah a false one? The answer, we recall, is arrogance.

Linkage of Keeping the Law and Coming of Messiah

The climax of the matter comes in an explicit statement that the practice of conduct required by the Torah will bring about the coming of the

Messiah. That explanation of the purpose of the holy way of life, focused now on the end of time and the advent of the Messiah, must strike us as surprising. The following contains the most striking expression of the viewpoint at hand.

Yerushalmi Taanit 1:1

X.J.   "The oracle concerning Dumah. One is calling to me from Seir, 'Watchman, what of the night? Watchman, what of the night?' (Isa. 21:11)."

K.   The Israelites said to Isaiah, "O our Rabbi, Isaiah, What will come for us out of this night?"

L.   He said to them, "Wait for me, until I can present the question."

M.   Once he had asked the question, he came back to them.

N.   They said to him, "Watchman, what of the night? What did the Guardian of the ages tell you?"

O.   He said to them, "The watchman says, 'Morning comes; and also the night. If you will inquire, inquire; come back again' (Isa. 21:12)."

P.   They said to him, "Also the night?"

Q.   He said to them, "It is not what you are thinking. But there will be morning for the righteous, and night for the wicked, morning for Israel, and night for idolaters."

R.   They said to him, "When?"

S.   He said to them, "Whenever you want, He too wants [it to be]—if you want it, He wants it."

T.   They said to him, "What is standing in the way?"

U.   He said to them, "Repentance: 'Come back again' (Isa. 21:12)."

V.   R. Aha in the name of R. Tanhum b. R. Hiyya, "If Israel repents for one day, forthwith the son of David will come.

W.   "What is the Scriptural basis? 'O that today you would hearken to his voice!' (Ps. 95:7)."

X.   Said R. Levi, "If Israel would keep a single Sabbath in the proper way, forthwith the son of David will come.

Y.   "What is the Scriptural basis for this view? 'Moses said, Eat it today, for today is a Sabbath to the Lord; today you will not find it in the field' (Exod. 16:25).

Z.   "And it says, 'For thus said the Lord God, the Holy One of Israel, "In returning and rest you shall be saved; in quietness and in trust shall be your strength." And you would not' (Isa. 30:15)."

What is new is at V–Z, the explicit linkage of keeping the law with achieving the end of time and the coming of the Messiah. That motif stands separate from the notions of righteousness and repentance, which surely do not require it. So the condition of "all Israel," a social category in historical time, comes under consideration, and not only the status of individual Israelites in life and in death.

We must not lose sight of the importance of this passage, with its emphasis on repentance, on the one side, and the power of Israel to reform itself, on the other. The Messiah will come any day that Israel makes it possible. If all Israel will keep a single Sabbath in the proper (Judaic) way, the Messiah will come. If all Israel will repent for one day, the Messiah will come. "Whenever you want . . . ," the Messiah will come. Two things are happening here. First, the system of religious observance, including study of Torah, is explicitly invoked as having salvific power. Second, the persistent hope of the people for the coming of the Messiah is linked to the system of Judaic observance and belief. Here we find an explicitly messianic statement that the purpose of the law of the Torah is to attain Israel's salvation: "If you want it, God wants it too." The one thing Israel commands is its own heart; the power it yet exercises is the power to repent. These suffice. The entire history of humanity will respond to Israel's will, to what happens in Israel's heart and soul. And, with the Temple in ruins, repentance can take place only within the heart and mind.

We should note, also, a corollary to the doctrine at hand, which carries to the second point of interest, the Messiah. Israel may contribute to its own salvation by the right attitude and the right deed. But Israel bears responsibility for its present condition, which has been brought about by the wrong attitudes, leading to deeds of rebellion against God. So what Israel does makes history. Any account of the Messiah doctrine of the Talmud of the Land of Israel must lay appropriate stress on that conviction: Israel makes its own history, therefore shapes its own destiny. This lesson, sages maintained, derives from the very condition of Israel even then, its suffering and its despair. How so? History taught moral lessons. Historical events entered into the construction of a teleology for the Talmud of the Land of Israel's system of Judaism as a whole. What the law demanded reflected the consequences of wrongful action on the part of Israel. So, again, Israel's own deeds defined the events of history. Rome's role, like Assyria's and

Babylonia's, depended on Israel's provoking divine wrath as it was executed by the great empire.

The paradox of the system of history and Messiah in the Talmud of the Land of Israel lies in the fact that Israel can free itself of control by other nations only by humbly agreeing to accept God's rule. The nations—Rome, in the present instance—rest on one side of the balance, while God rests on the other. Israel must choose between them. There is no such thing for Israel as freedom from both God and the nations, total autonomy and independence. There is only a choice of masters, a ruler on earth or a ruler in heaven. In the Talmud's theory of salvation, therefore, the framers provided Israel with an account of how to overcome the unsatisfactory circumstances of an unredeemed present, so as to accomplish the movement from here to the much-desired future. When the Talmud's authorities present statements on the promise of the law for those who keep it, therefore, they provide glimpses of the goal of the system as a whole. These invoked the primacy of the rabbi and the legitimating power of the Torah, and in those two components of the system we find the principles of the Messianic doctrine. And these bring us back to the argument with Christ triumphant, as the Christians perceived him.

But when would salvation come, and how could people hasten its arrival? These issues, in the nature of things, proved more pressing as the decades rolled by, becoming first one century, then another, while none knew how many more centuries, and how much more suffering, must still be endured. So the unredeemed state of Israel and the world, the uncertain fate of the individual, framed and defined the context in which all forms of Judaism necessarily took shape. The question of salvation presented each with a single ineluctable agendum. But it is not merely an axiom generated by our hindsight that makes it necessary to interpret all of a system's answers in the light of the single question of salvation. In the case of the Judaism to which the Talmud of the Land of Israel attests, the matter is explicitly stated.

The important fact is that the Talmud of the Land of Israel expressly links salvation to keeping the law. Sages maintained that keeping the law of the Torah now signified keeping the faith: the act of hope. This means that the issues of the law were drawn upward into the highest realm of Israelite consciousness. Keeping the law in the right way is represented as not merely right or expedient. It is the way to bring the

Messiah, the son of David. The messianic hope in concrete political terms also required neutralization, so that people's hopes would not be raised prematurely, with consequent, incalculable damage to the defeated nation. That was true in the second century, in the aftermath of Bar Kokhba's war, and in the fourth century, for obvious reasons, as well.

The Talmud of the Land of Israel treats the messianic hope as something gradual, to be worked toward, not a sudden cataclysmic event. That conception was fully in accord with the notion that the everyday deeds of people formed a pattern continuous with the salvific history of Israel.

Yerushalmi Yoma 3:2III

A. One time R. Hiyya the Elder and R. Simeon b. Halapta were walking in the valley of Arabel at daybreak. They saw that the light of the morning star was breaking forth. Said R. Hiyya the Elder to R. Simeon b. Halapta, "Son of my master, this is what the redemption of Israel is like—at first, little by little, but in the end it will go along and burst into light.

B. "What is the Scriptural basis for this view? 'Rejoice not over me, O my enemy; when I fall, I shall rise; when I sit in darkness, the Lord will be a light to me' (Mic. 7:8).

C. "So, in the beginning, 'When the virgins were gathered together the second time, Mordecai was sitting at the king's gate' (Esther 2:19).

D. "But afterward: 'So Haman took the robes and the horse, and he arrayed Mordecai and made him ride through the open square of the city, proclaiming, Thus shall it be done to the man whom the king delights to honor' (Esther 6:11).

E. "And in the end: 'Then Mordecai went out from the presence of the king in royal robes of blue and white, with a great golden crown and a mantle of fine linen and purple, while the city of Susa shouted and rejoiced' [Esther 8:15].

F. "And finally: 'The Jews had light and gladness and joy and honor' (Esther 8:16)."

The pattern laid out here obviously does not conform to the actual events of the Christianization of the Roman Empire. From the viewpoint of such fathers of the church as Eusebius and Chrysostom alike, the matter had come suddenly, miraculously. Sages saw things differently. We may regard the emphasis on the slow but steady advent of the Messiah's day as entirely consonant with the notion that the Messiah will come when Israel's condition warrants it. The improvement in standards of observing the Torah, therefore, to be effected by the nation's obedience to the clerks, will serve as a guidepost on the road to redemption. The moral condition of the nation ultimately guarantees salvation. God will respond to Israel's regeneration, planning all the while to save the saved—that is, those who save themselves.

Messianic Fulfillment Depends on Moral Regeneration

What is most interesting in the Talmud of the Land of Israel's picture is that the hope for the Messiah's coming is further joined to the moral condition of each individual Israelite. Hence the messianic fulfillment was made to depend on the repentance of Israel. The entire drama, envisioned by others in earlier types of Judaism as a world historical event, was reworked in context into a moment in the life of the individual and the people of Israel collectively. The coming of the Messiah depended not on historical action but on moral regeneration. So from a force that moved Israelites to take up weapons on the battlefield, the messianic hope and yearning were transformed into motives for spiritual regeneration and ethical behavior. The energies released in the messianic fervor were then linked to Judaic government, through which Israel would form the godly society. When we reflect that the message, "If you want it, He too wants it to be," comes in a generation confronting a dreadful disappointment, its full weight and meaning become clear.

The advent of the Messiah will not be heralded by the actions of a pagan or of a Christian king. Whoever relies on the salvation of a Gentile is going to be disappointed. Israel's salvation depends wholly on Israel itself. The message to a disappointed generation, attracted to the kin-faith, with its now-triumphant messianic fulfillment, and fearful of its own fate in an age of violent attacks on the synagogue buildings and faithful alike, was stern. But it also promised strength to the weak and hope to the despairing. No one could be asked to believe that the Messiah would come very soon. The events of the day testified otherwise. So the Talmud's sages counseled patience and consequential deeds.

People could not hasten things, but they could do something. The duty of Israel, in the meantime, was to accept the sovereignty of heavenly government.

Yerushalmi Sanhedrin 6:9.III

A.   R. Abbahu was bereaved. One of his children had passed away from him. R. Jonah and R. Yosé went up [to comfort him]. When they called on him, out of reverence for him, they did not express to him a word of Torah. He said to them, "May the rabbis express a word of Torah."

B.   They said to him, "Let our master teach us."

C.   He said to them, "Now if in regard to the government below, in which there is no reliability, [but only] lying, deceit, favoritism, and bribe taking—

D.   "which is here today and gone tomorrow—

E.   "if concerning that government, it is said, And the relatives of the felon come and inquire after the welfare of the judges and of the witnesses, as if to say, 'We have nothing against you, for you judged honestly' [Mishnah Sanhedrin 6:9],

F.   "in regard to the government above, in which there is reliability, but no lying, deceit, favoritism, or bribe taking—

G.   "and which endures forever and to all eternity—

H.   "all the more so are we obligated to accept upon ourselves the just decree [of that heavenly government]."

I.   And it says, "That the Lord . . . may show you mercy, and have compassion on you . . ." (Deut. 13:17).

Sage as Savior

The heavenly government, revealed in the Torah, was embodied in this world by the figure of the sage. The meaning of the salvific doctrine just outlined becomes fully clear when we uncover the simple fact that the rule of heaven and the learning and authority of the rabbi on earth turned out to be identified with each other. It follows that salvation for Israel depended on adherence to the sage and acceptance of his discipline. God's will in heaven and the sage's words on earth both constituted Torah. And Israel would be saved through Torah, so the sage was the savior—especially the humble one. The humblest of them all would be the sage-Messiah, victor over time and circumstance, savior of Israel.

Since Judaism lays such heavy stress on the right attitude, our attention is drawn to accounts of precisely what attitude is required to win from God the response that Israel desires. It is clear that God is not to be coerced, but God may take note and respond, according to the covenant, in a way that we may want. God cannot be manipulated, but God has the power to love, even as we do. God's power is no less than ours: to give or not to give what is wholly subject to one's own government—that is, love. The commandment to love is an appeal. Then what are the attitudes and actions that will elicit the response we hope from God? A set of stories answers that question, and these focus on the matter of *zekhut,* to which we now turn.

Zekhut: **Acts of Supererogatory Grace**

Here translated as "the heritage of virtue and its consequent entitlements," *zekhut* comes about through various supererogatory actions, which cannot be commanded or coerced but can only be freely given, actions that lay entirely beyond the measure of the law and represent pure love. To be sure, Torah study is one means of attaining access to that heritage, of gaining *zekhut.* There are other equally suitable means, and the merit gained by Torah study is no different from the merit gained by any other type of acts of supererogatory grace. And still more astonishing, a single remarkable action may produce *zekhut* of the same order as a lifetime of devotion to Torah study; through a noteworthy act of selfless behavior, a simple ass-driver may attain the same level of *zekhut* as a learned sage. The reason that *zekhut* forms so central a component of the doctrine of the coming (or bringing) of the Messiah has now to be made explicit.

Zekhut is not coerced and does not coerce, but forms a gift freely given, to which God, the ultimate recipient, freely responds. God cannot command or demand those acts of utter devotion to the other that yield *zekhut,* but God can and will respond to those acts. Just as the person who performs such an act gives what cannot be coerced, so God responds with an act of grace, and, in the end, the entire reconciliation of God and Israel is accomplished as that act of responsive grace that the sending of the Messiah embodies. For *zekhut* is the opposite of arrogance. *Zekhut* is gained for a person by an act of renunciation and self-abnegation, such that heaven responds with an act of grace. *Zekhut* defines the very opposite of coercion. It is an act that no one could anticipate or demand, but an act of such remarkable selflessness that heaven finds itself constrained to respond. That response is through an act of responsive grace on heaven's part, grace that by definition one cannot demand or compel, but only provoke.

Notice the contrast to Bar Kokhba's arrogance: "Just don't get in our way." When we make ourselves less, heaven makes us more, but we cannot force our will upon heaven. It is where heaven cannot force its will upon us that *zekhut* intervenes. It is that exquisite balance between our will and heaven's will that, in the end, brings to its perfect balance and entire fulfillment the exploration of the conflict of God's will and our will that began with Adam and Eve at their last hour in Eden, and our first hour on earth. In context, the fact that we may inherit a treasury of *zekhut* from our ancestors logically follows: Just as we inherit the human condition of the freedom to practice rebellion against God's word, so we inherit from former generations the results of another dimension of the human condition: our power to give willingly what none, not even God, can by right or rule compel.

What we cannot by our own will impose, we can by the act of renunciation of our own will evoke. What we cannot accomplish through coercion, we can achieve through submission. God will do for us what we cannot do for ourselves, when we do for God what God cannot make us do. And that means, in a concrete and tangible sense, to love God with all the heart, all the soul, all the might we have. God then stands above the rules of the created world, because God will respond not to what we do in conformity to the rules alone, but also to what we do beyond the requirement of the rules. God is above the rules, and we can gain a response from God when, on one unique occasion, we too do more than obey: We love, spontaneously and all at once, with the whole of our being. That is the conception of God that *zekhut*, as a conception of power in heaven and power in humanity, contains. In the relationship between God and humanity expressed in the conception of *zekhut*, we reach the understanding of what the Torah means when it tells us that we are in God's image and after God's likeness: We are, then, "in our image," the very mirror image of God. God's will forms the mirror image of ours: When we are humble, God responds; when we demand, God withdraws. The Temple was destroyed because of our—

Israel's—sin, the sin of arrogance. The Temple will be restored as an act of responsive grace, when we give freely what none can ask.

The final step in the path that began with God's profession of love for Israel, the response of the freely given, uncoerced act of love, *zekhut* stands for the empowerment, of a supernatural character, that derives from the virtue of one's ancestry or from one's own particular virtuous deeds. No single word in English bears the same meaning, nor is there a synonym for *zekhut* in the canonical writings. The difficulty of translating a word of systemic consequence with a single word in some other language (or in the language of the system's documents themselves) tells us we deal with what is unique, beyond comparison, and therefore beyond contrast and comprehension. What is most particular to and distinctive of the systemic structure and its functioning requires definition through circumlocution: "the heritage of virtue and its consequent entitlements."

The mark of the system's integration around *zekhut* lies in its insistence that all Israelites—even, or especially, women—not only sages, could gain *zekhut* for themselves and their descendants. A single remarkable deed, exemplary for its deep humanity, sufficed to win for an ordinary person the *zekhut* that elicits supernatural favor enjoyed by some rabbis on account of their Torah study. The centrality of *zekhut* in the systemic structure, the critical importance of the heritage of virtue together with its supernatural entitlements, therefore emerge in a striking claim: Even though a man may have been degraded, one action can suffice to win for him that heavenly glory to which rabbis in general aspire. The Judaic storyteller whose writing we shall consider next assuredly identifies with this lesson, since it is the point of his story and its climax.

In all three instances that follow, which define what the individual must do to gain *zekhut*, the point is that the deeds of the hero of each story make him worthy of having his prayers answered, which is a mark of the working of *zekhut*. Supererogatory, uncoerced deeds, those well beyond the strict requirements of the Torah, and even beyond the limits of the law altogether, transform the hero into a holy man, whose holiness served just like that of a sage who possessed great knowledge of the Torah. The following stories should not be understood as expressions of the mere sentimentality of the sages concerning the lower orders, for they deny in favor of a single action of surpassing power sages' lifelong devotion to what the sages held to be the highest value, knowledge of the Torah.

Yerushalmi Taanit 1:4.I

F.   A certain man came before one of the relatives of R. Yannai. He said to him, "Rabbi, attain *zekhut* through me [by giving me charity]."

G.   He said to him, "And didn't your father leave you money?"

H.   He said to him, "No."

I.   He said to him, "Go and collect what your father left in deposit with others."

J.   He said to him, "I have heard concerning property my father deposited with others that it was gained by violence [so I don't want it]."

K.   He said to him, "You are worthy of praying and having your prayers answered."

The point of K is a self-evident reference to the possession of entitlement to supernatural favor, and it is gained, we see, through deeds that the law of the Torah cannot require but must favor: what one does on one's own volition, beyond the measure of the law. Here is the opposite of sin. A sin is what one has done by one's own volition beyond all limits of the law. So an act that generates *zekhut* for the individual is the counterpart and opposite: what one does by one's own volition that also is beyond all requirements of the law.

In the next of these stories, we should not miss an odd fact. The story tells about the *zekhut* attained by a humble, poor, ignorant man. It is narrated to underline what he has done. But what provokes the event is an act of self-abnegation far greater than that willingly performed by the male hero: a woman's readiness to sell herself into prostitution to save her husband. That is not a focus of the story but a given. Nothing has compelled the woman to surrender her body to save her husband; to the contrary, the marital obligations of a woman concern only conventional deeds, which indeed the Mishnah's law maintains may be coerced; failure to do these deeds may result in financial penalties inflicted on the woman in the settlement of her marriage contract. So the story of the uncoerced act of selflessness is told about a man, but occasioned by a woman, and both actors in the story exhibit the same virtue.

When Torah stories are told, by contrast, the point is that a man attains *zekhut* by study of the Torah, and a woman attains *zekhut* by sending her sons and her husband off to study the Torah and sitting home alone—not exactly commensurate actions. Only *zekhut* stories represent the act of the woman as the counterpart and equivalent to the act of the man; and, in fact, even here, the fact that the woman's unco-erced gift is far greater than the man's—her body, merely his animal—should not go unnoticed. Once more, we find ourselves at the systemic center, where everything is reversed:

> L.   A certain ass-driver appeared before the rabbis [the context requires: in a dream] and prayed, and rain came. The rabbis sent and brought him and said to him, "What is your trade?"
>
> M.   He said to them, "I am an ass-driver."
>
> N.   They said to him, "And how do you conduct your business?"
>
> O.   He said to them, "One time I rented my ass to a certain woman, and she was weeping on the way, and I said to her, 'What's with you?' and she said to me, 'The husband of that woman [me] is in prison [for debt], and I wanted to see what I can do to free him.' So I sold my ass and I gave her the proceeds, and I said to her, 'Here is your money, free your husband, but do not sin [by becoming a prostitute to raise the necessary funds].'"
>
> P.   They said to him, "You are worthy of praying and having your prayers answered."

The ass-driver clearly has a powerful lien on heaven, so that his prayers are answered, even while those of others are not. What did he do to get that entitlement? He did what no law could demand: impoverished himself to save a woman from a "fate worse than death."

> Q.   In a dream of R. Abbahu, Mr. Pentakaka ["Five sins"] appeared, who prayed that rain would come, and it rained. R. Abbahu sent and summoned him. He said to him, "What is your trade?"
>
> R.   He said to him, "Five sins does that man [I] do every day, [for I am a pimp:] hiring whores, cleaning up the theater, bringing home their garments for washing, dancing, and performing before them."
>
> S.   He said to him, "And what sort of decent thing have you ever done?"
>
> T.   He said to him, "One day that man [I] was cleaning the

theater, and a woman came and stood behind a pillar and cried. I said to her, 'What's with you?' And she said to me, 'That woman's [my] husband is in prison, and I wanted to see what I can do to free him,' so I sold my bed and cover, and I gave the proceeds to her. I said to her, 'Here is your money, free your husband, but do not sin.'"

U.   He said to him, "You are worthy of praying and having your prayers answered."

Q moves us still further, since the named man has done everything sinful that one can do, and, more to the point, he does it every day. So the singularity of the act of *zekhut*, which suffices if done only one time, encompasses its power to outweigh a life of sin—again, an act of *zekhut* as the mirror image and opposite of sin. Here again, the single act of saving a woman from a "fate worse than death" has sufficed.

V.   A pious man from Kefar Imi appeared [in a dream] to the rabbis. He prayed for rain and it rained. The rabbis went up to him. His householders told them that he was sitting on a hill. They went out to him, saying to him, "Greetings," but he did not answer them.

W.   He was sitting and eating, and he did not say to them, "You break bread too."

X.   When he went back home, he made a bundle of faggots and put his cloak on top of the bundle [instead of on his shoulder].

Y.   When he came home, he said to his household [wife], "These rabbis are here [because] they want me to pray for rain. If I pray and it rains, it is a disgrace for them, and if not, it is a profanation of the Name of Heaven. But come, you and I will go up [to the roof] and pray. If it rains, we shall tell them, 'We are not worthy to pray and have our prayers answered.'"

Z.   They went up and prayed and it rained.

AA.   They came down to them [and asked], "Why have the rabbis troubled themselves to come here today?"

BB.   They said to him, "We wanted you to pray so that it would rain."

CC.   He said to them, "Now do you really need my prayers? Heaven already has done its miracle."

DD.   They said to him, "Why, when you were on the hill, did we say hello to you, and you did not reply?"

EE.   He said to them, "I was then doing my job. Should I then interrupt my concentration [on my work]?"

FF.   They said to him, "And why, when you sat down to eat, did you not say to us, 'You break bread too'?"

GG.   He said to them, "Because I had only my small ration of bread. Why would I have invited you to eat by way of mere flattery [when I knew I could not give you anything at all]?"

HH.   They said to him, "And why when you came to go down, did you put your cloak on top of the bundle?"

II.   He said to them, "Because the cloak was not mine. It was borrowed for use at prayer. I did not want to tear it."

JJ.   They said to him, "And why, when you were on the hill, did your wife wear dirty clothes, but when you came down from the mountain, did she put on clean clothes?"

KK.   He said to them, "When I was on the hill, she put on dirty clothes, so that no one would gaze at her. But when I came home from the hill, she put on clean clothes, so that I would not gaze on any other woman."

LL.   They said to him, "It is well that you pray and have your prayers answered."

The pious man of V, finally, enjoys the recognition of the sages by reason of his lien upon heaven, able as he is to pray and bring rain. What has so endowed him with *zekhut*? Acts of punctiliousness of a moral order: concentrating on his work, avoiding an act of dissimulation, integrity in the disposition of a borrowed object, his wife's concern not to attract other men, and her equal concern to make herself attractive to her husband.

In *zekhut* women find equality with men; with no role whatever in the study of the Torah and no possibility of attaining political sagacity, women find a critical place in the sequence of actions that elicit from heaven the admiring response that *zekhut* embodies. Indeed, a second reading of the stories shows that the hero is second to the heroine; it is the woman who, in each case, precipitates the occasion for the man's attainment of *zekhut*, and she, not he, exemplifies the highest pinnacle of selfless virtue. Just as Torah learning is subordinated, so man is subordinated; *zekhut*, the gift that can be given but not compelled, like love, in an unerring sense must be called the female virtue that sets atop a male structure and system: the crown of the Torah, exceeding the Torah in every dimension of the holy life—and that by definition.

Zekhut may be personal or inherited. The *zekhut* deriving from the prior generations is collective and affects all Israel. But one's own deeds can generate *zekhut* for oneself, with the simple result that *zekhut* is as much personal as it is collective. Specifically, Jacob reflects on the power that Esau's *zekhut* had gained for Esau. He had gained that *zekhut* by living in the land of Israel and also by paying honor and respect to his father, Isaac. Jacob then feared that, because of the *zekhut* gained by his brother, he (Jacob) would not be able to overcome Esau. So *zekhut* worked on its own; gained by proper action, it was credited to the person who had done that action. What made the action worthy of evoking heaven's response with an act of supernatural favor is that it was an action not to be required but if done to be rewarded, an act of will that cannot be coerced but must be honored. In Esau's case, it was the simple fact that he had remained in the Holy Land:

Genesis Rabbah LXXVI:II

2.   A.   "Then Jacob was greatly afraid and distressed" (Gen. 32:7): [This is Jacob's soliloquy:] "Because of all those years that Esau was living in the Land of Israel, perhaps he may come against me with the power of the *zekhut* he has now attained by dwelling in the Land of Israel.

B.   "Because of all those years of paying honor to his father, perhaps he may come against me with the power of the *zekhut* he attained by honoring his father."

C.   "So he said: 'Let the days of mourning for my father be at hand, then I will slay my brother Jacob' (Gen. 27:41).

D.   "Now the old man is dead."

The important point, then, is that *zekhut* is not only inherited as part of a collective estate left by the patriarchs; it is also accomplished by an individual in his or her own behalf. By extension, we recognize, the successor system opens a place for recognition of the individual (both man and woman) within the system of *zekhut*. As we shall now see, what a man or a woman does may win for that person an entitlement for supernatural favor of some sort from heaven. So there is space, in the system, for a private person, and the individual is linked to the social order through the shared possibilities of generating or inheriting an entitlement from heaven.

If we now ask, What are the sorts of deeds that generate *zekhut*? we realize that those deeds produce a common result of gaining for their doer, as much as for the heirs of the actor, an entitlement for heavenly favor and support when needed. And that fact concerning gaining and benefiting from *zekhut* brings us to the systemic message to the living generation, its account of what now is to be done. That message proves acutely contemporary, for its stress is on the power of a single action to create sufficient *zekhut* to outweigh a life of sin. Then the contrast between sin and *zekhut* gains greater depth. One sin of sufficient weight condemns, one act of *zekhut* of sufficient weight saves; the entire issue of entitlements out of the past gives way, then, when we realize what is actually at stake.

We recall that Torah study is one—but only one—means for an individual to gain access to that heritage, to get *zekhut*. There are other equally suitable means; the merit gained by Torah study is no different from the merit gained by acts of a supererogatory character. If one gets *zekhut* for studying the Torah, then we must suppose there is no holy deed that does not generate its share of *zekhut*. But when it comes to specifying the things one does to get *zekhut*, the documents before us speak of what the Torah does not require but does recommend: not what we are commanded to do in detail, but what the right attitude, formed within the Torah, leads us to do on our own volition. What is it that Israelites as a nation do to gain a lien upon heaven for themselves or entitlements of supernatural favor for their descendants? Here is one representative answer to that question.

Genesis Rabbah LXXIV:I

A. "If the God of my father, the God of Abraham and the Fear of Isaac, had not been on my side, surely now you would have sent me away empty-handed. God saw my affliction and the labor of my hand and rebuked you last night" (Gen. 31:41-42):

B. Zebedee b. Levi and R. Joshua b. Levi:

C. Zebedee said, "Every passage in which reference is made to 'if' tells of an appeal to the *zekhut* accrued by the patriarchs."

D. Said to him R. Joshua, "But it is written, 'Except we had lingered' (Gen. 43:10) [a passage not related to the *zekhut* of the patriarchs]."

E. He said to him, "They themselves would not have come up except for the *zekhut* of the patriarchs, for if it were not for the *zekhut* of the patriarchs, they never would have been able to go up from there in peace."

F.   Said R. Tanhuma, "There are those who produce the matter in a different version." [It is given as follows:]

G.   R. Joshua and Zebedee b. Levi:

H.   R. Joshua said, "Every passage in which reference is made to 'if' tells of an appeal to the *zekhut* accrued by the patriarchs except for the present case."

I.   He said to him, "This case too falls under the category of an appeal to the *zekhut* of the patriarchs."

So much for *zekhut* that is inherited from the patriarchs, a now-familiar notion. What about the deeds of Israel in the here and now?

J.   R. Yohanan said, "It was on account of the *zekhut* achieved through sanctification of the divine name."

K.   R. Levi said, "It was on account of the *zekhut* achieved through faith and the *zekhut* achieved through Torah."

Faith despite the here and now, study of the Torah—these are what Israel does in the here and now with the result that they gain an entitlement for themselves or their heirs.

L.   "The *zekhut* achieved through faith: 'If I had not believed...' (Ps. 27:13).

M.   "The *zekhut* achieved through Torah: 'Unless your Torah had been my delight' (Ps. 119:92)."

2.   A.   "God saw my affliction and the labor of my hand and rebuked you last night" (Gen. 31:41-42):

B.   Said R. Jeremiah b. Eleazar, "More beloved is hard labor than the *zekhut* achieved by the patriarchs, for the *zekhut* achieved by the patriarchs served to afford protection for property only, while the *zekhut* achieved by hard labor served to afford protection for lives.

C.   "The *zekhut* achieved by the patriarchs served to afford protection for property only: 'If the God of my father, the God of Abraham and the Fear of Isaac, had not been on my side, surely now you would have sent me away empty-handed.'

D.   "The *zekhut* achieved by hard labor served to afford protection for lives: 'God saw my affliction and the labor of my hand and rebuked you last night.'"

Here is as good an account as any of the theology of *zekhut*. The issue of the *zekhut* of the patriarchs comes up in the reference to the God of the fathers. The conception of the *zekhut* of the patriarchs is explicit, not general. It specifies what later benefit to the heir, Israel the family, derived from which particular action of a patriarch or matriarch. But acts of faith and Torah study form only one medium; hard labor, devotion to one's calling, defines that source of *zekhut* that will be accessible to the many Israelites unlikely to distinguish themselves either by Torah study and acts of faith, encompassing the sanctification of God's name, or by acts of amazing gentility and restraint.

The system here speaks to everybody, Jew and Gentile, past and present and future; *zekhut* therefore defines the structure of the cosmic social order and explains how it is supposed to function. It is the encompassing quality of *zekhut*, its pertinence to past and future, high and low, rich and poor, gifted and ordinary, that marks as the systemic statement the message of *zekhut*, now fully revealed as the conception of reciprocal response between heaven and Israel on earth, to acts of devotion beyond the requirements of the Torah but defined all the same by the Torah. As Scripture had said, God responds to the faith of the ancient generations by supernatural acts to which, on their own account, the moderns are not entitled, hence a heritage of entitlement. But those acts, now fully defined for us, can and ought to be done, also, by the living generation. As a matter of fact, no one today, at the time of the system-builders, is exempt from the systemic message and its demands: even steadfastness in accomplishing the humble work of the everyday and the here and now.

The systemic statement made by the usages of *zekhut* speaks of relationship, function, the interplay of humanity and God. One's store of *zekhut* derives from a relationship, that is, from one's forebears. That is one dimension of the relationships in which one stands. *Zekhut* also forms a measure of one's own relationship with heaven, as is attested in the power of one person, but not another, to pray and so bring rain.

Zekhut comes through deeds of a supererogatory character, to which heaven responds by deeds of a supererogatory character: supernatural favor to this one, who through deeds of ingratiation or self-abnegation or restraint exhibits the attitude that in heaven precipitates a counterpart attitude, hence generating *zekhut*, rather than to that one, who does not. The simple fact that rabbis cannot pray and bring rain, but a simple ass-driver can, tells the whole story. The relationship measured by *zekhut*—heaven's response by an act of uncoerced favor to a person's uncoerced gift, for example, an act of gentility, restraint, or self-abnegation—contains an element of unpredictability that is accounted for by appeal to the *zekhut* inherited from ancestors. So while one cannot coerce heaven, one can through *zekhut* gain acts of favor from heaven, by doing what heaven cannot require. Heaven then responds to one's attitude in carrying out one's duties—and more than those duties. That act of pure disinterest—as in giving away one's means of livelihood—is the one that gains heaven's deepest interest.

Here we find the ultimate reversal, which the moves from scarcity of real estate to abundance of Torah learning, from the legitimacy of power to the legitimacy of weakness, in perspective are shown merely to adumbrate. "Make God's wishes yours, so that God will make your wishes his. . . . Anyone from whom people take pleasure, God takes pleasure" (Abot 2:4). These two statements hold together the two principal elements of the conception of the relationship to God that *zekhut* conveys. Please others, do not impose your will but give way to the will of the other, and heaven will respond by giving a lien that is not coerced but evoked. By the rationality of discipline within, we have the power to form rational relationships beyond ourselves, with heaven; and that is how the system expands the boundaries of the social order to encompass not only the natural but also the supernatural world.

The conviction that, by dint of special effort, one may so conduct oneself as to acquire an entitlement of supernatural power turns one's commonplace circumstance into an arena encompassing heaven and earth. God responds to an individual's—and to holy Israel's—virtue, filling the gap, so to speak, about oneself and about one's entire family that one leaves when one forebears, withdraws, and gives up what is one's own: one's space, one's self. When one does so, then God responds; one's sacrifice then evokes memories of Abraham's readiness to sacrifice Isaac; devotion to the other calls up from heaven what cannot be coerced. What imparts critical mass to the conception of *zekhut*, that gaining of supernatural entitlements through the surrender of what is one's own, is the recasting, in the mold and model of that virtue of surrender, of the political economy of Israel in the Land of Israel. That explains why power in politics is weakness, economics is the rational increase of resources that are (but need not be) scarce, valued things that are capable of infinite increase.

Like Christ on the cross, Israel's God made manifest in the Torah ultimately breaks the rules, accords an entitlement to this one, who has done some remarkable deed, but not to that one, who has done nothing wrong and everything right. So a life lived in accord with the rules—even a life spent in the study of the Torah—is outweighed in heaven's view by a single moment, a gesture that violates the norm, extending the outer limits of the rule, for instance, of virtue. And who but a God who (like us) feels, not only thinks, who responds to impulse and sentiment, can be portrayed in such a way? No rule exhaustively describes a world such as this. Here the law of love is transcended, for love itself is now surpassed. Beyond love is the willing, uncoerced sacrifice of self: love of the other more than the love of self, love of the Other most of all.

What is asked of Israel and of the Israelite individual is truly godly restraint, supernatural generosity of soul that is "in [God's] image, after [God's] likeness": that is what sets aside all rules. The circumstance of genealogy dictated whether or not the moral entity, either the individual or the nation, would enjoy access to entitlements of supernatural favor without regard to the merit of either one. That is quite natural, in a society that traced its origin to a single couple, Abraham and Sarah, and that further regarded all of its members as equally responsible for the moral condition of the whole, as the prophets had insisted long ago. Hence "Israel" formed a single moral entity, and not only the individual person, but the entirety of the social order formed by Israel, constituted a moral actor, subject to God's judgment—but also to God's grace.

But, whether favored by a rich heritage of supernatural empowerment as was the nation, or deprived, by reason of one's immediate ancestors, of any lien upon heaven, in the end both the nation and the individual had in hand the power to shape the future. How was this to be done? It was not alone by keeping the Torah, studying the Torah, dressing, eating, making a living, marrying, procreating, raising a family, burying and being buried, all in accord with those rules.

That life in conformity with the rules, obligatory but merely conventional, did not evoke the special interest of heaven. Why should it? The rules describe the ordinary. But (in language of the Talmud of Babylonia), "the All-Merciful really wants the heart," and that is not an ordinary thing. Nor was the power to bring rain gained through a life of merely ordinary sanctity. Special favor responded to extraordinary actions, in analogy to special disfavor, misfortune deemed to punish sin. Just as culpable sin, as distinct from mere error, requires an act of will—specifically, arrogance—so an act of extraordinary character requires an act of will. But, as mirror image of sin, the act would reveal in a concrete way an attitude of restraint, forbearance, gentility, and self-abnegation. A sinful act, provoking heaven, was one that was done deliberately to defy heaven. An act that would evoke heaven's favor, so imposing upon heaven a lien that heaven freely gave, was one that, equally deliberately and concretely, displayed humility.

Zekhut is the power of the powerless, the riches of the disinherited, the valuation and valorization of the will of those who have no right to will. In the context of Christian Palestine, Jews found themselves on the defensive. Their ancestry called into question, their supernatural standing thrown into doubt, their future denied, they called themselves "Israel," and the land, "the Land of Israel." But what power did they possess, legitimately, if need be through violence, to assert their claim to form "Israel"? And, with the Holy Land passing into the hands of others, what scarce resource did they own that could take the place of that measure of value that now no longer was subjected to their rationality? How, when, and why will the Messiah come?

"Today, if you will it," found its final definition in the teaching: Today, if through sacrifice of will you offer God the ultimate gift within your power: the self. Israel saves itself by freely, willingly surrendering itself to God. The sending of the Messiah is an act of responsive grace, God's ultimate gesture of *zekhut*: what cannot be demanded or compelled, but only freely given, God's final gift for all eternity.

Messianic Virtues and
the Pleasure of God

BRUCE CHILTON

THE PROMISE OF THE MESSIAH, as a function of Israel's loyal adherence to the Torah, comports precisely with the equation between the kingdom and obeying the Torah, as described in chapter 3. The formative influence of the consequences of Simeon bar Kosibah's[1] revolt is plain (see the passage from Yerushalmi Taanit 4:5, cited on pp. 160–61, 167): the sometimes vague, sometimes vehement, not infrequently conflicting messianic teachings of early Judaism were rationalized by the fourth century. From that point on, there is a coherent emphasis on Israel's patient expectation of a usually Davidic (but always sage) king who would bring to completion the very obedience Israel had commenced.

The picture drawn within the Targum of Isaiah 53:5 is typical:[2]

And he *will build the sanctuary which was profaned* for our *sins, handed over* for our iniquities; *and by his teaching his peace will increase* upon *us,* and in *that we attach ourselves to his words our sins will be forgiven us.*

The degree of innovation in the rendering (indicated by the use of italics) is especially apparent when the passage is compared with any critical translation of the Hebrew text. The Messiah of the Targum is as solicitous of the status of the cult and correct teaching as Simeon bar Kosibah was reckless in his assassination of Eleazar of Modiin. The Messiah of Mishnah involves purity, and his words invoke that nexus of obedience, repentance, and forgiveness that will alone undo what had

188

been Israel's undoing. From that perspective, it is not surprising that the attributes of the Messiah as a sage would come to be heightened and specified (see the passages cited from Yerushalmi, Berakhoth 2:3 and 2:4, pp. 165–67).

The Rabbis framed a classic expectation of the Messiah not so much on the rubble of Simeon bar Kosibah's failure as in the midst of the rubble and with the rubble. The Psalms of Solomon, from the first century B.C.E., already portray the messianic son of David as establishing purity and true justice, even as he destroys Israel's enemies (17:21-46). The step to making him a royal Rabbi, complete with a temple of his endowment, was radical in the sense that it reached into the roots of messianic expectation, but the creativity involved was on the basis of elements already present.

Nonetheless, the Rabbis' creativity was of an order that demands a recasting of the way in which Christianity conceives of itself. The interest in Rabbinic Judaism that has been a hallmark of Christian scholarship since the Enlightenment has focused on the issue of the Messiah. To an extent, that focus has been part of a perennial interest in apologetics, but there is another interest as well. Because the scholarship of the Enlightenment concerned itself with the causal development of history, the Judaic antecedents of Christianity were seen to be of crucial concern to anyone who wished to understand Jesus and his movement.[3] But the assumption that history flowed from Judaism to Christianity (rather than within them both and between them both) produced the notion, still current today, that Judaism was characterized by a single concept of the Messiah, to which Jesus corresponded.

The mistake involved in that notion of history is as obvious as some of its results are appalling. Once "the Messiah" is conceived of as an evident, stable pattern within Judaism, then any delay to acknowledge that Jesus fits the pattern can only be ascribed to recalcitrance. Because sources of Judaism themselves refer to Israel as rebellious, once the messianic fallacy is accepted, "the Jews" may easily be cast in the role of God's conscious (and disloyal) opposition. The virulence of anti-Semitism in the modern period is partially attributable to the pseudo-historical judgment that "the Jews" should have known better than to crucify their own Messiah.

Once it is appreciated that messianic conceptions in the first century were as pluralistic as Judaism itself, and that the Rabbis demonstrated a commanding creativity from the second century onward, the messianic fallacy that has hampered scholarship and fed prejudice is revealed for what it is. But in that progress lies a certain threat to the manner in which Christian theology has typically been conducted. Our thinkers have found it convenient to cite sources of Judaism, or sources of ancient philosophy, or sources of modern ideology, and then claim a transcending fulfillment for Christianity. Matthew's Gospel sees Isaiah fulfilled by Jesus in that sense, Thomas Aquinas did much the same to Aristotle, and liberation theologians such as Leonardo Boff[4] perform the maneuver with Karl Marx. The systemic claim of Christianity is that we are transferred into God's kingdom by means of Christ, and therefore it is natural for us to proceed by the logic of transcending fulfillment: Whatever account of the world seems best, we must seek to better it in service of the world that is coming. The question that emerges is, Can we—without claims of transcending other systems, which today seem invidious—articulate the systemic assertion of the Christian faith?

The fact that our thought has typically proceeded by a dialectical opposition to other systems should itself give us pause. If it is the case, as seems incontrovertible, that the Christian ethos is to conduct ourselves in the manner of Christ, then our preference for arguments that dismiss other systems must seem out of character, however entrenched the habit may be. The picture of Israel's humility in Hullin 89a should be applicable to the church because humility is, as Professor Neusner remarks, a virtue that runs in tandem in the two systems: "The Christian parallel is the crucified Christ" (p. 162). Within such an understanding, the claim to be the Messiah is self-falsifying (p. 163): Jesus in the "little apocalypse" specifically cites just the principle that anyone who claims to be the Christ in triumph is a liar (see Matt. 24:4-6/Mark 13:5-7/Luke 21:8-9). If humility is a messianic virtue, then the claim of triumphant transcendence is self-falsifying.

"If Jesus is Christ, then history has come to its fulfillment and Israel is no longer God's people" (p. 164). That is an accurate characterization of many Christian claims, ancient and modern, but from within Christianity's system of religion the matter appears different. History is not over, because Jesus Christ marks the bodily invasion of the divine into our world, the change in our constitutions that makes a new sort of history possible. There is a fulfillment in the sense that we claim to understand the meaning of events, without asserting any special competence to predict the events themselves. But is Israel still Israel? Paul insisted, in a well-defined (if agonized) exposition devoted to just that question (Romans 9–11), that it was indeed, that the inclusion of non-Jews did not falsify the promise to and the covenant with Abraham. He even referred to the entirety of those to be included within the final disclosure of God's reign as "all Israel" (Rom. 11:26). For Paul, Jesus Christ represented the confirmation of the blessing of Abraham for all people, rather than the denial of Israel. The claim to know the meaning of history can degenerate and has degenerated into the claim to know history; the claim to inherit the promises to Israel can degenerate and has degenerated into the claim that "the Jews" are no longer Israel.

Anyone who has read of Jesus' warning against false Messiahs must be stunned by the heralding of Constantine by Eusebius as the political equivalent of the Christ, indeed of Jesus himself. That Eusebius initiated an epoch of triumphalist thinking within Christianity cannot reasonably be denied. R. Levi's famous statement, that keeping a single Sabbath would correspond to the arrival of the son of David (Yerushalmi, Taanit 1:1, cited on p. 168), is evocative of the difficulty of observing Judaism in unfavorable conditions, as well as of the hope of obedience in such conditions. Just as, within Judaism, "the system of religious observance, including study of Torah, is explicitly invoked as having salvific power" (p. 169), Christianity embarked on a quest of empire that is not yet finished.

The persistent challenge for Christianity has been to gain the world without losing its soul (see Matt. 16:26/Mark 8:36/Luke 9:25), and there has been no lack of communities of Christians, monastic and lay, that have explicitly renounced the attempt by turning away from the world. Numbers of such communities sought refuge in North America, where—ironically—their prosperity generated problems of governance that were cognate with those they had left behind in Europe. Because Christianity is a religion whose systemic center is in another world, this world is a perennial paradox for it. The attempt might be made to deny the paradox by embracing the world or rejecting it, but finally the world is where we live and yet beyond our control, and the paradox remains.

Paradox also attends our hope in the Parousia, Christ's ultimate coming in glory. The progressive view of the Yerushalmi (Yoma 3:2, cited on p. 171), that obedience and Messiah arrive in a "slow but steady advent" (p. 172), is a perspective we might yearn for. But for us, since the time of Augustine, it has seemed that the City of God is related only intermittently to the City of Man. Faith perceives the world to come, and we locate ourselves in that realm, but there is always at least a certain intransigence in the world we live in, and sometimes—even at its most "Christian"—the world for us is an alien place. Things might get worse before they get better, and better before worse, but when that good which is God alone might come, we cannot say. The Son himself disclaimed knowledge of that day and hour (see Matt. 24:36/Mark 13:32; cf. Acts 1:7).

Unease with the world is intrinsic to Christianity as a system of religion. Even when its influence is considerable, the sense of being adrift is more than a transient mood; it expresses the restless heart of a systemic commitment to transformation. The leading edge of that change is represented by those acts that one undertakes within the imitation of Christ. Precisely as this world is passing away, the one who performs the will of God remains (1 John 2:17). That performance, a walking in the footsteps of the Christ, is clearly related to the notion of *zekhut*, an innocence or virtue that is enacted freely and rejoices the heart of God. Latin *virtus*, in its reference to a warrior's power, perhaps approximates to *zekhut* as "the heritage of virtue and its consequent entitlements" (p. 174).

However *zekhut* is rendered, the centrality of "reciprocal response" (p. 184) between heaven and heaven's counterpart on earth (whether Israel or church) is common to Judaism and Christianity. Acts from the heart may warm the heart of God, because they prove to be enactments of God's own sympathy, the powerful love that can reach even to us. Within Christianity, a single, haunting parable has long and persistently resonated with that insight. It comes from Matthew (25:31-46), and in its present form is likely the composition of the Matthean community in Damascus. Here, as elsewhere, the Synoptic Gospel most conscious of Christian difference from Judaism is also most Judaic in its categories of expression, in this case the category of *zekhut*. In the parable, the Son of man is portrayed as attended by angels and sitting on his throne of glory; he gathers the nations and divides them, as a shepherd separates sheep and goats. The sheep inherit the kingdom prepared from the world's foundation, because—they are told—they have shown compassion to the Son of man. He was hungry, they fed him. He was thirsty, they gave him to drink. He was a stranger, they took him in. He was naked, they clothed him. He was ill, they cared for him. He was in prison, they visited him. The goats failed in all those respects, and are dispatched to the eternal fire prepared for the devil and his angels. For they failed in just the acts of compassion that vindicated the sheep. Both the sheep and the goats are puzzled: they ask, When did we (or did we not) provide you food and drink, take you in our homes, give you clothing, care for your illness, visit you in prison? It is the answer of the Son of man that haunts us: As much as you did for the least of my brethren, you did also for me, and as much as you did not do for them, you withheld from me.

The parable as it stands has little claim to be considered Jesus' own, but it perfectly expresses the Christian perspective on the reciprocity of the divine and human urgings of love. The messianic virtue of *zekhut* that evokes the pleasure of God is worked out in the relations between people, because they have been transferred, however partially, into the kingdom of God.

6

Christ: The Bodily Presence of God

Bruce Chilton

Why should not Christianity be accepted as rather like a liberal form of Judaism, not indeed requiring obedience to any rules such as Judaism requires, but believing as Jews do in a God of mercy and judgment, and looking back to Jesus as a Founder, rather as Jews look back to Moses?—C. F. D. Moule, *Times Higher Education Supplement*, 23 December 1977

IN AT LEAST TWO SENSES, Christianity can see no mystery about the Messiah, its Christ. Although many categories are used to understand Jesus within the New Testament, "Christ" predominates, and is so naturally associated with Jesus (and Jesus alone) that "Christ Jesus" and "Jesus Christ" indistinguishably refer to the church's Lord. And so one mystery of the Messiah—who he might be—is no mystery. His identity may be specified in a way that would satisfy the curiosity of anyone who is not obsessed with outdated notions of historical verification.[1] A second potential mystery—what the Messiah is to do—is also no mystery, because he is understood already to have performed his work in all its essentials. Specifically, he has accomplished what we have assessed in chapters 2 and 4. Christ releases a spirit in baptism that becomes available to the believer, such that prayer to God as Father is natural, behavior in the manner of Jesus is performed, and public thanksgiving with other Christians in eucharistic worship becomes a joy. He who proclaimed God's kingdom provides access to that kingdom, so we are transferred into a realm that is final in respect of time, transcendent in respect of space, perfect, holy, and inclusive of all those who enter its narrow gate. The entire system of Christian faith presupposes a familiarity with Christ Jesus, at least in narrative terms, and an awareness of the range of what he offers in the practice of the church and in the divine realm.

The mystery that the New Testament does not resolve, but in which it finds itself implicated, is: *How* can Jesus be Christ? What makes it possible for him, given his historical identity as a rabbi from Galilee during the first century, to provide full access to the power of God's spirit and gracious inclusion within the divine kingdom? That is the systematic question of Christology. Frequently attempts are made to answer that question by tabulating christological titles in the New Testament and identifying what is held to be their common denominator. By such a method, the term *prophet* is frequently isolated as the origin of Christology. Such exercises only prove in their results what should have been obvious from the outset: Early Christians could agree on no single title that they felt conveyed the identity of Jesus. "Prophet" puts Jesus in a category that was not widely used during his period, a category that in any case must be redefined in order to be applied to him, just as "Christ" itself, "Son of man" (inspired from Daniel 7), "Son of God," "Lord," "teacher," or "rabbi" must be redefined.

The number of such titles undermines the attempt to identify any one of them as the origin of Christology. Consideration of them individually reveals that each can in fact be applied misleadingly to Jesus. He is no prophet in the manner of Moses, in that Jesus was never a figure of truly national stature. If by "Messiah" we have in mind only the wise, forceful ruler of the Psalms of Solomon who subdues all comers with the word of his mouth (17:21-46), it is difficult to see how that term should be applied to Jesus at all. "Son of man," as referred to in Daniel 7, is a purely heavenly figure, whose precise connection with Jesus is not immediately obvious. "Son of God," on the other hand, seems almost too flexible to be informative: It might refer to an angel (Gen. 6:2), to all Israel (Exod. 4:22), to a righteous person (Wisd. of Sol. 2:18). "Lord," "teacher," and "rabbi" might similarly be titles of relative honor, or allusions to God's own attributes as master, instructor, and judge. If the history of research has shown plainly how much there might be in a name, it has also demonstrated that the welter of titles and allusions makes precision regarding Jesus' identity within Christianity problematic.

The phenomenon to hand is the aggregation and redefinition of a series of titles, with one of them ("Christ") emerging finally as the most widely used, although as a virtual synonym for Jesus himself. The best way to investigate the phenomenon is not to tabulate the titles, but to understand how the categories of early Judaism are taken up and framed in order to convey Jesus' identity. Following our usual approach, we will read examples of catechetical Christology, and then of Pauline and Johannine Christologies. On that basis, we will then proceed to the more advanced developments of the Revelation, Colossians, and the stories of Jesus' nativity.

A Question for Catechumens: Who do men say that I am?

The story of Peter's confession of Jesus (Matt. 16:13-20/Mark 8:27-30/Luke 9:18-21) is a classic of primitive Christology. The Petrine account has Jesus ask who people say he is. Common identifications are given (John the baptist, Elijah, one of the prophets). Jesus then asks who the disciples say he is, and Peter answers that he is the Christ.

The direction of the questioning leads away from the notion that a prophetic Christology is adequate; the disciples are implicitly encouraged by Jesus to try another category, which is precisely what Peter attempts. The response of Peter occasions a signal variation within the Synoptic tradition. Mark (8:30) and Luke (9:21) have Jesus admonish his disciples not to speak concerning his identity. Matthew (16:17-19), on the other hand, has Jesus praise Peter as the bearer of special revelation; the admonition to silence then follows (16:20). The peculiarly Matthean narrative makes explicit what the Synoptic Gospels generally presuppose: "Christ" is the designation that will ultimately triumph. Even so, Peter's confession is immediately qualified by Jesus' own prediction, the first in the Synoptics, that—as "the Son of man"—he is about to suffer, be condemned and executed (Matt. 16:21-23/Mark 8:31-33/Luke 9:22). The pericope as a whole is a magisterial demonstration that no single term, not even "Christ," may be accurately used of Jesus, unless it is redefined in the light of knowledge of Jesus himself.

The method of begging the question, of seeking a response to the issue of who Jesus might be, is also evident in the instructional source of Jesus' sayings. One dictum in particular has long attracted critical attention (Matt. 11:25b-27/Luke 10:21-22):

> I acknowledge to you, Father, Lord of heaven and earth, that you have hidden these things from the wise and intelligent, and revealed them to infants. Yes, Father, for so it was pleasing before you. Everything is given me by my Father, and no one knows the Son except the Father, neither does anyone know the Father except the Son, and anyone to whom the Son wishes to reveal him.

The setting in the instructional sources is a series of denunciations against those who have rejected the message of Jesus and his followers (Matt. 11:20-24/Luke 10:12-15, cf. vv. 16-20). In contrast to those whose arrogance blinds them to a simple truth, the saying contrasts the "infants" (*nepioi*).

The metaphor builds upon the axiom, well established within the Petrine catechesis, that in order to enter the kingdom, one must receive it as a child receives: without inhibition, completely absorbed by the vision of what is sought (Matt. 19:13-15 and 18:3/Mark 10:13-16/Luke 18:15-17).[2] What is commended about children in such sayings is not their romantic innocence (a theme that ill accords with the skepticism of antiquity); rather, their naive, single-minded desire is commended as a good model for how to enter the kingdom. A due sense of proportion is precisely what prevents the wise and intelligent from the revelation that the naifs might enjoy.

In chapter 2, it was found that the praise of poor, serving classes was a matter of proximity to Jesus, but that socioeconomic status in itself was not the point of the call to follow him. Rather, the call to discipleship is more readily heard among underclasses; response to the call itself will be manifest in selfless love, from whatever class one might derive. There is a certain analogy with the present saying from the instructional source, which is not a summons to undifferentiated naiveté. The "infants" are defined in a specific fashion as those to whom the son chooses to reveal the father. The relationship between father and son is the generative point of the saying. Each is the sole and sufficient criterion of who the other is; within that circle of intimacy, "infants" are only included by incorporation, because the son reveals the truth to them. By the time we come to the end of the saying, "infants" is no longer even a metaphor of human temperament, but a way of speaking of how believers are related to God the Father through Christ.

The whole of the teaching turns, then, around the circular relationship of mutual knowledge between father and son. In a manner even more radical than in the pericope concerning Peter's confession, any established category by which to measure Jesus (however exalted) is refused. Father and son are only truly intelligible to one another; anyone else is (at best) a fledgling adopted into the family circle. The pericope underscores its method by the lack of specification even as to whether the "son" is "of God" or "of man." The hearer is left to decide, and then to see that a decision between the alternatives is beside the point, because titles are deliberately transcended here. The instructional source joins the Petrine catechesis in insisting on the priority of a way of thinking about Jesus over any title that may be used of him. Both passages proceed from an insight concerning Jesus' relationship with God, which then becomes the basis on which categories that might be applied to him are rejected or qualified.

The new radicalism of the instructional source is its insistence on the mutuality of the relationship. One might have predicted, on the basis of the story concerning Peter's confession, that Jesus might say that no one knows the son truly except the father. God can be the only valid standard of God's own emissary. But the instructional source introduces what is not a corollary, but a statement of equivalent weight, that no one knows the father truly except the son. The Jesus of John's Gospel will say to his disciples (by way of a response to Thomas's question, 14:6-7):

> I am the way and the truth and the life; no one comes to the father except through me. If you knew me, you will know my father, and from this moment you do know him and have seen him.

The inescapable implication, that seeing Jesus is seeing the father, is spelled out in an exchange with Philip (vv. 8-9). Johannine Christology will concern us only at a later stage; for now, the issue of note is that the Fourth Gospel has picked up and expanded upon the symmetrical and mutual relationship of father and son that is a feature of Q.

The instructional saying manifests what is commonly regarded as a "high" Christology, precisely in that the relationship is fully mutual and not a matter of the subordination of Jesus to the father. Commentators for more than a century have come to call the passage the "Johannine meteorite," as if it were unexpected so early within the traditions behind the Gospels. The terminology betrays the Christology of the liberal critics themselves. They suppose that Jesus must originally have thought of himself simply as anointed by God, in the sense of being dispatched for a purpose, and that pious imagination provided the rest.

C. F. D. Moule has summarized the liberal consensus, and goes on to remark:

> And it does, at first sight, look like an easy bridge for the fancy to traverse: starting from a human, messianic Son, it crosses over to a divine, transcendental Son.[3]

There are, however, two gaping holes in the bridge. The first is that, as we have seen in the instance of Peter's confession, the tradition is especially slippery when it concerns using "Messiah" as an adequate category for Jesus. It could only be used as a title after it had been defined anew; Professor Moule observes that "Jesus could scarcely have been styled Messiah (or Christ) after his crucifixion at all unless his friends had already become convinced that he was Messiah in some unusual and transcendental sense."[4]

Because Professor Moule is both a skilled exegete and a theologian of Anglican doctrine, his terms of reference in the article (and elsewhere) are doctrinal. Specifically, he wishes to know whether the earliest of Christologies was "evolutionary," crossing the "easy bridge" he describes, or "transcendental," that is, animated by the conviction that Jesus is "'one in being' with God." His contribution to the study of Christology is one of the most important in this century, because he has revealed the reflexive recourse to an evolutionary point of view among interpreters, and he has suggested an exegetically viable alternative.[5] Perhaps the greatest tribute to his contribution is that it has been consistently sidestepped in the doctrinal discussion that has proceeded along the party lines of liberals and conservatives.

Here, then, is another example of the arid debate between liberals and conservatives to which we called attention in chapter 4. Liberals are so committed to an evolutionary approach, they ignore its exegetical problems. Conservatives are so afraid that critical inquiry will let them down, they prefer simply to assert inerrancy and leave the connection between Scripture and belief unexplored. In their respective campaigns of programmatic silence, an interpreter of the first order had been largely ignored just as he was making a most seminal contribution.

From the perspective of a generative exegesis in search of an understanding of Christianity as a system of religion, Professor Moule's critique of the liberal consensus is of the first importance. His own alternative, however, which he styles the "transcendental" Christology of Christian orthodoxy, must not be immediately invoked. The antinomy between the two is, to begin with, typical of the tension between science and orthodoxy that has entranced and obsessed intellectual observers since the nineteenth century. The antinomy may prove to be important within the New Testament, and therefore of merit in understanding the development of Christology, or it may turn out to be an artifact of a division between faith and reason that is only characteristic of intellectuals since the Enlightenment.

We would therefore reformulate Professor Moule's criticism of the liberal consensus. Instead of invoking an allegedly transcendental assessment of Jesus among the disciples, we have seen simply that the Petrine confession insists that no single term, not even *Christ,* may be accurately used of Jesus, unless it is redefined in the light of knowledge of Jesus himself. Jesus is the term of reference that determines the propriety of a title, not the reverse, because Jesus' relationship to God is what makes and unmakes the relevance of the title. For Jesus' relationship, the instructional source goes on to insist, is more *with* God than *to* God: Father and Son constitute a circle of intimacy in comparison with which all else is subsidiary, and into which one may only be included by the grace of revelation. The first hole in the evolutionary bridge is that the term *Messiah,* the postulated point of departure, offers no easy transition to such a notion. Indeed, we might go a bit further than Professor Moule and suggest that it is only possible to appreciate the Petrine confession and Jesus' acknowledgment of his Father when terms such as *Messiah* are qualified to the point of redefinition.

That brings us to the second hole in the evolutionary bridge, which is perhaps even more gaping than the first: There are simply too many titles applied to Jesus within too short a space of time to sustain the argument that one title spawned the rest. Moreover, there is no reason to suppose such titles would have been applied to Jesus simply because he was effective as a teacher or reputed for unusual deeds. Several brilliant rabbis taught during the first century, some of them skilled in healing and a few of them credited with an ability to influence natural phenomena; they managed to do so without being called "Messiah," "Son of God," "Son of man," or the like. A few revolutionary figures are styled "false prophets" by Josephus, and the famous messianic pretender of the second century, Simeon bar Kosibah, styled himself Bar Kokhba ("son of the star," after Num. 24:17) in order to proclaim his invincible might. But the untitled precedents far outweighed the titled, and insofar as titles are invoked, they tend to signal a political and military power that Jesus never commanded.

A doctrinal approach such as Professor Moule's infers from such evidence that Jesus must have been very different from his contemporaries, that there was a transcendental dimension within his person that escaped categorization and yet resonated (however partially) with the primary categories of how God was expected to act definitively through a single person on behalf of humanity. A systemic approach must eschew reference to the transcendent, except as such reference might emerge in the system to hand. The systemic impact of Peter's confession and Jesus' acclamation of his Father's revelation is to make the relationship between Jesus and God the point from which any assessment of Jesus is to be generated, and at the same time the only means of access to God.

A Question for Christians: What has God made of us with Christ?

A fundamental understanding of the primitive catechesis is that the intimate and mutual relationship between Father and Son is the key, not only to Jesus' identity, but to believers' identity before God. We know who we are as God's children in the light of our knowledge of Jesus as God's Son. A corollary of that understanding is that what God makes of his relationship with Jesus is an extension of himself to us. Christ and church are related, because the Son is related both intimately to the Father and constitutionally to believers.

A single confusion produces subordinationism, ancient and modern. When Christ is described in relation to God *in respect of believers,* the emphasis naturally falls upon a notion of dependence. In the fourth century, that led Arius to his claim that Christ was subordinate to the Father, in the sense that there was a time when the Son was not. From the nineteenth century, we have had the "evolutionary" Christology described by Professor Moule, according to which there was a time when the Christ was not. In both cases, the connection of Jesus to humanity is used to argue that, like humanity, Jesus Christ, the son of God, is temporally conditioned (or, in doctrinal terms, subordinate). But it ought to be obvious that, while Jesus may need to be described in temporal terms as a figure of the literary history of the New Testament, as Christ his intimate relationship with the Father is such that temporal references may be meaningless. Jesus Christ's unique status implies that categorical clarity must be preserved: He may be understood in respect of his humanity or in respect of his relationship to the divine, but the two sorts of reference must not be confounded. Paul and John provide good instances of self-conscious clarity in categorical development for the purposes of controversy and reflection. An example of Pauline Christology will here illustrate how Christ's identity is held to change our constitution as human beings, while John 1 will be read to suggest how a more purely theological reflection developed.

First Corinthians 15:24 has been cited in chapter 4 to demonstrate the importance for Paul of Christ's transfer of the believer (at baptism, and thereafter) from his or her previous condition into the realm of God. Consistent with that emphasis, Paul proceeds to posit a formal analogy between Adam and Christ (1 Cor. 15:45-49):

> So also it is written, "The first man, Adam, became a living psyche": the last Adam is life-giving spirit. The spiritual is not first, but the psychical is, then the spiritual. The first man was from earth—dust, the second man from heaven. As is the man of dust, such are those who are dust; as is the heavenly man, such are those who are heavenly. And just as we bore the image of the dust, so shall we bear the image of the heavenly.

Paul often speaks with less clarity than one might wish, but here the matter is put plainly.

Insofar as there has been confusion in regard to the statement, it has stemmed from attempts at translation, not from Paul's thought. Particularly, he adheres to two conventions that need to be honored in any rendering if he is to be understood. First, Paul thinks of "Adam" as the primordial human being, which he also calls "man." The meaning of the passage turns on the analogy that, just as the human constitution is laid down in the "first man" (Adam), it is seen to be changed in the "second man" (Christ). Another convention is equally significant. Paul is not demeaning "Adam," or humanity at large, when he calls him "psychical" (*psukhikon*): he means simply he was possessed of a "soul" (*psukhe*), complete with its animate self-consciousness and reason. Paul does not dismiss Adam as "physical" (so the Revised Standard Version) or as "natural" (so the King James Version) in order to praise Christ for the mere possession of human rationality. His point is rather that, just as "Adam" represents a constitutive act, enabling human life to flow forth thereafter, so "Christ" is a new creation, which makes possible a transition into spirit, the very world of God.

The transition into the realm of spirit is envisaged within 1 Corinthians 15 as at the resurrection, as has already been seen in chapter 4. But Paul also invokes the same image of Christ as a second Adam in association with baptism in Romans, written one or two years after the Corinthians correspondence, ca. 57. In an extended comparison, Paul contrasts the rule of sin from the transgression of Adam (compounded by the awareness of sin that the law of Moses occasioned) with the grace that flows from Jesus Christ (5:12-21).

His conclusion is as concise as what he wrote to the Corinthians (Rom. 5:18-21):

> Therefore as through one person's transgression there was condemnation for all men, so also through one person's justice there was exoneration unto life for all men. For just as through one man's disobedience many were made sinners, so also through the obedience of one many shall be made righteous. And law came in, in order that the transgression might abound: where sin abounds, grace overflows. So that just as sin ruled in death, grace might rule through righteousness unto eternal life through Jesus Christ our Lord.

Here, the insistence on the transference into a new realm by means of grace is equally emphatic, but the moment of the transfer is not resurrection, but baptism, which is the subject of the most pointed exposition in the whole of the Pauline corpus in Rom. 6:1-11.

The link between the two moments, baptism and resurrection, is Paul's conception of spirit. The very spirit that cries out "Abba!" in baptism (Rom. 8:15), after the manner of Jesus Christ, is also the principle that is to transform the lives and the existence of believers: "If the spirit of the one who raised Jesus from the dead dwells in you, the one who raised Christ from the dead will also make alive your mortal bodies through the spirit dwelling in you" (Rom. 8:11). Baptism and resurrection are joined by the single spirit of the Christ, who also teaches us to pray to our Father and to follow in his own path. Precisely when Paul may seem to be speaking of Christ within the terms of reference of humanity as we know it, the cutting edge of his Christology becomes apparent: Jesus Christ can be the second Adam, who offers humanity a new constitution of its existence both ethically and eschatologically, precisely as a function of his intimate and unique relation to God's Spirit.

The Fourth Gospel also develops a distinctive vocabulary in order to articulate Jesus' impact upon humanity, which is largely derived from the theological language of the Targumim. Jesus is explained in terms of God's "word," *logos* in Greek, *memra* in Aramaic. *Memra*, a nominal form of the verb "to speak" (*amar*), is the Targumic reference to God's activity of commanding. God might be thought of as simply commanding what is ordered when the term is used, but the emphasis might fall on how people respond to the order, or on what lies behind the divine order and the human response. *Memra* may convey a range of emphases, both interior to the act of commanding, informing the decision of command, and consequent upon the act, devolving from it. Context alone permits us to make a selection among its various senses. There is no such thing as a *concept* of God's *memra*, certainly not as personal being or hypostasis, nor even a systematic idea that is consistent from Targum to Targum. What links the Targumim, in their distinct usages of *memra*, is not a theological thought, but a theological manner of speaking of God in terms of divine commanding. *Memra* is not invoked haphazardly when some verb of speaking happens to be used of God in the rendering of the Hebrew text. The Targumim suggest that the usage of the term reflects the manner in which given interpreters conceived of God's intention in the command, or the human response to what is effected (or affected) by the command.

John's prologue presents a nuanced teaching of how Jesus Christ might be understood as a part of God's commanding *logos* or *memra*.[6] The first usage of *logos* in the Gospel simply establishes its identity with

God (not with Jesus, 1:1): "In the beginning was the word, and the word was related to God, and the word was God."[7] The word is identified as the creative, primordial source of what exists (1:2, 3), in a way consistent with the association of *memra* and creation within the Targumim.

The common notion that the *logos* is to be identified with Jesus in the prologue is to some extent based on a reading of the text in Greek that does not attend adequately to its obviously deliberate sequence. God's *logos* is said to be the place where "life" is, and that life is held to be the "light" of all humanity (v. 4). Insofar as a directly christological category is developed in the prologue, that category is "light," not "word." It is the "light" that shines in the darkness (v. 5), which enlightens every person (v. 9). Most crucially, the "light," a neuter noun in Greek (*to phos*), is identified as masculine and singular in v. 10: "In it was the world, and the world came into existence through it, and the world did not know *him*." From that moment, the usage of pronouns and the summary reference to Jesus' ministry (vv. 11-13, cf. vv. 6-8) makes it clear we are dealing with a person, not an entity. But, from the present point of view, the telling factor is that Jesus has been presented, precisely and grammatically, as the light that takes its origin in the *logos*, not as the *logos* itself.

We then come to the clause that has dominated the reading of the Fourth Gospel, and that has been taken as the cornerstone of a christological construction of the *logos* in Christian theology from the second century (v. 14a): "And the *logos* became flesh and dwelt among us. . . ." Once *logos* has been identified with Jesus, as it is for Clement of Alexandria and Irenaeus in the second century, the reference of the clause can only be to the incarnation. Indeed, the Latin text of the clause, *et verbum caro factum est*, is conventionally taken in association with the credal assertion that the "Son," understood as the second person of the Trinity, became incarnate (*incarnatus est*). But all such readings and construals are possible only on the assumption that the *logos* and Jesus are one; then he is a preexistent, personal entity come down from heaven. The problem with such an exegesis of the Johannine text is the care with which Jesus is *not* directly associated with the *logos* in vv. 1-13.

If v. 14 is not read as asserting a christological incarnation, what else can it be saying? An approach to that question guided by our discussion of the *memra* in the Targumim suggests an answer. *Memra* is essentially God's mighty command, vindicating and warning God's people; v. 14 refers to the *logos* as becoming flesh, and then explains that assertion by saying it "dwelt among us" (*eskenosen en hemin*). The verb *skenoo,* it is often observed, relates naturally to *shakhen* in Hebrew and Aramaic, from which *Shekhinah,* the principal term of reference to God's presence in the cult, is derived. To describe the *logos,* understood as *memra,* as dwelling among us such that we might behold its glory, is consistent with Targumic usage.

The "glory" beheld is subjected to a precise qualification at the end of the verse; it is "glory as of an only one with a father, full of grace and truth" (1:14c). At this point, elementary misreadings have obscured a complex statement. The assertion is *not* "we beheld his glory, glory as of the only Son from the Father," as in the Revised Standard Version; still less is it "we have seen his glory, the glory of the only Son, who came from the Father," as in the New International Version. The definite articles are conspicuously absent from the text in Greek; the glory spoken of is as of an only child, not "the only Son." The comparison is straightforwardly metaphorical, not doctrinal: the glory of *logos* was as a child's, reflecting the father's.

Now, however, comes the element of complexity: The glory of the *logos* is "as of an only one" (*hos monogenous*), and we know, as readers of the Gospel, that Jesus is God's Son. Indeed, we know explicitly from the body of the Gospel that Jesus, as God's "Son," speaks God's "word,"[8] and that the reaction to the one is congruent with the reaction to the other. The inference that the glory of the *logos* was "as of" Jesus is therefore precisely consonant with the presentation of the Gospel as a whole. Jesus speaks the word of God; as the Son who was sent by his Father, he permits God's voice to be heard.

The remainder of the prologue reflects the maintenance of the distinction between the *logos* and Jesus, and suggests the sense in which we should understand that the *logos* "became flesh." John, we are told, witnessed "concerning it" (*peri autou,* that is, the word) by saying of Jesus, "This was he of whom I said, He that becomes after me. . ." (v. 15). Fundamentally, the *logos* is still more the object of the prologue's attention than Jesus, and that continues to be the case in v. 16: "For from the fullness [*autou*] we have all received, even grace upon grace." *Autou,* whether taken of the *logos* or of Jesus, is a masculine pronoun, but the statement seems a resumption of what has been said in vv.

3-5: We live from devolutions of the *logos*, the dynamic structure of word, light, and life.

The understanding that God's "word" is still the essential issue in play makes the transition to the next topic straightforward (v. 17): "For the law was given through Moses, grace and truth came through Jesus Christ." The connection of *logos*, taken as *memra*, to the revelation through Moses is evident. Moreover, the syntax and logic of v. 17 cohere with that of v. 16; the coordination of God's activity in creation with God's donation of the law through Moses is established within Targumic usage.

The link between the verses is literal as well. The "grace" (*he kharis*) that came through Jesus Christ (v. 17) is akin to the "grace upon grace" (*kharin anti kharitos*) we have all received (v. 16). There is a constant and consistent activity of God's *logos* from the creation and through the revelations to Moses and to Jesus. The *logos* in John is simply a development of conventional notions of the *memra* in early Judaism. *At no point and in no way does the prologue present the revelation through Jesus as disjunctive with the revelation through Moses. Any such disjunction is an artifact of imposing an anachronistic Christology upon the text.* Verse 17 also provides guidance in regard to the reading of v. 14. The statement that grace and truth "came" (*egeneto*) through Jesus Christ is comparable to the assertion that God's word "became" (*egeneto*) flesh; in both cases, the underlying contention is that Jesus is the person in whom God's "word," God's activity in creating and revealing, is manifest.

The last verse of the prologue is also the last word of the present reading. Verse 18 makes an assertion that makes any formally incarnational reading appear nonsensical: "No one has at any time seen God; an only begotten, God, who was in the bosom of the father, that one has made him known." The first clause makes no sense whatever, if the prologue means to say that Jesus *is* the *logos*. If the *logos* is God (v. 1:1), and Jesus is that "word," v. 18 is more than paradoxical. But v. 18 makes eminent sense on the reading we have here suggested: No one has at any time seen God, provided the reader has followed the logic of God's revelation as the prologue outlines it. Jesus, as an only begotten (again, without the article), has made God known (*exegesato*). Just as we would expect on the basis of our reading of passages that refer to *logos* in the body of the Gospel, Jesus is presented as the exegesis of God, the one who speaks God's word. In that role, the Fourth Gospel can refer to Jesus as θεός just as Philo so refers to Moses:[9] not to make any ontological assertion, but to insist that the instrument of God's word is to be taken as divinely valued.

The Redeemer as Lord and God

John's Gospel points beyond the development of its own Christology to the bolder claims of its community in Ephesus. When Thomas, the famous doubter, encounters the risen Jesus, he exclaims, "My Lord and my God!" (John 20:28). Jesus replies, "Do you believe because you have seen me? Blessed are those who, without having seen, yet believe" (20:29).[10] In the final analysis, however nuanced the portrayal of Jesus in respect of God's eternal word of command, God's *memra* or *logos*, the Gospel concludes its narrative portrayal of Jesus' teaching and acting on God's behalf with the assertion that, substantially, Jesus *is* God. The ontological claim is made only at the close of the Gospel; after Jesus' instrumental representation of God, in the manner of Moses, is explored in the prologue, an entire Gospel pursues the matter further, until Jesus is treated, not only instrumentally but functionally, as God.

Within the Johannine circle, imagery of the Gospel was taken up in order to convey that claim ontologically, to the point that it becomes unmistakably plain. The Revelation of John is generally dated to around 100 C.E. The document itself is written in a Semitized Greek, with self-consciously bad grammar: The errors of case and tense, for example, are below a rudimentary level. And such attempts at archaism can scarcely convince, when a Jewish congregation is dismissed as a "synagogue of Satan" (2:9; 3:9). A formal distance from Judaism is assumed.

Likewise, Jesus as the divine lamb is now explicitly an object of worship. The *amnos* of John 1:29, 36 has become a surreal "little lamb (*arnion*) standing as slain" (Rev. 5:6). The attribution to the *arnion* of divine status is obvious both in its placement, in the midst of the throne, the living creatures, and the elders, and in its possession of seven eyes, "which are the spirits of God sent out into all the earth." Although the term *arnion* in Koine appears unequivocally to connote the helplessness of a lamb, so that the fact of its slaughter is emphasized, the focus of the Revelation is the power that proceeds from the lamb after its slaughter. Indeed, the lamb is worthy of heavenly and human worship (5:8, 13; 7:9-10) precisely as slain (5:12). That is what provides it the authority to open the seals (6:1f.) and exercise judgment with God (6:15-16; cf. 14:10; 17:12-14).

The essential focus of the Synoptic catechesis regarding Eucharist, the solidarity of believers in the witness of a faithful martyr, is also assumed in the Revelation. Indeed, that solidarity is combined with the imagery of Jesus as a sacrifice for sin in the portrayal of Christian martyrs as those who have whitened their robes in the blood of the lamb (7:14): They indeed enjoy the presence of the lamb in their midst, now portrayed as shepherding them (7:17). The notion of whitening in blood is no paradox, once it is understood that the underlying issue is the purification effected by a sacrifice for sin. And the imagery of the lamb's blood is explicitly linked with the theme of Christian witnessing in 12:11.

There is genuine creativity, however, in the assertion that the lamb is best regarded as slain from the foundation of the world (13:8). That conviction is expressed in the same verse that regards the book of life as belonging to the lamb. The association of the two ideas is no coincidence. Jesus' death is now viewed as an eternal sacrifice that both gives him access to the divine throne and offers his followers solidarity with his triumphant purity. For that reason, those followers—or at least 144,000 of them, marked especially for purity—are to appear with the lamb on Mount Zion and offer worship in the presence of the throne, the four beasts, and the elders (14:1-5). Ultimately, however, all those who conquer the beast and its image are to join in the song of Moses and of the lamb (15:2-4; cf. 21:22-27).

The festal quality of the solidarity of faithful followers with the lamb leads to the (at first sight) unlikely imagery of the marriage of the lamb with his bride, an image of the Jerusalem that is to come (21:1-14). The earlier blessing pronounced on those who are called to "the wedding supper of the lamb" (19:9, cf. v. 7 also, and the context from v. 1) locates the occasion that produced the imagery: Reference to the parable of the wedding feast has joined with a conception of the Eucharist in which union is effected by participation. It is a union that even makes the seer, and any faithful Christian, a fellow servant with the angelic host (cf. 19:9-10), a citizen of the new Jerusalem whose purpose is the worship of God and the lamb (22:1-5).

Perhaps because the idiom of the Revelation is visionary, it is possible for it to express openly and trenchantly what even the Gospel according to John only intimates. The discourse of vision also does not require that the obviously important systematic question to be posed: If Jesus is God, are there two Gods? The situation is similar in the exalted language of Philippians (ca. 90). It closes its praise of Jesus' example (2:5f, discussed in chapter 2, pp. 78–79) with a doxological conclusion (2:10-11):

> So that at the name of Jesus every knee should bow,
> in heaven and earth and in the depths,
> and every tongue acknowledge that Jesus Christ is Lord,
> to the glory of God, the Father.

What Thomas can stammer in recognition of the resurrected Jesus, and the Johannine seer can see in a rhapsody of spirit, Timothy's Paul can echo in an exaltation of praise.[11]

Stammering, rhapsody, and exaltation, however, may not be dismissed as "merely" emotional outbursts or epiphenomenal exaggeration. Feelings are part of the totality of any religious system of which we are aware,[12] and the affective engagement of diverse documents, at just the moment when Jesus Christ's status as God is asserted, must give us pause. Timothy's Paul enables us to pursue the matter further, in that Colossians (ca. 90) is taken up largely with the issue of a Christology of Jesus' being as God.

The interface between redemption and such a Christology is clearly signaled: The introduction of the key passage refers to God's transfer of the believer "into the kingdom of the son of his love" (1:13), a passage that took up our attention in chapter 4 (pp. 147–48). In him, the text proceeds, "we have redemption, the forgiveness of sins" (v. 14). Colossians then goes on to make a christological statement comparable to the Johannine prologue, in that Christ is portrayed in terms of the creational imagery of Genesis 1.

But Timothy's Paul directly asserts Jesus' existence prior to any historical appearance (1:15-20):

> He is the invisible God's image, firstborn of all creation, because everything was created by him, in heaven and on earth, visible and invisible.

Be they angelic thrones or lordships or principalities or authorities, everything has been created through him and for him.

He is before all things, and all things consist in him, and he is
the head of the body, the church.

He is the beginning, firstborn of the dead, that he might personally be precedent in all things. For in him all the fullness was
pleased to dwell, and through him—and for him—to reconcile all
things (whether on earth or in heaven), as he made peace through
the blood of his cross.

The advanced nature of the passage is manifest, not only in its development of the language of John's Gospel, but in its development of typically Pauline expressions. The church as the body of Christ, which had
been used by Paul to insist that all Christians belong to one another in
Christ,[13] here is applied in the sense of a hierarchy, to insist that Christ is
the head. And the Pauline emphasis upon the importance of reconciliation between people as a function of their salvation in Christ[14] here
reaches into the truly cosmic dimensions of the powers behind the visi-
ble world.

Colossians reaches into the treasury of early Christian theology in
order to fashion a true Christology: an ontology of Jesus Christ as God.
The very person who died on the cross is the origin and the goal of the
entire creation; he is the primordial first instance, the inherent principal
of order, and the proleptic end point of all things. Orthodox Christianity in the centuries after the formation of the New Testament would
avail itself of the language and thought of Colossians in order to agree
upon credal confessions of Christology. The length, complication, and
violence of the struggle for credal unity amount to an old story, which
cannot be rehearsed here. But the canonical system we are describing
directly indicates why that struggle began, why it endured, and why it is
far from over. Jesus, personally and historically, is there identified with
God in the creation, in the maintenance and the redemption of humanity and everything connected with humanity. The canonical system does
not explain how that confession is to be reconciled with monotheism; it
does not specify how divinity is to be claimed for Jesus; it does not even
(as we have seen) concern itself directly with the biography of the person for whom so much is claimed. Although those questions are left to
be worked out, the stakes involved in how they are answered are incal-
culably high. After all, the person of whom we speak is our origin, our

destiny, the very face of God. The Christian dispute concerning Christology, no less than the Christian quest for ecumenical unity, is a vital and necessary aspect of its canonized system of religion.

Uncompromising and trenchant though Colossians is in its claim of Jesus' divinity, at one point there is a certain obscurity. Which "fullness" is it that chooses to dwell in him (1:19)? It would seem to be the divine fullness, which also is to reconcile all things in Christ, but there may be a certain ambiguity. If so, Colossians later removes it, in a passage that begins by discussing the ethical implications of baptism (2:6-11a):

> As you, then, received Christ Jesus the Lord, walk in him, rooted and built up in him and established in faith—just as you were taught, abounding in thanksgiving. See to it lest anyone make prey of you by means of philosophy and empty deceit: the tradition of men and the elements of the world, and not Christ. For in him all the fullness of deity dwells bodily, and you are fulfilled in him, who is the head of every principality and authority. In him also you were circumcised with a circumcision made without hands. . . .

If there were some ambiguity in the earlier statement about the "fullness," now it is exploited, because it is asserted both that believers are fulfilled in Christ Jesus, and—more dramatically—that deity resides bodily in him.

For all that the claim is plain, it is also not without complexity. The language of "body" has already been deployed to speak of the church of which Christ is head (see also 1:24, 2:10, and 2:16-19) so that believers' endowment with "Christ in you" (1:27) is also an indwelling of God in their midst. But the "bodily" indwelling of God is not merely a metaphorical way to speak of the church. "Body" is also meant literally, as when Colossians states that Christ has "reconciled [you] by the body of his flesh through death" (1:22). Deity is first of all resident there "bodily," and on that basis may be said to dwell in the church as well.

The fundamental response to the issue of Christology, then, is ontological. Jesus Christ speaks of God, teaches God's way, conveys divine grace, transforms human life, offers access to the kingdom, simply because he is God. There is a functionally infinite variety of ways to speak of Christ's being as God, and the reverse, and—as we have already remarked—serious differences are bound to emerge as that variety is realized. But that the range of ways God is reflected in Christ can only be explained fully by relating Christ and deity essentially—and not simply by representing Christ as correct in certain of his opinions about God[15]—is characteristic of Christianity.

At the time the Gospels according to Matthew and Luke were produced, narrative versions of the nativity were available in Damascus and Antioch. There is not sufficient agreement between the two versions to make them appear to have been part of the generally available catechesis represented by the Synoptics, and the divergences between them make it impossible to construct anything approaching a harmonized, historical account. Nonetheless, scholarship has doggedly read the opening chapters of Matthew and Luke as if the self-evidently appropriate aim were to discover what sort of historical information regarding Jesus' birth may have been available in Damascus and Antioch. An approach more suitable to the interests that produced the texts would see in them both, rather than scraps of reminiscence organized by pious imagination, serious investigations in narrative form of what it means for deity to dwell bodily in Jesus, and from that place to shine in the life of believers.

Matthew's story has Joseph told by an angel not to fear to take Mary as his wife, because what has been begotten in her is from the Holy Spirit (1:18-20). The angel goes on to command Joseph to name the child Jesus, because he will save his people from their sins,[16] and the events are said to have fulfilled a passage from Isaiah that speaks of the child Emanuel, "God with us" (1:21-23). The Matthean understanding of Joseph's place in the proceedings is ambivalent: Joseph is troubled in the first place because he knows he is not Jesus' father (1:18-19), and yet Jesus' Davidic ancestry comes through him (1:2-17).[17] The only resolution the text offers is at the level of what results from whatever happened: that which is begotten is from spirit, and the child will save his people as God in our midst.

Luke's nativity account is framed more from early Christian hymns of praise than from reflections on specifiable passages of the Hebrew Bible, and the whole of the narrative is focused on Mary more than on Joseph. Here the angel Gabriel announces to Mary what is to take place (1:30b-31):

> Fear not, Mary, for you have found favor with God.
>   And behold, you will become pregnant and bear a son, and you will call his name Jesus.

He shall be great, and will be called Son of the Most High, and the Lord God will give him the throne of David his father, and he will reign over the house of Jacob forever and of his kingdom there will be no end.

The perplexity concerning how this could be is Mary's in this case (1:34), and once again the angel explains, in a canticle that shows some of the formal signs of poetry (v. 35):

Holy spirit will come upon you,
and (God) most high's power will overshadow you: therefore that which is begotten shall be called holy, God's Son.

The psalmic language of Luke gives the appearance of being more explicit than Matthew's, and yet the central assertion is the same: By one means or another, he who is the source of divine Spirit in baptism is himself of God's Spirit from the outset. Just that union of physical body and divine presence constitutes the central assertion of the nativity, in either version. In that it occurs within the womb of Mary, her place as the bearer of God (the *theotokos* of later orthodoxy) is implicit, and yet receives its notice. There is no coincidence in the popularity of observing Christmas even among those who would decline to be identified as Christians: The claim that human nature has been deified, however proleptically and exceptionally, is a deeper force within our culture than the issue of how we choose to describe ourselves in religious terms.

The mystery of the Messiah within Christianity concerns how it is that Jesus Christ, a rabbi from Galilee who came to grief and rose again, can offer us communion with God (by means of baptism in his name, prayer in his manner, ethics after his example, and Eucharist), access into a divine kingdom that is also his, and partnership in a body of believers who contest the finality of race, history, time, and death. The solution of the mystery is a riddle over which we insist on puzzling, because in the puzzling our faith rejoices. Jesus is the Christ because he is God himself, bodily in an instant of human experience that can be located historically, bodily also in an eternal moment of God's own destiny that can be described theologically. He who was born of a woman, within the constraints of humanity, was then and has been forever the divine force that our restless natures seek, the bodily fullness that answers the pangs of our vacancy.

The Question of Incarnation

JACOB NEUSNER

~

WHERE CHRISTIANITY PARTS COMPANY from all other religions, including Judaism, signifies the systemic center of Christianity—all Christianities. That point, of course, is Jesus Christ. What, in particular, about Jesus Christ matters (from the perspective of Judaism in particular) is not the claim that he was and is the Messiah, or that he was and is God incarnate, or that he taught and teaches Torah over and above the Torah of Sinai and in fulfillment of that first Torah. What matters is that Jesus Christ for Christianity uniquely is the Messiah, uniquely is God incarnate, uniquely reveals Torah against which all other Torah falls short. These claims of uniqueness come to expression in simple ways: "Christ," Messiah, joins only the name of Jesus, but the Judaism of the dual Torah uses "Messiah" in a variety of ways; incarnation speaks only of Jesus, anthropomorphism of all others; and for Christianity, when quoting from the Torah of Moses, only one says, "You have heard it said . . . but I say to you. . . ."

In these ways Christianity insists that only one is incarnate, only one is the Messiah, and only one ascends the mount and bears authority to speak as did Moses at Sinai. We cannot address the claim of Jesus Christ by itself but only in the context of the claim of Jesus Christ as God incarnate. Professor Chilton's citation of C. F. D. Moule makes that point with ample authority: ". . . starting from a human, messianic Son, it crosses over to a divine, transcendental Son." I need not enter into the theological debates so ably summarized by my coauthor if I observe that, seen from a distance, the space between God incarnate and the Messiah appears slender indeed—and narrower still when we remember that the language before us pertains to one person only, uniquely and incomparably.

Here is where Judaism and Christianity, in all their dazzling varieties, must part company, and without regret on either side. Christianity stands or falls on the claim of the uniqueness of Jesus Christ. No Christian discourse, from antiquity to our own day, bears weight or substance without bearing the burden of that point of insistence. The yoke may be easy, the burden light, but the Christian has no more a choice about undertaking to bear that cross than the Israelite—the Jew who is a Judaist and accepts the yoke of the kingdom of heaven and the yoke of the Torah—may decide to leave off the burden of the Torah and yet remain a member in good standing of holy Israel.

When for the Christian Jesus Christ becomes merely a reformer, merely a rustic wonder-worker, merely a wise teacher, then the Christian enters a strange twilight realm of gathering darkness, a realm also occupied by the Jew who practices not the commandments of the Torah but the customs and ceremonies of ethnic Jewry because he prefers the flavor of the food or the warmth of the family. The Talmud says, "Greater is the one who acts by reason of being commanded than the one who acts not by reason of being commanded," but by personal preference; so too, Jesus not Christ, the Messiah, Jesus, not God incarnate, hardly commands attention. After all, everyone knows, when it comes to mere mortal sages, we of holy Israel have hundreds who compare in wisdom and piety and supernatural insight; and prophets, priests, and martyrs to compare as well. What we do not have is God incarnate in one person only, and what we have not known is the Messiah in any one person—at least, not yet. These minimal definitions of the two faiths seem to me to stand for a broad consensus: Jesus Christ as God incarnate formulates the one side, which insists upon the supernatural character of the founder of Christianity; the Torah, come from heaven, formulates with equal precision the generative and definitive principle of Judaism, as we noted at Mishnah Sanhedrin 10:1: "All Israelites have a share in the world to come, and these are the ones who have no portion in the world to come: He who says, 'the resurrection of the dead is a teaching which does not derive from the Torah,' (2) and 'the Torah does not come from Heaven. . . .'"

It seems fair, therefore, to underscore the generative point of provocation, the specific point of difference from which all other disagreements naturally flow. And it is not only fair but necessary. On both sides of the abyss, people of good will have tried to formulate what separates them in merely rational terms, turning their backs on the mystery of faith that takes over and transforms each side into what that side insists God wants it to be. When Professor Chilton and I agree to disagree, as we must, but to do so with enormous affection and esteem for the religion of the other, it is a disagreement not by reason of good will. It is a disagreement compelled by the mystery of the other, one that we have no choice but to endure as the consequence of what, all parties concur, God has made of us. Too much has happened for us of holy Israel to continue to deny the presence of not merely one more other, but the Christian Other, who by their own word stand at Sinai with us and by their own faith believe (in the language of the Mishnah) that "the Torah does come from Heaven," and manifestly maintain that "the resurrection of the dead is a teaching that does derive from the Torah." Christians really are different from Gentiles in general. And every word of Professor Chilton's chapters in this book—every word!—is animated by profound respect for the Torah; that is, for Judaism.

What does it mean to maintain that Jesus Christ is uniquely God incarnate? For long centuries, the Judaic party to the Judeo-Christian dialogue has answered that question in a disdainful manner. What it means—so Christians have heard from us—is that God is physical and has a body and looks like us, and we find that conception manifestly absurd. A review of the medieval disputations will turn up ample evidence that the Judaic party regarded the claim of incarnation as decisive proof of Christianity's implausibility—indeed, incomprehensibility. So it must follow that the parties parted company at incarnation, and that judgment, if substantiated, would set aside my insistence that at issue are not the details but the main point: the insistence that only Jesus is Christ and only Jesus is God incarnate. If through this ongoing dialogue of ours, Professor Chilton and I are able to focus on the main point of difference, we shall have made a contribution to the strengthening of the bonds of amity and good will that in our own generation have begun to take shape. We shall have said, Here we differ, and here we understand why we differ: It is God's mystery, God's will be done (in the language of Kaddish and the Lord's Prayer) in the world that God has created in accordance with God's will.

To make the point stick that the most distinctive conception of Christianity—the notion that God takes human form and walks among us as Jesus Christ—finds a perfectly reasonable counterpart in the Judaism of the dual Torah, a simple procedure is called for. I have to cite evidence to show that our sages of blessed memory have understood the claim of Christianity, even while rejecting that claim as not absurd or irrational but only wrong as to the case at hand. I state very simply: Our sages of blessed memory have not objected to the principle that God takes human form (that is, the doctrine of incarnation stated in its neutral terms), because they took the same view and said so. For them, Israel knows God as a person and, at the end of the formation of the oral Torah, even as a fully embodied personality. Sages know God in four aspects: (1) principle or premise; that is, the one who created the world and gave the Torah; (2) presence; for example, supernatural being resident in the temple and present where two or more persons engaged in discourse concerning the Torah; (3) person; for example, the one to whom prayer is addressed; and (4) personality, a God we can know and make our model.[1]

When God emerges as a personality, God (1) is represented as corporeal; (2) exhibits traits of emotions like those of human beings; (3) does deeds that women and men do, in the way in which humans do them. Let me turn directly to this final stage, the one that is relevant to the argument at hand. In the final documents of the dual Torah as it emerged in the formative age of Judaism, God becomes incarnate as a vivid and highly distinctive personality, actor, conversation partner, hero. In references to God as a personality, God is given corporeal traits. God looks like God in particular, just as each person exhibits distinctive physical traits. Not only so, but in matters of heart and mind and spirit, well-limned individual traits of personality and action alike endow God with that particularity that identifies every individual human being. When God is given attitudes but no active role in discourse, referred to but not invoked as part of a statement, God serves as person. When God participates as a hero and protagonist in a narrative, God gains traits of personality and emerges as God like humanity: God incarnate.

The Hebrew Scriptures had long ago portrayed God in richly personal terms: God wants, cares, demands, regrets, says, and does—just as human beings do. In the written Torah God is not merely a collection of abstract theological attributes and thus rules for governance of reality,

nor a mere person to be revered and feared. God is not a mere composite of regularities, but a specific, highly particular personality, whom
people can know, envision, engage, persuade, impress. Sages painted
this portrait of a personality through making up narratives, telling stories in which God figures like other (incarnate) heroes. When therefore
the authorship of documents of the canon of the Judaism of the oral
half of the dual Torah began to represent God as personality, not merely
premise, presence, or person, they reentered that realm of discourse
about God that Scripture had originally laid out. It was not inevitable
that some sages, represented by the authorship of the Babli, should have
done so.

For sages God and humanity are indistinguishable in their physical
traits. They are distinguished in other, important ways. The issue of the
Talmud of Babylonia is the re-presentation of God in the form of
humanity, but as God. Let us begin with the conception that God and
the human being are mirror images of one another. Here we find the
simple claim that the angels could not discern any physical difference
whatever between man—Adam—and God:

> A.   Said R. Hoshaiah, "When the Holy One, blessed be He,
> came to create the first man, the ministering angels mistook Him
> [for God, since man was in God's image,] and wanted to say before
> Him, 'Holy, [holy, holy is the Lord of hosts].'
> B.   "To what may the matter be compared? To the case of a
> king and a governor who were set in a chariot, and the provincials
> wanted to greet the king, 'Sovereign!' But they did not know which
> one of them was which. What did the king do? He turned the gover-
> nor out and put him away from the chariot, so that people would
> know who was king.
> C.   "So too when the Holy One, blessed be He, created the
> first man, the angels mistook Him [for God]. What did the Holy
> One, blessed be He, do? He put him to sleep, so everyone knew
> that He was a mere man.
> D.   "That is in line with the following verse of Scripture:
> 'Cease you from man, in whose nostrils is a breath, for how little is
> he to be accounted' (Isa. 2:22)."
>
> *Genesis Rabbah VIII:X*

Here, I maintain, we find an ample counterpart to the conception of
God incarnate, that is to say, God in fully human form. Still, it is in the
Talmud of Babylonia in particular that God is represented as a fully ex-
posed personality. There we see in a variety of dimensions the single

characterization of God as a personality that humanity can know and love.

Telling stories provides the particular means by which theological traits that long generations had affirmed are portrayed as qualities of the personality of God, who is like a human being. It is one thing to hypostatize a theological abstraction—for example, "The quality of mercy said before the Holy One, blessed be He. . . ." It is quite another to construct a conversation between God and, say, David, with a complete argument and a rich interchange, in which God's merciful character is spelled out as the trait of a specific personality. And that is what we find in the Babli— and, so far as my survey suggests, not in any prior document. Specifically, it is in the Babli that the specification of an attribute of God, such as being long-suffering, is restated in the following by means of narrative. God then emerges not as an abstract entity with theological traits but as a fully exposed personality. God is portrayed as engaged in conversation with human beings because God and humanity can understand one another within the same rules of discourse. When we speak of the personality of God, we shall see, traits of a corporeal, emotional, and social character form the repertoire of appropriate characteristics. To begin with, we consider the particular means by which, in the pages of the Talmud of Babylonia, in particular, these traits are set forth.

In the Babli's stories God not only looks like a human being but also does the acts that human beings do. For example, God spends the day much as does a mortal ruler of Israel, at least as sages imagine such a figure. That is, he studies the Torah, makes practical decisions, and sustains the world (meaning, administers public funds for public needs), just as (in sages' picture of themselves) sages do. What gives us a deeply human God is that for the final part of the day, God plays with his pet, leviathan. Some correct that view and hold that God spends the rest of the day teaching youngsters. In passages such as these we therefore see the concrete expression of a process of the personality of God:

> A.   Said R. Judah said Rab, "The day is twelve hours long. During the first three, the Holy One, blessed be He, is engaged in the study of the Torah.
>
> B.   "During the next three God sits in judgment on the world and when He sees the world sufficiently guilty to deserve destruction, He moves from the seat of justice to the seat of mercy.
>
> C.   "During the third He feeds the whole world, from the horned buffalo to vermin.

D. "During the fourth he plays with the leviathan, as it is said, 'There is leviathan, whom you have made to play with' (Ps. 104:26)."

E. [Another authority denies this final point and says,] "What then does God do in the fourth quarter of the day?

F. "He sits and teaches schoolchildren, as it is said, 'Whom shall one teach knowledge, and whom shall one make to understand the message? Those who are weaned from milk' (Isa. 28:9)."

G. "And what does God do by night?

H. "If you like, I shall propose that He does what He does in daytime.

I. "Or if you prefer: He rides a light cherub and floats in eighteen thousand worlds . . .

J. "Or if you prefer: He sits and listens to the song of the heavenly creatures, as it is said, 'By the day the LORD will command His loving kindness and in the night His song shall be with me'" (Ps. 42:9).

Babli Abodah Zarah 3B

The personality of God encompasses not only physical, but also emotional or attitudinal traits. In the final stage of the Judaism of the dual Torah, God emerged as a fully exposed personality. The character of divinity, therefore, encompasses God's virtue, the specific traits of character and personality that God exhibits above and here below. The humanity of God emerges in yet another way. As in the written Torah, so in the oral Torah, the covenant prevails. God enters into transactions with human beings and accords with the rules that govern those relationships. God exhibits precisely the social attributes that human beings do. A number of stories, rather protracted and detailed, tell of God as a social being, living among and doing business with mortals. These stories provide extended portraits of God's relationships—in particular, arguments—with important figures, such as angelic figures, as well as Moses, David, and Hosea. In them God negotiates, persuades, teaches, argues, exchanges reasons. The personality of God therefore comes to expression in a variety of portraits of how God engages in arguments with men and angels, and so enters into the existence of ordinary people. God is represented as accepting accountability, by the standards of humanity, for what God does.

A. Said R. Isaac, "When the temple was destroyed, the Holy One, blessed be He, found Abraham standing in the Temple. He said to Him, 'What is my beloved doing in my house?'

B.   "He said to Him, 'I have come because of what is going on with my children.'

C.   "He said to him, 'Your children sinned and have been sent into exile.'

D.   "He said to Him, 'But wasn't it by mistake that they sinned?'

E.   "He said to him, 'She has wrought lewdness' (Jer. 11:15).

F.   "He said to Him, 'But wasn't it just a minority of them that did it?'

G.   "He said to him, 'It was a majority' (Jer. 11:15).

H.   "He said to Him, 'You should at least have taken account of the covenant of circumcision [which should have secured forgiveness despite their sin]!'

I.   "He said to him, 'The holy flesh is passed from you' (Jer. 11:15).

J.   "And if You had waited for them, they might have repented!

K.   "He said to him, 'When you do evil, then you are happy' (Jer. 11:15).

L.   "He said to Him, 'He put his hands on His head, crying out and weeping, saying to them, "God forbid! Perhaps they have no remedy at all!"'

M.   "A heavenly voice came forth and said, 'The LORD called you "a leafy olive tree, fair with excellent fruit"' (Jer. 11:16).

N.   "'Just as in the case of an olive tree, its future comes only at the end [that is, it is only after a long while that it attains its best fruit], so in the case of Israel, their future comes at the end of their time.'"

Babylonian Talmud Menahot 53b

God relates to Abraham as to an equal. That is shown by God's implicit agreement that God is answerable to Abraham for what has taken place with the destruction of the Temple. God does not impose silence on Abraham; that, God says, is a decree not to be contested but only accepted. God as a social being accepts that He must provide sound reasons for His actions, as must any other reasonable person in a world governed by rules applicable to everyone. Abraham is a fine choice for the protagonist, since he engaged in the argument concerning Sodom. His complaint is expressed at B: God is now called to explain Himself. At each point then Abraham offers arguments in behalf of sinning Israel, and God responds, item by item. The climax has God promising Israel a future worth having. God emerges as both just and merciful, reasonable but sympathetic. The transaction attests to God's conformity to rules of reasoned transactions in a coherent society.

The status of sage, expressed in rituals of proper conduct, is attained through knowing how to participate in argument about matters of the Torah, particularly the law. Indeed, what makes a sage an authority is knowledge of details of the law. Consequently, my claim that God is represented as a particular sort of human being, namely, as a sage, requires evidence that God not only follows the arguments (as above, "My sons have conquered me!") and even has opinions that God proposes to interject, but also participates in debates on the law. Ability to follow those debates and forcefully to contribute to them forms the chief indicator. That this ability joins some humans to God is furthermore explicit. So the arguments in the academy in heaven, over which God presides, form the exact counterpart to the arguments on earth, with the result that God emerges as precisely consubstantial, physically and intellectually, with the particular configuration of the sage:

> A.   In the session in the firmament, people were debating this question: If the bright spot came before the white hair, the person is unclean. If the white hair came before the bright spot, he is clean. What about a case of doubt?
> B.   The Holy One, blessed be He, said, "Clean."
> C.   And the rest of the fellowship of the firmament said, "Unclean."
> D.   They said, "Who will settle the matter?"
> E.   It should be Rabbah b. Nahmani, for he is the one who said, "I am an expert in the laws of plagues and in the effects of contamination through the overshadowing of a corpse." . . .
> F.   A letter fell down from the sky to Pumbedita: "Rabbah b. Nahmani has been called up by the academy of the firmament . . ."
> *Babylonian Talmud Baba Mesia 86a*

God in this story forms part of the background of action. Part of a much longer account attached to the academy of Pumbedita of how Rabbah b. Nahmani was taken up to heaven, the story shows us how God is represented in a session of the heavenly academy studying precisely those details of the Torah, here chapter 13 of Leviticus as restated in Mishnah-tractate Negaim, as were mastered by the great sages of the day. That the rest of the heavenly court would disagree forms an essential detail, because it verifies the picture and validates the claim, to come, that heaven required the knowledge of the heroic sage. That is the point of B-C-D. Then Rabbah b. Nahmani is called to heaven—that is, killed and transported upward—to make the required ruling. God is not the center-piece of the story. The detail that a letter was sent from the heavenly academy to the one on earth, at Pumbedita, then restates the basic point of the story: the correspondence of earth to heaven on this matter.

But while the sage is in God's image, God is not in the sage's image. For our sages of blessed memory, God is always God, and what makes God God is God's sovereignty, even over matters that for us yield only mystery. God has the power to tell us to shut up, even before the Torah that is ours and God's alike. Though in the image of the sage, God towers over other sages, disposes of their lives and determines their destinies. Portraying God as sage allowed the storytellers to state in vivid ways convictions on the disparity between sages' great intellectual achievements and their this-worldly standing and fate. But God remains within the model of other sages, takes up the rulings, follows the arguments, participates in the sessions that distinguish sages and mark them off from all other people:

> A.   Said R. Judah said Rab, "When Moses went up to the height, he found the Holy One, blessed be He, sitting and tying crowns to the letters [of the Torah]."
>
> B.   "He said to Him, 'Lord of the universe, why is this necessary?'
>
> C.   "He said to him, 'There is a certain man who is going to come into being at the end of some generations, by the name of Aqiba b. Joseph. He is going to find expositions to attach mounds and mounds of laws to each point [of a crown].'
>
> D.   "He said to Him, 'Lord of the universe, show him to me.'
>
> E.   "He said to him, 'Turn around.'
>
> F.   "[Moses] went and took his seat at the end of eight rows, but he could not understand what the people were saying. He felt weak. When discourse came to a certain matter, one of [Aqiba's] disciples said to him, 'My lord, how do you know this?'
>
> G.   "He said to him, 'It is a law revealed by God to Moses at Mount Sinai.'
>
> H.   "Moses' spirits were restored.
>
> I.   "He turned back and returned to the Holy One, blessed be He. He said to Him, 'Lord of the universe, now if you have such a man available, how can you give the Torah through me?'

> J.   "He said to him, 'Be silent. That is how I have decided matters.'
>
> K.   "He said to Him, 'Lord of the universe, you have now shown me his mastery of the Torah. Now show me his reward.'
>
> L.   "He said to him, 'Turn around.'
>
> M.   "He turned around and saw people weighing out his flesh in the butcher-shop.
>
> N.   "He said to Him, 'Lord of the universe, such is his mastery of Torah, and such is his reward?'
>
> O.   "He said to him, 'Be silent. That is how I have decided matters.'"

Babylonian Talmud Menahot 29B

This is the single most important narrative in the Babli's repertoire of allusions to, and stories about, the personality of God. For God's role in the story finds definition as hero and principal actor. God is no longer the mere interlocutor, nor does God simply answer questions of the principal voice by citing Scripture.

Quite to the contrary, God is always God, never humanity. God makes all the decisions and guides the unfolding of the story. Moses then appears as the straight man. He asks the questions that permit God to make the stunning replies. Moses, who is called "our rabbi" and forms the prototype and ideal of the sage, does not understand. God then tells him to shut up and accept God's decree. God does what God likes, with whom God likes. And the task of humanity, at the ultimate moment, is to accept the decree: "Be silent. That is how I have decided matters." That is an appropriate point for concluding a book on the Judeo-Christian debate. God clearly has not wanted holy Israel to take leave of humanity, nor has it been God's will that the Torah be left in its ark, not declaimed, not celebrated, not responded to. But, after two thousand years, it surely is equally self-evident that Christianity is here to stay and has made a difference in the world. The same reasoning that appeals to the facts of history to validate Israel's enduring existence— "God has willed it"—imposes assent to the claim that the cross has changed the world, too. To these conflicting facts, silence is the response our sages' example commands: Let the mystery be ours, so too our task, which is to respond to mystery with the certain faith that God will clarify matters in due course. And in the interim, we shall be, all of us, what God has made of us: "in our image, after our likeness."

Notes

~

Preface

1. Josef van Ess, "Teaching and 'Universities' in Medieval Islam," *Diogenes* 150 (1991): 66.

2. The three complementary volumes are: Jacob Neusner and Bruce Chilton, *Christianity and Judaism: The Formative Categories*; vol. 1, *Revelation: The Torah and the Bible* (Valley Forge, Pa.: Trinity Press International, 1995); vol. 2, *The Body of Faith: Israel and Church* (Valley Forge, Pa.: Trinity Press International, 1996); and vol. 3, *God in the World* (Harrisburg: Trinity Press International, 1997).

3. In addition to the joint authors' companion works listed in note 2, Jacob Neusner has published the following works on the Judeo-Christian dialogue, past and present:

Aphrahat and Judaism: The Christian Jewish Argument in Fourth Century Iran (Leiden: Brill, 1971).

The Bible and Us: A Priest and a Rabbi Read the Scriptures Together, with Andrew M. Greeley (New York: Warner Books, 1990; trade paperback edition: 1991. Jewish Book Club alternative selection.

Jews and Christians: The Myth of a Common Tradition (New York: Trinity Press International, and London: SCM, 1990).

Judaism in the Beginning of Christianity (Philadelphia: Fortress Press, 1983; British edition, London: SPCK, 1984; 2d printing 1988, 3d printing 1990).

Judaism and Christianity in the Age of Constantine: Issues of the Initial Confrontation (Chicago: University of Chicago Press, 1987).

Judaism in the Matrix of Christianity (Philadelphia: Fortress Press, 1986;

British edition, Edinburgh: T. & T. Collins, 1988; 2d printing, with a new introduction, Atlanta: Scholars Press for South Florida Studies in the History of Judaism, 1990).

Judaism without Christianity: An Introduction to the Religious System of the Mishnah in Historical Context (Hoboken: Ktav Publishing House, 1991). Abbreviated version of *Judaism : The Evidence of the Mishnah.*

A Rabbi Talks with Jesus: An Intermillennial, Interfaith Exchange (New York: Doubleday, 1993).

Telling Tales: Making Sense of Christian and Judaic Nonsense: The Urgency and Basis for Judaeo-Christian Dialogue (Louisville: Westminster-John Knox Press, 1993).

Bruce Chilton has written several volumes that discuss the emergence of early Christianity, and some that characterize the Judaism(s) of that period. Among them are:

Beginning New Testament Study (London: SPCK, 1986, and Grand Rapids: Eerdmans, 1987).

A Feast of Meanings: Eucharistic Theologies from Jesus through Johannine Circles; Supplements to *Novum Testamentum* (Leiden: Brill, 1994).

A Galilean Rabbi and His Bible: Jesus' Use of the Interpreted Scripture of His Time (Wilmington: Glazier, 1984); also published with the subtitle, *Jesus' own Interpretation of Isaiah* (London: SPCK, 1984).

The Isaiah Targum: Introduction, Translation, Apparatus, and Notes; The Aramaic Bible (Wilmington: Glazier; Edinburgh: Clark, 1987).

Jesus and the Ethics of the Kingdom, with J. I. H. McDonald; Biblical Foundations in Theology (London: SPCK, 1987); also published in the United States not as part of a series (Grand Rapids: Eerdmans, 1988).

Jesus' Prayer and Jesus' Eucharist: His Personal Practice of Spirituality (Valley Forge, Pa.: Trinity Press International, 1997).

The Kingdom of God in the Teaching of Jesus, editor, translator, and author of introduction (London: SPCK; and Philadelphia: Fortress, 1984).

Profiles of a Rabbi: Synoptic Opportunities in Reading about Jesus; Brown Judaic Studies 177 (Atlanta: Scholars Press, 1989).

Pure Kingdom: Jesus' Vision of God: Studying the Historical Jesus (Grand Rapids: Eerdmans, 1997).

The Temple of Jesus: His Sacrificial Program within a Cultural History of Sacrifice (University Park: Pennsylvania State University Press, 1992).

Chapter 1

1. Ingolf U. Dalferth, *Theology and Philosophy* (Oxford: Basil Blackwell, 1988), vii.

Response to Chapter 1

1. Benedict Viviano, *Study as Worship: Aboth and the New Testament* (Leiden: Brill, 1978).

2. See Rudolf Otto, *The Idea of the Holy*, trans. J. W. Harvey (London: Oxford University Press, 1931); Mircea Eliade, *The Sacred and the Profane*, trans. W. R. Trask (New York: Harcourt Brace, 1959); Joseph Campbell and M. J. Abadie, *The Mythic Image* (Princeton, N.J.: Princeton University Press, 1974).

3. See William Robertson Smith, *Lectures on the Religion of the Semites* (New York: Macmillan, 1927); Emile Durkheim, *The Elementary Forms of the Religious Life*, trans. J. W. Swain (London: Allen and Unwin, 1915); Clifford Geertz, *Local Knowledge: Further Essays in Interpretive Anthropology* (New York: Basic, 1983).

4. "Jacob Neusner and the Philosophy of Mishnah," in *Jewish Law from Jesus to the Mishnah* (London: SCM; Philadelphia: Trinity Press International, 1990), 309–31. The unfortunate reference to double talk appears on p. 316.

5. The most important thinker in the process, whose reputation is a measure of the victory of synthesis, is Thomas Aquinas.

6. Among Goodenough's many works, see *An Introduction to Philo Judaeus* (New Haven: Yale University Press, 1940). Moore's famous contribution is *Judaism in the First Centuries of the Christian Era* (Cambridge: Harvard University Press, 1962).

7. Aristotle was mediated to the West by Islam, which could therefore be viewed from the angle of a philosophy. The story of Christianity's relations with Islam still needs to be told from a systematic perspective. But two strands of a truly ambivalent Christian attitude may be cited: (1) the impulse to engage Islam as a philosophy, and (2) the will to conquer Islam as a primitive religion. For all that Edward Said's *Orientalism* (New York: Pantheon, 1978) has usefully laid bare the colonial stamp of Western attitudes, there is curiously scant attention paid to the philosophical engagement with Islam that preceded—and survived—the Crusades. Said himself has ironically played into the hands of the triumphalist West he wishes to criticize, by an unquestioning acceptance of a historiography and hermeneutical stance that only a Westerner could conceive, much less approve.

8. The counterpoint of Robert Frost's poem, "Mending Wall," is the comment, "Good fences make good neighbors"; dismissed as prosaic, the laconic remark may be more incisive than the poem itself.

9. As Paul says in 2 Cor. 5:7, "we walk by faith, not by sight."

Chapter 2

1. He here refers to Isa. 49:15, initially in Latin.

2. For discussion and a table (pp. ix–xi), see Bruce Chilton, *Beginning New Testament Study* (London: SPCK, 1986; Grand Rapids: Eerdmans, 1987).

3. For what follows, cf. Bruce Chilton, *Profiles of a Rabbi: Synoptic Opportunities in Reading about Jesus*; Brown Judaic Studies 177 (Atlanta: Scholars Press, 1989).

4. Agreement in order is a measure of common catachesis; deviations indicate local variation. Contact among the communities may be assumed to be both by oral and by written means, given the evidence regarding communication within early Christianity.

5. The same verb will refer to the tear in the veil of the Temple after Jesus' crucifixion (Mark 15:38).

6. The Gospel even lets slip that Jesus baptized others (John 3:22), but then in 4:2 denies what is explicitly affirmed in the earlier passage.

7. Because the incident concerning the waters of Meribah is reported in Num. 20:2-13 as well, Paul's supposition is that the rock was following the Israelites, somewhat in the manner of the cloud and pillar of fire.

8. God's name as "Father" itself features in the Targumim, early Judaic, liturgical prayers, and the Pseudepigrapha. Cf. Bruce Chilton, "God as Father in the Targumim, in Non-canonical Literatures of Early Judaism and Primitive Christianity, and in Matthew," in *The Pseudepigrapha and the New Testament: Comparative Studies*, ed. J. H. Charlesworth and C. A. Evans (Sheffield: JSOT, 1993), 151–69.

9. The German word for "source," *Quelle*, has led to the conventional designation, Q.

10. Such sources also fed the development of Rabbinic literature and were designed for the expert transmission of a master's teaching.

11. See "Early Christian and Rabbinic Liturgical Affinities: Exploring Liturgical Acculturation," *New Testament Studies* 30 (1984): 63–90, 74; and Aboth 2.4; Berakhoth 29b, 38a; Yoma 53b; Megillah 27b. One analogy (in the Yerushalmi, Berakhoth 7d) is even linked to a request "to vanquish and remove from our hearts the inclination to do evil."

12. See Mark 11:25; Matt. 6:14-15, 18:23-25; Luke 17:3-4.

13. See Matt. 5:21-26, 18:15-18; Luke 12:57-59.

14. The latter issue is the context that precedes (rather than follows) the Lord's Prayer in *The Didache* 8.

15. In the Masoretic text, v. 6.

16. See Bruce Chilton, *The Temple of Jesus: His Sacrificial Program within a Cultural History of Sacrifice* (University Park: Pennsylvania State University Press, 1992), "Sacrifice in 'Classic' Israel," 45–67.

17. See also Ps. 103:13, together with its reference to forgiveness in v. 3 and to God's kingdom in v. 19.

18. For a discussion of such elements, see Bruce Chilton, *A Galilean Rabbi and His Bible* (Wilmington: Glazier; London: SPCK, 1984); Chilton,

The Isaiah Targum: Introduction, Translation, Apparatus, and Notes; The Aramaic Bible (Wilmington: Glazier, 1987); and Joseph A. Fitzmyer, *The Gospel According to Luke (X–XXIV)*, The Anchor Bible (Garden City, N.Y.: Doubleday, 1985), 896–909; Chilton, *Jesus' Prayer and Jesus' Eucharist: His Personal Practice of Spirituality* (Valley Forge, Pa.: Trinity Press International, 1997).

19. Cf. J. Heinemann and J. J. Petuchowski, *Literature of the Synagogue*, Library of Jewish Studies (New York: Behrman, 1975), 29–36; and D. W. Staerk, *Altjudische liturgische Gebete ausgewahlt und mit Einleitungen: Kleine Texte* (Bonn: Marcus and Weber, 1910), 11, 12. The latter nine "benedictions" are here excluded, since they are specifically related to the history and ultimate fate of Israel, which became especially pressing concerns after the Roman arson of the Temple in 70 C.E.

20. The form of those elements are themselves appeals, in the imperative, third person, unlike what we read in the Eighteen Benedictions. But they comport quite well with the Kaddish, in which the imperfect is associated with the kingdom and with the magnification of God's name: "May his great name be magnified and hallowed in the world he created in his pleasure, and may his kingdom rule in your lifetime." Texts are proved in Staerk, *Altjudische liturgische Gebete*, 30–32; Heinemann and Petuchowski, *Literature of the Synagogue*, 81–84.

21. The Markan community therefore seems no less familiar with Jesus' model of prayer than the Matthean and Lukan communities were.

22. The classic expression was to come later, in the devotional manual of the fourteenth century attributed to Thomas à Kempis.

23. Although conservative scholars still place the epistle within Paul's actual ministry, and therefore about thirty years earlier, the mention of Timothy as cowriter (1:1), the absence of a definite purpose for writing, and the conscious style of exalted praise for Christ all comport better with the later period.

24. The key in which rewards are promised varies from Gospel to Gospel. That issue cannot concern us here, but it does confirm the observation that the catechetical tradition is construed distinctively in the community of each Gospel.

25. Cf. Bruce Chilton and J. I. H. McDonald, *Jesus and the Ethics of the Kingdom* (Grand Rapids: Eerdmans, 1988; London: SPCK, 1987), 1–3, 5, 7–8, 13, 37–38, 92–95, 101–2, 113–14.

26. *A Feast of Meanings: Eucharistic Theologies from Jesus through Johannine Circles*, Supplements to *Novum Testamentum* (Leiden: Brill, 1994).

27. See *The Temple of Jesus*, "Jesus' Occupation of the Temple," 91–111.

28. See Matt. 26:26-28/Mark 14:22-24/Luke 22:19, 20 (with v. 17 in respect to the original order)/1 Cor. 11:24, 25.

29. Matt. 17:1-9/Mark 9:2-10/Luke 9:28-36.

30. See Matt. 26:28/Mark 14:24/Luke 22:20.

31. See Matt. 26:17-20, 30/Mark 14:12-17, 26/Luke 22:7-14.

32. See Matt. 26:1-5; Mark 14:1-2; Luke 22:1-2, 15-16.

33. See Matt. 26:28/Mark 14:24/Luke 22:20; Heb. 9:11-22; 13:10-16, with Leviticus 4.

34. In Matthew, the blood is "poured out for many for the forgiveness of sins"; the wording fastens upon the issue of forgiveness, which is developed particularly within Matthew (cf. 18:15-18, 23-35). In Mark, the blood is simply "poured out for many"; "many" here refers to those, whether Jews or Gentiles, for whom the servant Son of man will give himself as a ransom (10:45). In Luke, the blood is "for you," which puts the promise in precisely the same key as the address to the "you" who have endured with Jesus in Luke 22:24-30, a discourse referred to during the supper only in the third Gospel. Jesus is the heroic *hata'at* in Matthew, Mark, and Luke, then, but that identification is achieved by means of narrative and discourse unique to each Gospel. The forgiveness of Matt. 26:28 relates to the Matthean concern over forgiveness; the "many" of Mark 14:24 to the Markan emphasis on the ransoming death of the "son of man"; the "you" of Luke 22:20 to the Lukan theme of discipleship.

35. Paul in 1 Cor. 10:3 tentatively suggested a similar exposition.

36. The last meal of Jesus with his disciples in chapter 13 is a symposial gathering, in which heroic service is exemplified, rather than the institution of what for John is an eternal reality. In that John appears to have been composed on the basis of familiarity with the Hellenistic catechesis that crystallized in the Synoptic Gospels, the form of chapter 13 may be taken to confirm the reading of the Synoptic last supper as a heroic symposium.

Response to Chapter 2

1. All translations in this and in chapters 3 and 5 are taken, with some minor revisions, from Jules Harlow, ed., *Weekday Prayerbook* (New York: Rabbinical Assembly of America, 1962), pp. 42ff.

Chapter 3

1. Abraham J. Heschel, *The Sabbath: Its Meaning for Modern Man* (New York: Farrar, Strauss & Young, 1951), p. 8.

2. Ibid., 10.

3. Ibid., 10.

4. Harlow, ed., *Weekday Prayerbook*, pp. 42ff.

Response to Chapter 3

1. T. W. Manson, *The Teaching of Jesus: Studies of Its Form and Content* (Cambridge: Cambridge University Press, 1955), 201. It should be noticed that

Manson goes on to claim that Jesus' innovation lay in the way he saw the kingdom as related to people.

2. Ibid., 235.

3. Ibid., 283.

4. See Bruce Chilton and J. I. H. McDonald, *Jesus and the Ethics of the Kingdom* (Grand Rapids: Eerdmans, 1988; London: SPCK, 1987), 24–47.

5. Manson, *The Teaching of Jesus*, 312.

Chapter 4

1. In any case, a separate study offers a comprehensive discussion. See Bruce Chilton, *Pure Kingdom: Jesus' Vision of God; Studying the Historical Jesus* (Grand Rapids: Eerdmans, 1997).

2. For a more detailed consideration of what follows, see Bruce Chilton, *The Kingdom of God in the Teaching of Jesus* (London: SPCK; Philadelphia: Fortress, 1984), and "The Kingdom of God in Recent Discussion," in *Studying the Historical Jesus*, ed. Bruce Chilton and C. A. Evans (Leiden: Brill, 1994).

3. See Chilton, *The Kingdom of God*, 6.

4. See, for example, G. R. Beasley-Murray, *Jesus and the Kingdom of God* (Grand Rapids: Eerdmans; Exeter: Paternoster, 1986).

5. As I have discussed elsewhere (see *The Kingdom of God*, 7–8). Weiss perceived the problem, while Schweitzer did not, but even Weiss failed to develop any program for the study of other aspects of the kingdom.

6. When the wider context of each passage is considered, the observation is all the more valid.

7. Types of meaning within the Psalms, which correspond to their historical development, are analyzed in Chilton, *Pure Kingdom,* pp. 146–63.

8. For a detailed analysis of the saying, see Bruce Chilton, *God in Strength: Jesus' Announcement of the Kingdom* (Sheffield: Sheffield Academic Press, 1987), reprinted from *Studien zum Neuen Testament und seiner Umwelt* 1 (Freistad: Plöchl, 1979): 179–201.

9. See the discussion in Bruce Chilton, *A Galilean Rabbi and His Bible* (Wilmington: Glazier; London: SPCK, 1984), 58–59.

10. In the Targum, the oppressor of Israel is apparently Rome and the reference is distributed through the chapter; see Bruce Chilton, *The Isaiah Targum: Introduction, Translation, Apparatus, and Notes*; The Aramaic Bible (Wilmington: Glazier; Edinburgh: Clark, 1987), 47–51.

11. See Bruce Chilton and J. I. H. McDonald, *Jesus and the Ethics of the Kingdom* (Grand Rapids: Eerdmans, 1988; London: SPCK, 1987), 31–37.

12. In my own opinion, the statement originally meant that there are figures, such as Moses and Elijah, who did not die, but remain with God and stand surety that the kingdom will indeed come; see Bruce Chilton, "The

Transfiguration: Dominical Assurance and Apostolic Vision," *New Testament Studies* 27 (1980): 115–24.

13. It will be recalled from chapter 2 that the concept of covenant was the contribution of the Petrine group to the Eucharist. The group had a particular tendency to reinterpret sayings of the form "X will not occur, until Y"; that is why their activity is especially evident around Matt. 16:28, Mark 9:1, Luke 9:27; and Matt. 26:29, Mark 14:25, Luke 22:18. That the Semitic idiom was not originally temporal in either case is shown in Bruce Chilton, *A Feast of Meanings: Eucharistic Theologies from Jesus through Johannine Circles*; Supplements to *Novum Testamentum* (Leiden: Brill, 1994), appendix 1, "The construction οὐ μή . . . ἕως [ἄν] in asseverations of Jesus."

14. Chilton, *A Galilean Rabbi and His Bible*, 90–97.

15. Matt. 4:17, 23; 9:35; 12:28; Mark 1:15; Luke 4:43; 8:1; 9:2; 10:9, 11; 11:20.

16. Matt. 5:3, 10, 19, 20; 6:10, 33; 7:21; 8:11, 12; 11:12; 13:11, 19, 24, 31, 33, 38, 41, 43, 44, 45, 52; 16:19; 18:1, 3, 4, 23; 19:12, 14, 23: 20:1; 21:31, 43; 22:2; 23:14; 24:14; 25:1, 34; Mark 4:11, 26, 30; 9:1, 47; 10:14, 15, 23, 24, 25; 12:34; Luke 6:20; 7:28; 8:1, 10; 9:11, 27, 60, 62; 11:2; 12:31: 13:18, 20, 28, 29; 16:16; 17:20, 21; 18:16, 17, 24, 25, 29; 21:31.

17. The history of such speculation is impressively given objective standing by referring to it as "the Synoptic Problem," as if it were a phenomenon of texts, rather than a disturbance among interpreters. Cf. Bruce Chilton, *Profiles of a Rabbi: Synoptic Opportunities in Reading about Jesus*; Brown Judaic Studies 177 (Atlanta: Scholars Press, 1989).

18. See Bruce Chilton, "The Son of Man: Human and Heavenly," in *The Four Gospels: 1992 Festschrift Frans Neirynck*, ed. F. van Segbroeck, C. M. Tuckett, G. van Belle, and J. Verheyden; BETL 100 (Leuven, 1992), 203–18.

19. *Anothen* might be taken to be "again," but that is how Nicodemus is presented in v. 4 as understanding the term, and he is a paradigm of how to misconstrue Jesus' teaching.

20. It is rooted in a pattern of usage exemplified by Luke 12:32, where the kingdom is presented as an apocalyptic promise. Cf. Chilton, *God in Strength*, 231–50. That is a development from the mid-first century (see also Matt. 19:28; Luke 22:28-30).

21. For usages during the same general period, see Rev. 11:15; 12:10 (cf. 1:9); 2 Pet. 1:11. The turn of phrase seems to have influenced the Gospel according to John, as well, when Jesus refers to "my kingdom" (18:36).

Response to Chapter 4

1. *The Fathers according to Rabbi Nathan*, trans. Jacob Neusner (Decatur, Ga.: Scholars Press, 1986).

Chapter 5

1. T. Zahavy, *The Talmud of the Land of Israel I. Berakhot* (Chicago: University of Chicago Press, 1992).

Response to Chapter 5

1. Simeon bar Kosibah was the name of the revolutionary, as actual letters from him, recently discovered, demonstrate. He took the name of Bar Kokhba, "son of a star," an allusion to Num. 24:17. Later Rabbis called him Bar Kozebah or Bar Kozibah, "son of a lie."

2. See Bruce Chilton, *The Isaiah Targum: Introduction, Translation, Apparatus, and Notes;* The Aramaic Bible 11 (Wilmington: Glazier, 1987).

3. A curious result of that expectation is that Christian scholars apparently anticipate that non-Christian scholars of Judaism will come up with adequate Christologies in their descriptions of Jesus. They even complain when that is not the result; see Donald A. Hagner, *The Jewish Reclamation of Jesus: An Analysis and Critique of Modern Jewish Study of Jesus* (Grand Rapids: Zondervan, 1984). Were we to see a book by a Jewish scholar entitled *The Christian Appropriation of Hillel*, I think we would guess that ideological claims intrinsic to Judaism were at issue, as well as texts concerning Hillel. Such exercises may be worthwhile, but it is unrealistic to expect a scholar of one system of religion to make convincing sense within the ideology of another.

4. See Leonardo Boff, *Passion of Christ, Passion of the World: The Facts, Their Interpretation, and Their Meaning Yesterday and Today*, trans. R. R. Barr (Maryknoll: Orbis, 1987); Leonardo Boff and Clodovis Boff, *Introducing Liberation Theology*, trans. P. Burns (Tunbridge Wells: Burns & Oates, 1987).

Chapter 6

1. It is commonplace to observe that the historical canons of the eighteenth and nineteenth centuries, designed largely to deal with official, public events, were not the appropriate instruments for understanding folk sources such as the New Testament. The redefinition of Jesus in history over the past fifty years manifests literarily historical criteria that are more suitable for the topic at hand. See Bruce Chilton, *Profiles of a Rabbi: Synoptic Opportunities in Reading about Jesus;* Brown Judaic Studies 177 (Atlanta: Scholars Press, 1989).

2. For a consideration, see McDonald's treatment in Bruce Chilton and J. I. H. McDonald, *Jesus and the Ethics of the Kingdom;* Biblical Foundations in Theology (London: SPCK, 1987; Grand Rapids: Eerdmans, 1988), 83–89.

3. "Incarnation: Paradox That Will Not Go Away," *Times Higher Education Supplement* (23 December 1977): 11.

4. Ibid.

5. It should be added that one of the few liberal exegetes self-consciously and effectively to engage in debate with Professor Moule was Bishop John A. T. Robinson.

6. For a detailed discussion of the present reading, see Bruce Chilton, "Typologies of *Memra* and the Fourth Gospel," *Targum Studies* 1 (1992): 89–100.

7. The preposition *pros* in Greek unequivocally means "to." The verse has been rendered in the past, "and the word was with God." That translation is flawed, however, because it is a function of later Christian theology, in which *logos* was simply identified with Jesus, conceived of as the preexistent second person of the Trinity.

8. In John's Gospel, the underlying perspective that the *logos* may be God's in particular, not only Jesus' or even God's in Jesus', turns out to be fundamental. It is precisely on that basis that Jesus can claim that the word he speaks will judge anyone who rejects him and does not accept his utterances (12:48-50): It is neither Jesus himself, nor whatever he says, that will judge such a person on the last day, but the *logos*. The *logos* spoken by Jesus is held to have a dynamic property here, as in 15:3, where it is held to have purified those who belong to Jesus. But it is Jesus, and no other, who is understood to speak the *logos*, and the treatment of the disciples is to reflect people's response to his word (15:20).

9. Cf. *Legum Allegoria* I.40; *De Sacrificiis Abelis et Caini* 9; *Quod Deterius Potiori insidiari soleat* 161, 162; *De Migratione Abrahami* 84; *De Mutatione Nominum* 19; *De Vita Moses* I.158; *Quod Omnis Probus Liber sit* 43.

10. The incident is located eight days after Jesus' earlier appearance (v. 26), a symbolic reference to the eighth day on which circumcision was once to occur, before it was superseded by baptism as the preeminent sign of the covenant.

11. Indeed, it is one indication of the pseudepigraphy of Philippians that the logical implications of the outburst are not worked out. The contrast with 1 Corinthians 15 is instructive.

12. The affective aspect as integral within a typology of sacrifice is analyzed in Bruce Chilton, *The Temple of Jesus: His Sacrificial Program within a Cultural History of Sacrifice* (University Park: Pennsylvania State University Press, 1992), chapter 3, "Towards a Typology of Sacrifice."

13. See 1 Cor. 12:12-27; Rom. 12:4-7.

14. See 2 Cor. 5:14-21; Rom. 5:10. The term Paul preferred was *katalasso*; in Ephesians (2:16) and Colossians (1:20, 22) it becomes *apokatalasso*.

15. Indeed, an adequate Christology will easily accommodate any demonstrable mistakes in his views, without recourse to the expedient of saying that he knew better to say what he did, but did not wish to appear out of step with his contemporaries. If deity is indeed "bodily" resident in the case of

Jesus Christ, then deity has taken the risk of temporality and other human limi-
tations.

16. In Hebrew or Aramaic, he is to be named *Yeshua'*, because he will
yasha'.

17. Notably, four other women are mentioned in the genealogy (Tamar,
Rachab, Ruth, and Bathsheba) whose sexual experiences made them unconventional. Tamar conceived Phares and Zara from her father-in-law; Rachab, at
least, shared her name with a harlot; Ruth maneuvered Boaz into marriage by
means of a local celebration of fertility; David committed adultery with
Bathsheba.

Response to Chapter 6

1. I give a brief summary of my book *The Incarnation of God: The Character of Divinity in Formative Judaism* (Philadelphia: Fortress Press, 1988)
(reprinted: Atlanta: Scholars Press for South Florida Studies in the History of
Judaism, 1992). For the context, see also my *Doubleday Anchor Reference
Library: Rabbinic Judaism. An Historical Introduction* (New York: Doubleday, 1995).

Index